TESTIMONIALS
CONTRACT & PROCUREMENT FRAUD INVESTIGATION GUIDEBOOK

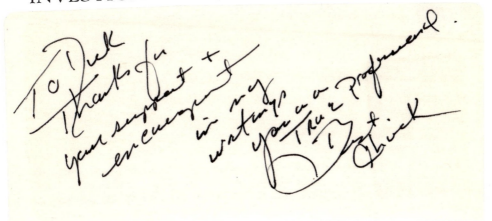

TESTIMONIALS

"No organization operates in isolation. In order to function, every entity must procure goods and services. Large organizations negotiate contracts worth hundreds of millions each year; therefore, the potential losses due to fraud, collusion and corruption can be enormous—if you don't know what to look for. Charles Piper is a seasoned fraud examiner. In this book, he breaks down the common schemes, how to spot them, and how to conduct effective investigations. Piper's *Contract and Procurement Fraud Investigation Guidebook* is a vital resource for fraud investigators as well as businesses and government organizations that want to ensure the integrity of their acquisition systems."

James D. Ratley, CFE, CEO & President, Association of Certified Fraud Examiners

"I served over 40 years conducting investigations, including white collar and major fraud, for the U.S. Department of Defense. Charles Piper's *Contract and Procurement Fraud Investigation Guidebook* is the ultimate investigation guidebook on all things related to contract and procurement fraud, collusion and corruption. I wish such a manual was available when I first started. This book should be required reading for all current and future fraud fighters, contracting officials, business owners and politicians worldwide."

Richard L. Messersmith
(Retired) Resident Agent in Charge, Defense Criminal Investigative Service, Department of Defense, Office of Inspector General
& (Retired) Special Agent, Air Force Office of Special Investigations

"Charles Piper's *Contract and Procurement Fraud Investigation Guidebook* describes the contract, procurement and acquisitions process and the types of schemes that take place before, during and after contracts are awarded. It also provides a step-by-step process on how to thoroughly investigate these matters. Had this book been written years ago, a lot of governments and businesses would have saved money and many bad individuals and vendors would have been brought to justice. 'The Piper Method' of conducting thorough and complete investigations needs to become the preventive remedy to stamp out procurement fraud, collusion, and corruption. This book should be required reading in any class or lecture on contracting and it will greatly assist investigators and others in the field."

Scott Amey, J.D. General Counsel
Project on Government Oversight
Washington, D.C.

"Investigators should put Charles Piper's *Contract and Procurement Fraud Investigation Guidebook* front-and-center on their resource shelf. Piper's described investigative techniques and personal 'War Stories' make this book an enjoyable and informative read."

Andy Wise
Chief Consumer Investigator, WMC Action News 5
Memphis, Tennessee

"Whether you are new to white collar crime investigations or a seasoned professional, you will find Charles Piper's *Contract and Procurement Fraud Investigation Guidebook* is an educational, fascinating and useful read. Most experts agree that investigating white collar crime (especially contract and procurement fraud and corruption) can be extremely challenging even for the most experienced investigators. Readers will find Piper's expertise in this field is unparalleled and his shared personal investigative 'War Stories' are educational, entertaining and inspiring. In this writing, he identifies the schemes and shares his proven successful, 'Piper Method of Conducting Thorough and Complete Investigations' so that fraud fighters can solve more cases and prevent future fraud, waste and abuse. I highly recommend this book for veteran, new and upcoming fraud investigators, examiners, auditors, business owners and others."

Gregory Mohr, CFS
(Retired) Federal Special Agent
Security Consultant, Licensed Investigator & Adjunct Professor
Owner: Criminal Justice Training & Consulting, LLC
Scottsdale, Arizona

"While serving as federal special agents, Charles Piper and I worked several cases jointly. I consider him an expert on investigating contract and procurement fraud. He's investigated multi-million dollar fraud cases, some of which involved high profile players. His integrity is beyond reproach and he fights for justice regardless of the source or power of the resistance—and he gets results! Piper's *Contract and Procurement Fraud Investigation Guidebook* details the contracting, procurement and purchasing process; the schemes used before, during and after acquisitions; and describes in detail how to thoroughly investigate these matters. The 'War Stories' he provides are based on his firsthand experiences and make this book an especially enjoyable read. Piper's *Contract and Procurement Fraud Investigation Guidebook* should be considered 'the go to book' on investigating contract and procurement fraud, collusion and corruption."

Bruce Durbin
(Retired) Federal Special Agent
U.S. Department of Homeland Security

"In today's world of billion-dollar international government and private sector procurements, there is a dire need for Charles Piper's *Contract and Procurement Fraud Investigation Guidebook*. The author exposes the many different types of fraud schemes and wrongful actors that can beset contracting and procurements. He also provides a step-by-step list of protocols to be followed while investigating, which provides readers with a distinct advantage. Truly, every fraud investigation should incorporate 'The Piper Method of Conducting Thorough and Complete Investigations.' Procurement and contracting, whether in government or in the private sector, stands to be greatly and positively affected by this book and its adoption by investigation authorities. It should be used as core course and be required reading for every fraud investigator."

Gilbert R. Jimenez, JD, CIG, LPD
Licensed Illinois Private Investigator
Principal—Insight Investigation Services of Chicago, Illinois
Attorney
Former Deputy Inspector General—Illinois

"I've personally worked cases jointly with Charles Piper. He's all about hard work, integrity and accomplishing objectives. He conducts investigations with enthusiasm and passion. Those same qualities along with his expertise are shared in his latest book, *Contract and Procurement Fraud Investigation Guidebook*. It is a must read for all fraud fighters as well as all business owners and government officials that are responsible for expenditures involving contracting, procurements, purchases or acquisitions."

Thomas Terry, CFE, Private Investigator & Consultant
(Retired) U.S. Postal Inspector
Founder and Owner of Silent Service Financial Investigations
Memphis, Tennessee

"For over 20 years, Charles Piper and I both previously investigated contract and procurement fraud, collusion and corruption while serving as Federal Special Agents. Piper was one of the most thorough and determined agents I had the pleasure of working with and he epitomized the agency's slogan of 'dogged pursuit of the truth', wherever it may lead. His *Contract and Procurement Fraud Investigation Guidebook* illustrates the meticulous way he pursued his cases and the theoretical meets the practical in his *War Stories*. This book should be considered the *'new tool'* for those responsible for investigating and prosecuting contract, procurement or vendor fraud and I highly recommend it."

Craig A. Brueckman, CFE-Retired
(Retired) Special Agent
Defense Criminal Investigative Service,
Office of Inspector General, Department of Defense

Contract and Procurement Fraud Investigation Guidebook

Contract and procurement fraud, collusion, and corruption are worldwide problems. Such wrongdoing causes federal, state, and local governments, as well as private-sector corporations and businesses, to lose funds and profits, while the wrongdoers unjustly benefit. Bid riggers conspire to eliminate fair and open competition and unjustly increase prices, allowing some to monopolize industries. Too often, contracting officials and others responsible for placing orders or awarding contracts compromise their integrity and eliminate fair and open competition to favor vendors offering bribes or gifts. This results in unfair playing fields for vendors and causes financial losses for businesses, government agencies, and taxpayers.

Charles Piper's *Contract and Procurement Fraud Investigation Guidebook* educates readers on fraud and corruption schemes that occur before, during, and after contracts are awarded. This book teaches not only how to identify such wrongdoing, but also how to investigate it and prevent reoccurrence. Piper shares *The Piper Method of Conducting Thorough and Complete Investigations*, his innovative and proven method of investigating contract and procurement fraud,* and demonstrates its principles with personal, on-the-job examples (which he calls "War Stories") woven throughout the text. Intended for criminal justice students as well as investigators, auditors, examiners, business owners, policy-makers, and other professionals potentially affected by fraud, this book is a must-read guide to effective procurement and contract fraud investigations from inception to testimony.

Charles E. Piper, CFE, CRT, is an award-winning investigator and author. He served for over 30 years in law enforcement, including 20 years as a special agent-criminal investigator with the U.S. Department of Defense (DoD). He has successfully conducted numerous internal and external contract and procurement fraud investigations, as well as investigations involving collusion and public corruption (bribes and kickbacks). As a federal agent, he led interagency investigations and worked jointly with some of the most experienced and well-trained fraud fighters in the world. His investigations have resulted in millions of dollars in recoveries as well as criminal convictions and civil judgments against fraudsters. Piper also served seven years in the U.S. Army in the Military Police Corps and additional years as a city police officer and supervisory detective.

Currently the owner of Charles Piper's Professional Services, which provides investigative, consulting, and training services, Piper is a Certified Fraud Examiner (CFE), Certified in the Reid Technique of Interview and Interrogation (CRT), and a graduate of three law enforcement-investigative academies (federal, state, and military).

Charles Piper, CFE, CRT, has received numerous awards and recognition while serving in law enforcement, including *Special Agent of the Year*. He was also the recipient of the 2014 Association of Certified Fraud Examiners' (ACFE) *Hubbard Award* and has written several antifraud and investigative articles for the ACFE's *Fraud Magazine* and for other publications.

In 2014, Piper authored *Investigator and Fraud Fighter Guidebook: Operation War Stories** to assist investigators around the globe. The book introduced *The Piper Method of Conducting Thorough and Complete Investigations.** This unique methodology assists investigators in solving more cases and detecting, preventing, and reducing criminal activity and other wrongdoing as well as waste and abuse. This method is also used in Piper's approach to investigating contract and procurement fraud, collusion, and corruption and is provided in this *Contract and Procurement Fraud Investigation Guidebook*.

In 2016, Piper authored the *Healthcare Fraud Investigation Guidebook* (published by CRC Press), which is currently being used by others to fight fraud, waste, and abuse in the healthcare industry.

Charles Piper is a member of:

- The Association of Certified Fraud Examiners;
- The Federal Law Enforcement Officers Association;
- The Reid Institute;
- The Tennessee Association of Investigators.

For more information, visit www.piper-pi.com.

**Investigator and Fraud Fighter Guidebook: Operation War Stories* by Charles E. Piper, Copyright © 2014 by John Wiley & Sons, Inc. All rights reserved.

Charles E. Piper, CFE, CRT (Retired Federal Agent)
Photo Credit: Ben Hubbard

Contract and Procurement Fraud Investigation Guidebook

Charles E. Piper, CFE

Routledge
Taylor & Francis Group
NEW YORK AND LONDON

First published 2017
by Routledge
711 Third Avenue, New York, NY 10017

and by Routledge
2 Park Square, Milton Park, Abingdon, Oxon, OX14 4RN

Routledge is an imprint of the Taylor & Francis Group, an informa business

© 2017 Taylor & Francis

The right of Charles E. Piper to be identified as author of this work has been asserted by him in accordance with sections 77 and 78 of the Copyright, Designs and Patents Act 1988.

All rights reserved. No part of this book may be reprinted or reproduced or utilized in any form or by any electronic, mechanical, or other means, now known or hereafter invented, including photocopying and recording, or in any information storage or retrieval system, without permission in writing from the publishers.

Trademark notice: Product or corporate names may be trademarks or registered trademarks, and are used only for identification and explanation without intent to infringe.

Library of Congress Cataloging in Publication Data
A catalog record for this book has been requested

ISBN: 978-1-138-04496-8 (hbk)
ISBN: 978-1-138-04498-2 (pbk)
ISBN: 978-1-315-17222-4 (ebk)

Typeset in Goudy
by Deanta Global Publishing Services, Chennai, India

Contents

Preface		*xiii*
Acknowledgments		*xvi*
1	Introduction to Contracts, Procurements, and Related Fraud	1
2	Corruption in Contracting	28
3	Source Selection and Competition Schemes	40
4	Contractor and Vendor Performance Schemes	62
5	Contractor and Vendor Payment Schemes	69
6	Investigators, Enforcers, and Statutes	79
7	Investigative Sources and Resources	88
8	Investigative Tools and Techniques	103
9	Interviews and Interrogations	112
10	Investigative Reports and Evidence	133
11	Investigative Case Planning, Goals, and Strategies: The Piper Method of Conducting Thorough and Complete Investigations*	144
12	Case Presentations and Testifying	157

* *Investigator and Fraud Fighter Guidebook: Operation War Stories*; Charles E. Piper: Copyright © 2014 by John Wiley & Sons, Inc. All rights reserved.

13	Post-Adjudicative Action	162
14	Sample Case Study: Story #1	166
15	Sample Case Study: Story #2	182
16	Sample Case Study: Story #3	190

Conclusion 197
Appendix: Samples of Visual Aids for Presentations on Contract and Procurement Fraud, Collusion and Corruption Investigations 198
Index 205

Preface

Theodore Roosevelt once said, "A man who has never gone to school may steal from a freight car; but if he has a university education, he may steal the whole railroad." Things haven't changed much since Roosevelt's time, except more people now have college degrees and the dollar amount of fraud, waste, and abuse across the globe has skyrocketed.

Contract and procurement fraud cause tremendous dollar losses worldwide in all industries and also cost consumers directly and indirectly. From an investigative standpoint, contracts and procurements often go hand in hand with collusion and corruption. When it comes to getting awarded contracts, there are lots of people and entities fighting for the same pieces of pie and some will do almost anything to get their share. Yes, greed plays a big role in it all.

For 20 years, I served as a federal special agent with the U.S. Department of Defense (DoD), Office of Inspector General (OIG) investigating contract and procurement fraud and related collusion and corruption. The DoD spends billions of dollars annually and purchases everything from paper clips to planes, from glue to guns and from hammers to Humvees. They also award contracts for services, supplies, goods, research and development, construction, manufacturing, and other needs.

Today, large corporations, small businesses, as well as governments worldwide—including federal, state, and local—fall victim to many of the same fraud and corruption schemes involving their own procurements and acquisitions. As a result of those schemes, taxpayers' funds and many profits go down the tube, or perhaps more accurately, go into the pockets of unscrupulous individuals.

This book describes contract and procurement fraud schemes as well as the often-related collusion and corruption. The pages also include many of my own firsthand relevant experiences, which I call "War Stories." You'll probably find many of the stories enlightening as they share insight into the real world of white-collar investigations. There's some light humor and sarcasm in the book which will hopefully also keep you entertained.

I've included much information about U.S. federal and DoD contracting in this book. But the schemes, information, and investigational guidance should prove beneficial to those responsible for the integrity in contracting and procurements in all government agencies and industries in both the public and private sectors.

You may have read another crime-fighting book I wrote, titled *Investigator and Fraud Fighter Guidebook: Operation War Stories.** If not, I highly recommend that you consider reading it because those pages detail how to conduct thorough and complete investigations and actually solve more cases—even with fewer resources. It details my own unique method of conducting investigations, called *The Piper Method of Conducting Thorough and Complete Investigations,** and includes a one-page diagram that outlines the method.

That same diagram of *The Piper Method** follows the preface of this book. My unique method of conducting thorough and complete investigations is also detailed in this *Contract and Procurement Fraud Investigation Guidebook*. It's my hope that you'll consider using this methodology (or at least elements of it) in your future investigations so that you might enjoy the same investigative success that I have, or even better results.

One of the great pleasures I take in this book's publication is that, after reading it, you and all the other readers should be able to deter, detect, and successfully identify and investigate contract and procurement fraud and related schemes as well as collusion and corruption. As a result of this knowledge and your hard work, the "bad guys" are going to wonder in frustration why the heck they are all of sudden getting caught and why they can't get away with their misdeeds the way they previously did. I applaud your efforts!

**Investigator and Fraud Fighter Guidebook: Operation War Stories* by Charles E. Piper. Copyright © 2014 by John Wiley & Sons, Inc. All rights reserved.

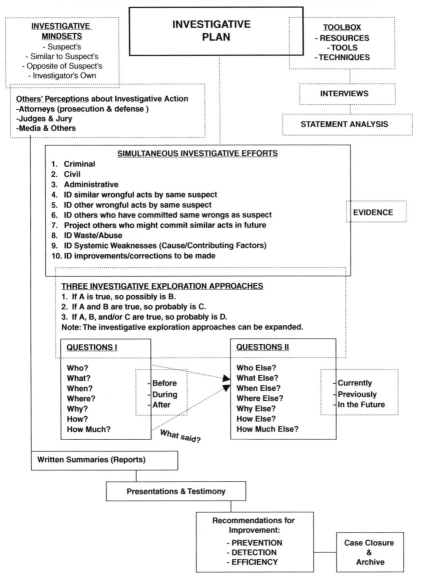

(Reprinted from *Investigator and Fraud Fighter Guidebook: Operation War Stories*; Charles E. Piper: Copyright © 2014 by John Wiley & Sons, Inc. All rights reserved.)

Acknowledgments

I was only able to write this book because of the many opportunities I've had serving others, first as a member of the U.S. Army as a military policeman and investigator, then as a city police officer, a supervisory detective, for 20 years as a Federal Special Agent—Criminal Investigator, and now as a private investigator and consultant. During my career, I've had the pleasure of working with some of the finest law enforcement officers and investigators in the world. I'm grateful for the camaraderie we shared and the many friendships we developed.

Because of lessons learned over the years and my continued determination to stop criminal activity and other injustices, I've enjoyed a tremendous amount of success in the investigative profession. I've been lucky because, more often than not, I've had fun doing the job.

In my post—law enforcement career, I've written books and articles which share my knowledge so that others might benefit from the lessons I learned over the years. The positive feedback and recognition received led me to write this book, for which I'd like to express my sincere appreciation to the following:

The Association of Certified Fraud Examiners (ACFE), including Dr. Joseph Wells, Jim Ratley, Dick Carozza, and the entire crew at the ACFE.

All of the dedicated fraud fighters I've had the pleasure of working with over the years, including federal agents and auditors from various law enforcement agencies (particularly the Department of Defense, the Federal Bureau of Investigation, the U.S. Postal Inspection Service, the many Federal Offices of Inspector General, and many others), state and private insurance investigators, federal prosecutors in both the criminal and civil divisions (particularly in Orlando and Tampa, Florida; Las Vegas, Nevada; Nashville and Memphis, Tennessee; and attorneys with the Department of Justice in Washington, D.C.).

My wife and daughters, older brother, and other family members for all of their support and encouragement along the way.

I thank the publisher of this book, Routledge, a subsidiary of the Taylor & Francis Group, particularly Ellen Boyne, acquisition editor; Eve Strillacci, editorial assistant; and all others who assisted in putting this book together.

I'd also like to thank the readers of this book. I hope my suggested investigative guidance, tips, and shared experiences will benefit you and all those that you strive to assist.

1 Introduction to Contracts, Procurements, and Related Fraud

One of the most gratifying experiences as a fraud fighter is identifying and proving cases against white-collar criminals. Although it's also gratifying to prevent and deter such wrongdoing, catching bad guys is just downright fun. Interviewing and confronting the suspects about their misdeeds is also enjoyable. During the two decades I served as a U.S. federal agent with the Department of Defense (DoD) investigating contract and procurement fraud, collusion, and corruption, I found that just about every wrongdoer I confronted with evidence of their misdeeds attempted to rationalize their illegal and/or improper actions. Common excuses offered by the suspects included:

- "There was no harm in what I did;"
- "Everyone else does it;"
- "We needed the items ASAP;"
- "I deserve this because…;"
- "It's just the way the game is played;"
- "If I don't pay, I can't play;"
- "I did what I was told to do."

Author's Note: *Throughout this book, I'll often use the words vendor and contractor interchangeably.*

WAR STORY 1.1

The evidence showed that a government contracting officer accepted bribes in return for eliminating competitors' bids, thereby circumventing contract award procedures. The contracting officer then awarded purchase orders to a favored vendor. When I confronted the contracting officer about his corrupt activity, he replied, "But I made sure the Government always paid the lowest prices when I awarded those purchase orders to that vendor."

The contracting officer told me that he slept well at night because he could rationalize his contract award decisions. What the contracting officer didn't realize was that after that vendor was awarded the government purchase orders, the vendor submitted invoices and got paid for goods that the vendor never actually shipped.

> Well, the contracting officer didn't sleep very well after my investigation was completed because he got sent to prison! In fact, the idiot even involved his stay-at-home wife in a scheme to launder the bribe payments, so his wife ended up pleading guilty to felony offenses too.
>
> What about the vendor that paid the bribes and submitted false invoices for payment? Well, that knucklehead also got sent to prison and two of his companies eventually went belly-up. The local press wasn't very forgiving either, so the criminals had to also face public humiliation. The vendor's fall from grace was especially hard because he was very well respected in his community as a generous donator to various charitable causes and his children all attended prestigious schools and universities.
>
> A few years later, after the vendor had served his time in prison, he unexpectedly knocked on my office door. To be honest, when I first saw him, my first reaction was to grab my handgun because I assumed he was angry with me. But he actually extended his hand to shake mine and thanked me for doing my job. He said his time spent in prison changed his life and he was a better person because of it. Well, that made me feel pretty good. But I still locked the door after he left, just in case he changed his mind.

Although this book will not focus entirely on government contracting, before we move on, I'll provide some general background information about how the federal government awards contracts and some of the problems encountered. I'll also provide a few basic definitions about contracts, procurements, fraud, collusion, corruption, etc. This chapter will not provide all of the intricate details about every type of contract that can be awarded and/or what rules and regulations might dictate how and when contracts can be awarded or modified, etc. (*Yes, that means you should be able to stay awake.*)

Corporate executives and even small business owners should especially find this book interesting because all too often greed plays a role in diminishing business owners' profits, even among those entities that don't award many contracts. For example, before World War II, my grandfather owned a small meat market on the southside of Chicago. Business was pretty good but he found profits weren't what they should be. What was the reason for the losses? He learned that some of his own employees were stealing meat out the back door! Later, during World War II, the U.S. Government rationed meat, which forced my grandfather to look for a new line of work. He closed his meat market business and became an investigative auditor for the state of Illinois. Even back then there was a need for fraud fighters.

Depending on what entity or organization you work for and/or are investigating, it's worth noting that the rules for acquisitions can range from being simple to complex or may not exist at all. Maybe whoever provides the best lunches, dinners, or use of condos gets awarded the contracts and orders. Maybe whoever retired from the buyer's enterprise and opened their own business gets priority over everyone else. A common determination as to which company gets awarded a contract is, "That's who we've always used."

Businesses, countries, states, counties, municipalities, and small towns also have their own rules and regulations for contracting. One politician told me he believed his small town's method of awarding contracts consisted of just utilizing "The Good Ole' Boy Network." After he told a few stories about contracts awarded, I opined he was probably right.

One large county in Tennessee previously allowed its mayor to award contracts valued at less than $100,000 without any competition. A county chairman stated that he noticed instances where several contracts valued at $99,999 were signed with the same company over just a few days. Those contracts seemed to have been "split" to avoid competition. Such instances certainly do not pass the smell test. By law, the mayor was legally permitted to do exactly what he did. In October 2015, the county commission approved a 10–2 resolution that cut the dollar amount on contracts that the mayor could sign from $100,000 to $50,000. Call me cynical, but it makes me wonder how many new contracts have since been signed by the mayor for $49,999—perhaps on the same day. That same county allows contracts for under $5,000 to be awarded without any advertising and without any competition!

In 2015, the City of Memphis, Tennessee, wanted to hurriedly award a multimillion-dollar contract to procure body cameras for its city police officers. This was during the time frame when politicians and law enforcement nationwide were especially under the microscope for their handling of police shootings of black males. Understandably, those under pressure were looking for quick fixes and in Memphis, there was an upcoming mayoral election on the horizon. The city's contract rules required that 10 percent of the total contract award price be subcontracted to a minority or female-owned business. To accommodate this requirement, the large company that was awarded the multimillion city contract to supply the cameras awarded a subcontract worth almost $900,000 to a company headed by the city mayor's campaign manager to provide "public awareness" about the body cameras.

Once again this didn't pass the smell test and the local press was all over the story. Many wondered if the total contract price was inflated to accommodate the 10 percent subcontract work that seemed totally unrelated to the acquisition of the body cameras. Many also wondered if that approximately $900,000 expense for public awareness was even needed in the first place. Some argued that press conferences and billboards probably would have done just fine to promote awareness. At least in part due to the negative publicity, the $900,000 subcontract was quickly canceled. Perhaps not surprisingly, the mayor lost his re-election bid not long after that.

In October 2015, the former head of the Chicago public school system pled guilty to steering more than $23 million in no-bid contracts to her previous employers in exchange for kickbacks worth millions of dollars. It was reported that the former school chief expected to receive a job, and that the kickbacks (10 percent of the value of the contracts) were to be disguised as a one-time signing bonus.

By and large, the same types of schemes used to defraud government agencies are conducted in the private and public sector alike—perhaps with a slight tweaking of different contracting rules or the lack thereof.

The Contract Award Process

As stated, the contract award process can vary greatly depending on the buyer's entity and the rules which dictate their contract award procedures. Obviously, the public and private sectors have different requirements. When anything but small dollars is involved, a typical contract process might resemble the following:

- Determine a need, ensure funding is available and that the funds are obligated to the acquisition.
- Advertise and specify exactly what is needed and solicit and obtain price quotes.
- Review the price quotes and make a determination of the reasonableness of the lowest price and/or "the best value," and evaluate the seller's track record of being "responsible."
- Award a contract for the goods, services, supplies, etc.
- Inspect and accept delivery (or refuse if unacceptable).
- Make payment(s) as agreed to in the contract.
- Note: The contract may usually be modified and/or terminated (in writing) if necessary and permissible as described in the contract.
- Note: Applicable rules may dictate that a percentage of contracts should be awarded to (and/or percentages of work/services be provided by) small businesses, female or minority-owned businesses, disabled veteran-owned businesses, and/or others.

Procurement and Administrative Contracting Officers

Large organizations (like the DoD) may utilize a Procurement Contracting Officer (PCO) to be responsible for all pre-award aspects of the contract, the awarding of the contract, and perhaps any amendments, modifications, and change orders. They may also utilize an Administrative Contracting Officer (ACO) to be responsible for evaluating subcontractors and their plans and for monitoring, evaluating, and documenting contractor performance. Very often, the PCOs and ACOs are located in completely different offices and sometimes in completely different regions or states. Therefore, pre- and post-award contract-related documents might be located in different offices.

The Federal Acquisition Regulation

To illustrate just how detailed and complex the acquisition process can be, let's consider the Federal Acquisition Regulation (FAR), which provides uniform acquisition policies and procedures for use by all U.S. executive agencies. There

are 53 parts to the FAR. One useful website describing the FAR is powered by the U.S. General Services Administration (GSA). To view a hyperlinked index and each part of the FAR, visit https://www.acquisition.gov/?q=browsefar.
The GSA website reads,

> "The Department of Defense (DoD), GSA, and the National Aeronautics and Space Administration (NASA) jointly issue the Federal Acquisition Regulation (FAR) for use by executive agencies in acquiring goods and services."
>
> (Source: http://www.gsa.gov/portal/content/101126.)

The U.S. Small Business Administration's (SBA) website also describes the FAR:

> The Federal Acquisition Regulation (FAR) is a substantial and complex set of rules governing the federal government's purchasing process. Its purpose is to ensure purchasing procedures are standard and consistent, and conducted in a fair and impartial manner. So whether you are a small business owner or the contracting official, it is important to understand FAR. There are many costly pitfalls if you don't take the time to understand the provisions in your contract, which often reference areas of the FAR.
>
> The FAR is issued and maintained jointly under the statutory authorities granted to the Secretary of Defense, Administrator of General Services and the Administrator, National Aeronautics and Space Administration. Statutory authorities to issue and revise the FAR have been delegated to the Procurement Executives in DOD, GSA and NASA.
>
> Government contracts are different from commercial contracts in many important ways. Federal contracts contain or reference many provisions unique to the government. These provisions include requirements for:
>
> - Changing the scope of work
> - Terminating contracts
> - Making payments
> - Conducting inspection, testing, and acceptance of delivered goods and services...
>
> (Source: https://www.sba.gov/content/federal-acquisition-regulations-far.)

DFARS and Other Supplements to the FAR

The DoD also has a supplement to the FAR called the Defense Federal Acquisition Regulation Supplement (DFARS), and the U.S. military branches and other government agencies have their own supplements. Listed here are some of them:

- AFARS (Department of the Army)
- AFFARS (Department of the Air Force)
- AGAR (Department of Agriculture)
- AIDIR (Agency for International Development)

- CAR (Department of Commerce)
- DARS (Defense Information Systems Agency)
- DEARS (Department of Energy)
- DFARS (Defense Federal Acquisition Regulation Supplement)
- DIAR (Department of Interior)
- DLAD (Defense Logistics Agency)
- DOLAR (Department of Labor)
- DOSAR (Department of State)
- DTAR (Department of Treasury)
- EDAR (Department of Education)
- EPAAR (Environmental Protection Agency)
- GSAM (General Services Administration)
- HHSAR (Health and Human Services Administration)
- HSAR (Department of Homeland Security)
- HUDAR (Department of Housing and Urban Development)
- IAAR (Broadcasting Board of Governors)
- JAR (Department of Justice)
- LIFAR (Office of Personnel Management [OPM], Federal Employees Group Life Insurance)
- NMCARS (Department of Navy)
- NFS (National Aeronautics and Space Administration)
- NRCAR (Nuclear Regulatory Commission)
- SOFARS (U.S. Special Operations Command)
- TAR (Department of Transportation)
- TRANSFARS (U.S. Transportation Command)
- VAAR (Department of Veterans Affairs)

A great website which has links to the FAR and the supplemental regulations is http://farsite.hill.af.mil/vfdfara.htm.

Example of FAR Clause

The U.S. Government strives to be fair when awarding contracts to ensure that the big and powerful companies are not the only ones that get awarded federal contracts. To assist in this effort, the government sets aside a percentage of contracts that must be awarded to small, minority-owned, disabled veteran-owned, and other businesses. FAR clause 52.219-14 places limits on subcontracting. For example, if a contract is awarded to a minority-owned business on a set-aside basis, the minority company is not authorized to just outsource 100 percent of the work and make a profit for shuffling papers around and subcontracting all the work to another company.

FAR 52.219-14: Limitations on Subcontracting

Source: http://farsite.hill.af.mil/vffahttp://farsite.hill.af.mil/vffara.htm ra.htm.

As prescribed in 19.508(e) or 19.811-3(e), insert the following clause:

Limitations on Subcontracting (Nov 2011)

(a) This clause does not apply to the unrestricted portion of a partial set-aside.
(b) *Applicability.* This clause applies only to—

   (1) Contracts that have been set aside or reserved for small business concerns or 8(a) concerns;
   (2) Part or parts of a multiple-award contract that have been set aside for small business concerns or 8(a) concerns; and
   (3) Orders set aside for small business or 8(a) concerns under multiple-award contracts as described in 8.405-5 and 16.505(b)(2)(i)(F).

(c) By submission of an offer and execution of a contract, the Offeror/Contractor agrees that in performance of the contract in the case of a contract for –

   (1) *Services (except construction).* At least 50 percent of the cost of contract performance incurred for personnel shall be expended for employees of the concern.
   (2) *Supplies (other than procurement from a nonmanufacturer of such supplies).* The concern shall perform work for at least 50 percent of the cost of manufacturing the supplies, not including the cost of materials.
   (3) *General construction.* The concern will perform at least 15 percent of the cost of the contract, not including the cost of materials, with its own employees.
   (4) *Construction by special trade contractors.* The concern will perform at least 25 percent of the cost of the contract, not including the cost of materials, with its own employees.

Obviously, the FAR and supplements help to ensure that government contracting officials and contractors follow the rules and ensure fairness. They also help ensure that the contractors can't later claim they did not know that they could or couldn't do something, because the clauses are referenced in their signed contract(s) or agreement(s).

WAR STORY 1.2

I investigated many contracts awarded by one particular military contracting office in which several contracting officials and their supervisors just *kicked-to-the-curb* many of the rules governing federal contracting so that they could award contracts to whomever they wanted. They did this even when more experienced competitors could provide the same services or goods at less cost. Their alleged motive was simply to please their own superiors by steering contracts to a recently retired U.S. four-star general's brand new company and/or the general's associates' companies. I'll call the general's company "Four Stars, Inc." (a fictional name).

At first, the contracting officials were helping the recently retired general get his business started by awarding several contracts (under $100,000 each) to favored contractors. Those contracts later led to the awarding of a 5-year contract worth about $50 million to Four Stars, Inc. Ironically, prior to the awarding of the smaller dollar contracts, Four Stars, Inc. had never before had a government contract and the company didn't seem to have any employees (besides the executives).

The taxpayers got screwed because they overpaid for the services and the rules for fair and open competition were completely circumvented. In fact, one experienced vendor said they could have provided the same service for about $25 million, but the government officials instead decided to pay $50 million to Four Stars, Inc.

Author's Note: *See Chapter 3's War Story 3.6, which describes how the Limitations on Subcontracting clause can be circumvented.*

Definition of a Contract

There are many legal definitions that describe what a contract is. Some of the definitions might put you to sleep. To keep it simple, I'll just quote a couple sources.

- "A contract is a binding agreement between two or more persons or parties; *especially*: one legally enforceable ..."
(Source: http://www.merriam-webster.com/dictionary/contract.)

- "A contract is an agreement creating obligations enforceable by law. The basic elements of a contract are mutual assent, consideration, capacity, and legality. In some states, the element of consideration can be satisfied by a valid substitute. Possible remedies for breach of contract include general damages, consequential damages, reliance damages, and specific performance."
(Source: https://www.law.cornell.edu/wex/contract.)

Types of Contracts

There are more types of contracts than Forrest Gump's friend Bubba knew ways to cook shrimp. If everyone acted in an ethical manner, the type of contract selected as the vehicle to acquire goods, services, etc. would serve the best interests of the customer(s), the government(s) or stockholder(s) or owner(s). But this book's focus is not on the actions of people that act ethically.

Too often programs, rules, and regulations that were established with good intentions are manipulated or used to the advantage of unscrupulous individuals and businesses. Although Chapter 2 details common contract and related corruption schemes, some different types of contracts awarded are described here. Many people wrongfully assume the type of contract utilized always protects the customer's own interests. Although the type of contract usually protects the customer's interests, it doesn't always.

Firm-Fixed Priced Contract

Firm-fixed priced (FFP) contracts are sometimes referred to as *Stipulated Price Contracts* or *Lump-Sum Contracts*. When an FFP contract is awarded, the contractor will only receive a set price (no more and no less) for whatever is being acquired. For example, if an FFP contract was awarded to Vendor A to supply 1,000 widgets at $500 each for a total cost of $500,000.00 (perhaps plus shipping costs), that contractor would not get paid any more if the contractor later determined that it was going to cost more than $500 to produce each widget. Many contract and procurement courses profess that an FFP contract puts all the risk on the contractor. That sounds like a good thing if you are the customer, right?

But what if the $500 per widget price is inflated to begin with? What if the widgets could actually be produced for $250 each? Then how is all of the risk on the contractor?

Some might argue that the contracting official has an obligation to perform due diligence and secure additional bid quotes and/or check price histories to determine if the proposed contract award price is "reasonable" before actually awarding the contract. If several competitors submitted bids with similar prices, then it might be logical to assume their prices are reasonable, right?

But what if the bidders acted in collusion to rig the bids? For example, Vendors A, B, and C could have conspired to submit similar bid prices, knowing in advance which bidder would submit the lowest bid price. For future contracts, the vendors could alternate submitting the lowest bid price. That scheme is called *bid rigging* and it's very common (*although not often detected*).

Sometimes, in this type of scenario, an unexpected bidder will submit a proposed bid price that is much higher or much lower than the other bidders. Sometimes the contracting official(s) will totally dismiss the unexpected proposal price because it's not in line with the others. It's kind of like, "the majority rules." It's often just assumed that if most bidders are bidding close to the same price, then their prices must be reasonable. It's also usually assumed that all or most of the bidders are not working in collusion. Unfortunately, the out-of-line (honest) bidder's price is often dismissed as if there must be something wrong with their bid price or something wrong with the quality of their product/service.

10 Chapter 1

The FAR actually has a clause which permits contracting officials to determine the reasonableness of a bid price based on the bids of competitors. A portion is copied and pasted here.

FAR 15.402 Pricing policy (Adequate Competition and Price Reasonableness)

Contracting officers shall:

(a) Purchase supplies and services from responsible sources at fair and reasonable prices. In establishing the reasonableness of the offered prices, the contracting officer-
(1) Shall obtain certified cost or pricing data when required by 15.403-4, along with data other than certified cost or pricing data as necessary to establish a fair and reasonable price; or
(2) When certified cost or pricing data are not required by 15.403-4, shall obtain data other than certified cost or pricing data as necessary to establish a fair and reasonable price, generally using the following order of preference in determining the type of data required:
  (i) No additional data from the offeror, if the price is based on adequate price competition, except as provided by 15.403-3(b).

Author's Note: *The last entry provides that price reasonableness can be determined by adequate price competition. It just assumes that there is no bid rigging taking place.*

WAR STORY 1.3

One day I received a call from a reputable government contractor that worked in the electronic cable industry. He complained that for the past couple years he could not get awarded any contracts from the DoD even though his bids were priced low and he'd make a minimal profit. He learned that a competitor (Company B) regularly submitted extremely low bid prices for the same type of cable and kept getting awarded DoD contracts.

The caller knew that Company B's prices were unreasonably low because the cable could not be produced for such low dollar amounts and still meet the required military specifications. In the most recent contract awarded to Company B, the cable procured was intended to be installed on U.S. military nuclear aircraft carriers and submarines.

The caller said he previously complained to federal investigators and contracting officials. But to the best of his knowledge, no one acted on his complaints because Company B kept getting awarded more DoD contracts.

After speaking with the complainant, I checked the bid abstract from the most recent contract awarded to Company B. (*Bid abstracts list all the bidders on individual contracts along with their bid prices.*) After my review, I found that the caller was correct. Company B's price was almost three times lower than all of its competitors.

I asked the contracting officer why he awarded the contract to a vendor whose bid was out of the norm of all the others. The contracting officer said he simply awarded the contract to the lowest-priced qualified bidder.

I couldn't help but wonder if the cable provided to the government had passed all required inspections before being accepted. I was surprised to learn that, although the cable was supposed to be inspected, it never was! I next asked why the cable wasn't inspected. About a week later, a contracting supervisor provided a response in the form of a memorandum. The memo baffled me. It said something like, "Due to the excellent quality history of this item, the inspection requirement is waived."

So I checked the history for the DoD's purchases of this cable and found that type of cable had not been purchased by the DoD in several years. Then I checked the date on the memorandum which waived the inspection requirement and found it was dated several weeks *after* the cable had already been accepted by the government. That memo had obviously been prepared as a CYA (cover your ass) (*and the idiot didn't even have enough sense to backdate it*).

So I requested that the cable be tested at a government laboratory. Months later, the lab determined that the cable was defective and could have caused a fire if it was installed onboard a nuclear aircraft carrier or submarine, as intended.

Because the cable was found to not meet the required military specifications, I asked to see the vendor's certifications that the cable would meet the required military specifications. I then learned that the vendor had certified that the cable would meet the government's previous (10-year-old) specification but not the more recently revised specifications. I also learned that the government contracting officer failed to include the most recent military specifications in the advertisement for the cable or in the contract itself. In short, the government (specifically the contracting officer) dropped the ball. Since the most recent specifications were not listed in the solicitation or the contract, the vendor was not required to provide cable that would meet the newer specifications.

The government's own stupidity troubled me. And that CYA supervisory memo which removed the inspection requirement really ticked me off. I guess the supervisor that signed the memo arrogantly (and wrongfully) assumed that no one would compare the date of his memo with the date the cable was accepted.

Because the government employees screwed up so many times before and during the acquisition process, the contractor could not be considered for criminal prosecution for providing inferior cable.

Author's Note: *This is an example of why it is important for investigators to not only investigate for "criminal violations" but also for "civil violations" as well as simultaneously searching for waste, abuse, and systemic weaknesses which caused or contributed to the problem or wrongdoing being investigated.*

In this case, with assistance from the U.S. Attorney's Office, we were able to secure a civil judgment on this matter and I also made recommendations for improvement regarding the contracting office's poor contract award and inspection procedures. It's probably worth mentioning that the contracting office personnel (especially that supervisor who wrote the memo) were not very happy with my constructive criticism about the way they did (or didn't do) their jobs. But, as you know, an investigator's job is not to make everybody happy.

Checking Price Histories

Some contracting officials will check the price history for the item they intend to purchase and, as a result, a bidder's price might be deemed reasonable based on the prices historically paid. Well, what if the price history is inflated? In other words, what if the customer has historically been paying too much for the item?

WAR STORY 1.4

Government contracting personnel responsible for awarding contracts to obtain medical items researched price histories for all the items before awarding contracts and purchase orders for the items. I checked the price history for many of the medical items and found that some individual prices for common items had skyrocketed over an 18-month period. Items that previously sold for about $20 many months before were suddenly selling for about $200 each. If a contracting official or anyone else only looked at the recent price history, it would seem perfectly acceptable and reasonable to award the next contract for the same item for $200 to $225 because that was the trend.

But I established that the reason the prices were escalating was because many purchase orders were awarded by contracting officers who were accepting bribes in return for awarding contracts. Because of that, the contracting officials often accepted the first bid prices (which were inflated) that the bribe payers offered. Over time, the prices of many items unnecessarily went through the roof.

In short, just because a contract is Firm-Fixed-Priced (FFP), don't assume that it was/is the best price and/or will result in the best quality. Also, contrary to many teachings, don't assume that all of the risk on a fixed-priced contract is on the contractor that was awarded the contract.

Cost-Plus Contract

Many contract training programs profess that there is more risk for the customer/buyer (the one paying the costs) in cost-plus contracts because of the uncertainty of the cost of labor, supplies and materials, etc. My experience is that this is true. In cost-plus contracts, the customer has no certainty of how much they will pay until invoices are received. Two examples of cost-plus contracts are cost-plus labor and cost-plus materials. An example of why these types of contracts are needed might be when a housing project, aircraft, or ship is built. It could be that the price and quantity of materials might increase more than expected and/or the amount of labor needed might be more than expected. Perhaps the reason the contract must be awarded on a cost-plus basis is because no contractor is willing to risk losing big money on a fixed-priced contract due to the many variables. A good example of a commodity varying in price that we all can relate to is fuel.

WAR STORY 1.5

For a multimillion-dollar contract award, I established that a team of bid evaluators favored one vendor over all the others. I'll call that favored company "Vendor Buddy." In other words, the bid evaluators gave terrible ratings to most vendors and superb ratings to Vendor Buddy. Because Vendor Buddy knew the bid evaluators were favoring it, it sometimes snubbed its nose at the requirements to prove it was capable of completing the contract. Vendor Buddy knew the "fix was in" and that it would be awarded the contract no matter what.

For example, Vendor Buddy was a brand new company that was required to prove that it was financially solvent before the government could award it the large dollar contract. The contract term that describes that the vendor was financially solvent was "responsible." Vendor Buddy and a competitor (Vendor B) were both asked to provide their bank statements to prove they were responsible.

Vendor B didn't have any financial statements to provide, so the bid evaluators kicked Vendor B out of the competition and reported that Vendor B was "non-responsive" to the requirement to provide financial statements.

Well, good ole' Vendor Buddy sent the bid evaluators an e-mail which read something like, "Although I understand that I am required to provide financial statements, I will not provide them because I believe my word is good enough."

Guess what the bid evaluators wrote about Vendor Buddy? They wrote that Vendor Buddy was considered to be "responsible" because it "understood the requirement to provide financial statements."

But in reality, Vendor Buddy (just like Vendor B) failed (refused) to provide the required financial statements and therefore neither company should have been further considered to be awarded the multimillion-dollar contract. Regardless, the contract was still awarded to Vendor Buddy!

> The contracting official had a legal obligation to ensure that the contract was awarded to the vendor that met all the requirements and presented "the best value" for the government. I later interviewed the contracting official who made the final decision to award the contract to Vendor Buddy.
>
> I let him read out loud the FAR clause (subpart 9.1) that described that a contracting officer could only award a contract after ensuring the vendor was responsible. I asked him a question like, "So Vendor B was not considered responsible because he failed to provide required financial statements, right?"
>
> The contracting officer said that was correct. I asked if Vendor Buddy provided the financial statements. The contracting officer said that Vendor Buddy did not.
>
> So I politely asked, "So why the hell did you award the contract to Vendor Buddy? And why the hell did you only write that Vendor Buddy understood the requirement, when in fact he refused to provide the financial statements just like Vendor B?!"
>
> Ok, maybe I wasn't really polite. But you should have seen the look on that contracting officer's face after I asked him those questions. He just sat stone-faced in his chair, in silence. It was later proven that his high-ranking supervisor put pressure on him to award the contract to Vendor Buddy.

Certification of Cost and Pricing Data

In cost-plus contracts (and sometimes in FFP contracts), contractors might be required to certify to their cost and pricing data. In other words, they will have to provide proof of their costs and expenses and be subjected to audits during the contract's performance to verify their expense information.

Contractors would prefer not to have to certify to their cost and pricing data. That way, they do not have to support the costs they include on their invoices. Undetected bid-rigging can help ensure that contractors will not have to submit cost and pricing data.

As previously mentioned, FAR 15.402 (Pricing Policy: Adequate Competition and Price Reasonableness) allows a contracting officer to not require a vendor to certify to cost and pricing data if there is adequate competition (two or more bidders) and price comparability. Therefore, having a second bidder submit a complementary bid with a similar bid price could eliminate the requirement to certify to cost-and-pricing data. (Conspiring to and submitting a complementary bid is illegal.)

As you can already see, the federal government has rules to ensure that the government's own interests are protected and that contracts are awarded fairly. But, as I've described, the rules are relatively easy to manipulate or violate—especially when someone on the inside is willing to compromise his or her own integrity.

Guaranteed Maximum Price or Not to Exceed Contract

A guaranteed maximum price contract is often referred to as a GMP or GMAX. Sometimes it is referred to as a not to exceed price, or NTE or NTX contract. These are often used for construction contracts. Typically, the contractor is paid for their actual costs plus a fixed fee. The benefit to the customer is that the contractor is responsible for any price overruns.

Sometimes, GMP contracts are amended and/or receive change orders during contract performance that are agreed to by the customer and the contractor. Sometimes those amendments and change orders are worthy of scrutiny because the process can be corrupted or could have been corrupt from the very beginning if it was known (before the contract was awarded) that the contract would be amended and/or modified and result in significant price increases.

If the customer wants the contractor to try to save money, the contractor must have some incentive to do so. Depending on the terms of the contract, the savings may go to either the customer or the contractor. Sometimes it's stipulated in the contract that a percentage of savings will go to the contractor and the remaining back to the customer.

Fraud can occur if the costs and/or expenses the contractor provides are inflated or false. A careful review of costs should be completed by the customer before, during, and after the contractor's performance. During the performance of a construction contract, the contractor will usually be required to provide a breakdown of the costs incurred to date.

Schedule of Values

A Schedule of Values is a breakdown of costs/prices by allocation and is often provided before the contract is awarded and during the contract performance (perhaps monthly). One of the benefits of a Schedule of Values for the customer is that the customer will get to review the costs to determine if they are reasonable and accurate and to ensure that the money won't run out before the project is completed.

It's a red flag if the contractor says they won't provide a Schedule of Values until after the contract is signed. It's also a red flag if the contractor bills for three-fourths of the cost of the contract before the project is even one-third completed. In short, GMP contracts are not always the best value for the customer and do not always ensure that the customer won't spend more than they needed to.

Purchase Order Contracts

Purchase orders are like mini-contracts that are awarded for lower dollar amounts, often with little or no competition. Sometimes the value of the purchase order may be less than a specified dollar threshold—perhaps under $25,000. Perhaps orders for $25,000 and over will require actual signed contracts which require advertising the need and more formal bid submission requirements. Sometimes purchase orders are awarded by getting price quotes over the phone or, nowadays, through electronic bid submissions.

> ## WAR STORY 1.6
>
> I investigated a contracting directorate responsible for awarding millions of dollars in government contracts. They also awarded a lot of "small purchase orders" that were less than $25,000 each. Orders under $2,500 could be awarded with no competition, as long as the price was considered reasonable.
>
> Orders over $2,500 but under $25,000 required the assigned contracting officer to obtain at least three competitive bids (usually over the phone), and the lowest offer would win.
>
> While reviewing the purchase order files, I found evidence that contracting officials were manipulating the award procedures. When an order was for a quantity of items with a total price over $2,500, one contracting officer often "split" the large order into several smaller purchase orders under $2,500. By doing this, the contracting officer was not required to obtain three competitive quotes. Instead, he/she could just obtain one price quote and if the quoted price was "reasonable," the purchase orders could be awarded without competition.
>
> I asked myself, "Why would a contracting officer split the orders?" Initially, I thought that perhaps it would be less work and quicker to award several smaller dollar purchase orders.
>
> But I found evidence to the contrary. One particularly careless contracting officer left his handwritten notes inside the contract files and there was white liquid correction fluid covering his handwritten numbers. I was curious why someone would white-out their own notes, so I held the pages up to a light and could then see what was previously written. I found that the contracting officer repeatedly changed prices and quantities to ensure that the final purchase order prices would be under $2,500 and that therefore he would not have to call more than one vendor.
>
> He was not saving time at all. In fact, he was wasting time and eliminating fair competition. Why was he doing that? Because he was getting paid bribes by the vendors that were awarded the purchase orders.

Blanket Purchase Agreement Contract

A Blanket Purchase Agreement (BPA) is a contract with one vendor for repeated orders for the same item(s) with a set price per item. For example, the buyer might have several different organizations or units under their control that frequently need the same item(s) at different times and the quantity might vary. An example of this could be a hospital with the repeated need for a certain type of bandage or a company that might have a frequent need for a certain type of widget. So they might award a 1-year BPA to a vendor to provide those items at agreed-upon prices. Sometimes, a single BPA might cover many different items. Because of the large number of orders to be placed on the BPA, vendors are encouraged to submit bids with their best (lowest) prices because the lowest-priced responsible bidder will usually be awarded the contract.

Shipping Costs

As consumers, most of us have purchased items off the internet. When we shop and compare prices, we sometimes find that an item might be less expensive at one store but later find that they also charge for shipping. Also, some stores don't charge state sales tax. Although one store might have a lower list price, the consumer might find that after paying shipping costs and/or state taxes, it's actually more expensive than its competitors. Shipping costs and/or state taxes must be factored in when deciding which vendor to select. In the contracting world, it's important to understand the difference between Free On Board (FOB) origin and FOB destination.

FOB Origin and FOB Destination

FOB essentially identifies who will pay the cost of shipping. FOB origin means the buyer will pay shipping costs and FOB destination means the shipper will pay. In North America, the FOB point is also used to determine responsibility for ownership and liability, which could play a huge role if theft or damage occurs.

Definition: www.businessdictionary.com defines Free On Board as:

> "1. Term of sale under which the price invoiced or quoted by a seller includes all charges up to placing the goods on board a ship at the port of departure specified by the buyer. Also called collect, freight collect, or freight forward.
>
> 2. Used in shipping to indicate that there is no charge to the buyer for goods placed on board a carrier at the point of shipment. Typically followed by the name of a port or city, e.g., F.O.B. San Francisco."

WAR STORY 1.7

When analyzing some telephonic quotes provided by vendors competing to be awarded purchase orders, I noticed some anomalies. Three vendors' quotes were listed side by side. At first glance, it appeared that one vendor's prices were always lower than its competitors. For example:

- Vendor "A" bid: $97.00
- Vendor "B" bid: $98.00
- Vendor "C" bid: $96.50

On the surface, it would seem that Vendor "C" offered the lowest price. And because of that, Vendor "C" was awarded the purchase order for 100 items.

> However, when I looked closer, I saw that both Vendors "A" and "B" quoted FOB destination, which meant that they would pay the shipping costs. But Vendor "C" quoted FOB origin, which meant the buyer paid the shipping costs.
>
> Once shipping costs were added, Vendor "C's" price per item was actually higher than both Vendors "A's" and "B's." Therefore, Vendor "C's" price quotation did not represent the best value for the buyer.

I call such an act of performing misdeeds, as used by the contracting official to favor Vendor "C" when awarding those purchase orders, "shenanigans." *(That's not a contracting term.)*

Definition: Merriam-webster.com defines shenanigans as:

1. a devious trick used especially for an underhand purpose
2a: tricky or questionable practices or conduct—usually used in plural
2b: high-spirited or mischievous activity—usually used in plural

Research and Development Contract

One reason that brand-name prescription drugs often have high prices when they first enter the market is because the manufacturer must try to recapture the costs incurred for having done the research and development (R&D) which led to the creation of the product. That certainly makes sense. A single pill might not cost much to produce but it took quite a bit of experimental effort to get the pill to do what it does—and get approval from the Food and Drug Administration (FDA). As we all know, the cost of the medication often (but not always) becomes much cheaper once the same type of medication is later released in a generic form by other manufacturers that did not have to invest in the R&D time and expense. As consumers, we sometimes conclude that the more expensive name brand is still more effective than the generic version, but it's nice to have options. Some insurance companies, however, won't cover the cost of the name brand medication if the generic version is available.

An example of the use of R&D contracts can be found on the U.S. Department of Health and Human Services National Institutes of Health website, pertaining to the National Institute of Allergy and Infectious Diseases.

(See: http://www.niaid.nih.gov/researchfunding/contract/pages/about.aspx.)

It reads, in part:

> About NIAID Research and Development Contracts
>
> The National Institute of Allergy and Infectious Diseases (NIAID), Office of Acquisitions (OA) supports the Institute's mission through planning, soliciting, negotiating, awarding, and administering biomedical and behavioral Research and Development (R&D) contracts, contracts for the

direct support of R&D, station support contracts, and simplified acquisitions.

NIAID OA uses R&D contracts to address critical needs, such as the acquisition of clinical trials, vaccine development, statistical and data coordinating centers, animal models, and maintaining reagent and specimen repositories.

R&D contracts do not include grants and cooperative agreements.

Overview of R&D Contracting Process

Concept Review: NIH Scientific Peer Review regulations require peer review and approval of all biomedical and behavioral R&D project Concepts and proposals before contract award. Peer review of R&D project concepts evaluates the basic purpose, scope, and objectives of the projects and establishes relevance, priority, and need to accomplish NIH objectives. After the peer review and approval of project concept, the Office of Acquisitions works with NIAID program staff to create a solicitation.

Solicitation: The solicitation contains all the elements necessary for prospective offerors to submit a proposal. It includes the following: schedule, contract clauses, lists of documents, exhibits, and other attachments, representations and instructions, evaluation factors for award.

Prospective offerors should carefully review each element of the solicitation to ensure that they understand the requirements and are able to fully respond. Solicitations are advertised in FedBizOpps and the NIH Guide to Grants and Contracts. See NIAID's Requests for Proposals list.

Factually, the federal government (and others) sometimes awards contracts and/or provides funds through other legal means so that contractors may perform R&D to manufacture or create items. The DoD is the biggest U.S. Government investor in R&D, mainly because it has such a large budget.

The Congressional Research Service completed a fascinating 27-page report on April 30, 2015, titled *Defense Acquisitions: How and Where DoD Spends Its Contracting Dollars.*

(See: https://www.fas.org/sgp/crs/natsec/R44010.pdf.)

Listed here are just a few highlights:

The Department of Defense (DOD) has long relied on contractors to provide the U.S. military with a wide range of goods and services, including weapons, food, uniforms, and operational support. Without contractor support, the United States would be currently unable to arm and field an effective fighting force. Understanding costs and trends associated with contractor support could provide Congress more information upon which to make budget decisions and weigh the relative costs and benefits of different military operations—including contingency operations and maintaining bases around the world.

Obligations occur when agencies enter into contracts, employ personnel, or otherwise commit to spending money. The federal government tracks money obligated on federal contracts through a database called the Federal Procurement Data System-Next Generation (FPDS). There is no public database that tracks DOD contract outlays (money spent) as comprehensively as obligations.

In FY2014, the U.S. federal government obligated $445 billion for contracts for the acquisition of goods, services, and research and development. The $445 billion obligated on contracts was equal to approximately 13% of FY2014 federal budget outlays of $3.5 trillion.... In FY2014, DOD obligated more money on federal contracts ($284 billion) than all other federal agencies combined. DOD's obligations were equal to 8% of federal spending.

In the early 1960s, the federal government funded approximately twice as much R&D as U.S. industry and thus played a substantial role in driving U.S. and global technology pathways. Today, U.S. industry funds more than twice as much R&D as the federal government. This transformation has had, and continues to have, implications for federal R&D strategy and management and for the efficacy of the DOD acquisition system. As one general officer stated, whereas the military used to go to industry and tell them to create a technology to meet a requirement, increasingly the military is going to industry and asking them to adapt an existing commercial technology to military requirements.

The United States remains the world's single largest funder of R&D, spending more than the next two highest funders combined (China and Japan) in 2012.

In FY2014, 45% of total DOD contract obligations were for services, 45% for goods, and 10% for research and development (R&D). This is in contrast to the rest of the federal government (excluding DOD), which obligated a significantly larger portion of contracting dollars on services (68%) than on goods (22%) or research and development (9%).

Research and Development contracting is but a portion of overall DOD investment in developing technology. For example, more than half of DOD's basic research budget is spent at universities and represents the major contribution of funds in some areas of science and technology.

Despite increased spending on R&D from FY2000 to FY2007, adjusted for inflation, DOD obligated less money on R&D contracts in FY2014 ($28 billion) than it invested more than 15 years earlier ($31 billion in FY1998). In contrast, over the same period, DOD obligations to acquire both goods and services are substantially higher than they were 15 years ago.

Sole Source Contract

FAR Part 6 provides definitions and requirements for awarding contracts. Sometimes federal contracts are awarded without competition if the customer has a need and only one source can provide what is needed. It's hard to imagine that only one source can provide what is needed but sometimes that is the case (especially within the DoD).

FAR 6.302-1 states, "When the supplies or services required by the agency are available from only one responsible source, or, for DoD, NASA, and the Coast Guard, from only one or a limited number of responsible sources, and no other type of supplies or services will satisfy agency requirements, full and open competition need not be provided for." An example might be if a particular name brand is needed.

> ### WAR STORY 1.8
>
> I reviewed a contract that was awarded to a company without competition because the company was said to be the "sole source" for the product. But when I flipped through the pages inside the contract file, I found the contracting officer's notes and some website printouts indicating two other vendors could have provided the same product. When I asked the contracting officer why she awarded the contract as a sole source contract, she said her supervisor instructed her to award the contract to a specific company. She added that her boss assigned her to award the contract after another contracting officer was previously assigned responsibilities for awarding that same contract, but refused to follow her boss's (illegal) demands.
>
> I next interviewed the contracting officer who was originally assigned responsibilities for awarding the contract. She said her supervisor ordered her to award the contract to a specified source, but she refused. Her supervisor then threatened to have her demoted for not following instructions. The honest contracting officer still refused. So her supervisor reassigned responsibilities to another contracting officer who would do what she was told.

Urgent Need Contract

FAR 6.302-2 describes when contracts can be awarded without competition if there is an "unusual and compelling urgency." The FAR reads, "When the agency's need for the supplies or services is of such an unusual and compelling urgency that the Government would be seriously injured unless the agency is permitted to limit the number of sources from which it solicits bids or proposals, full and open competition need not be provided for." Obviously, during times of war or during natural disasters, there is not time to advertise needs and review and evaluate proposals when items are desperately needed.

> ### WAR STORY 1.9
>
> I knew one commander in a military unit who always wanted things done "now." In my personal and professional life, I'm pretty guilty of that myself. In fact, I have a low tolerance for people that for no valid reason delay

accomplishing things that could be accomplished. While reviewing one contract file, I saw the contract was awarded without competition and the reasoning provided was because there was an unusual and compelling urgency.

However, I learned that there was no real urgency except that the commander (as usual) wanted it done "now." The government contracting officer was not supposed to allow the commander's rank to take precedent over established federal rules in the FAR. In fact, by law, the contracting officer was supposed to follow the rules of FAR to the letter.

But in the real world, people want to keep their jobs, make their bosses happy, and get promoted. So the rules went out the window! I later learned that the commander also insisted that the contract be awarded to a specified contractor and the contracting officer was instructed to find a way to make it happen. The contracting officer improvised, swallowed his integrity, and awarded the contract to the contractor that his superior wanted.

Set-Aside Contracts and the Small Business Administration (SBA)

There are many types of contracts used by the federal government and others. Percentages of contracts are specifically set aside for small businesses and businesses owned by women, minorities, disabled veterans, and others.

Small Business 8(a) Business Development Program

The SBA has established a development program to help small disadvantaged businesses compete in the marketplace. Some of the highlights from the SBA's website about the program are copied below.

(Source: https://www.sba.gov/contracting/government-contracting-programs/8a-business-development-program/about-8a-business-development-program.)

What is the 8(a) Business Development Program?

- The 8(a) Business Development Program is a business assistance program for small disadvantaged businesses. The 8(a) Program offers a broad scope of assistance to firms that are owned and controlled at least 51% by socially and economically disadvantaged individuals.
- The 8(a) Program is an essential instrument for helping socially and economically disadvantaged entrepreneurs gain access to the economic mainstream of American society. The program helps thousands of aspiring entrepreneurs to gain a foothold in government contracting.
- Participation in the program is divided into two phases over nine years: a four-year developmental stage and a five-year transition stage.

Benefits of the Program

- Participants can receive sole-source contracts, up to a ceiling of $4 million for goods and services and $6.5 million for manufacturing. While we help 8(a) firms build their competitive and institutional know-how, we also encourage you to participate in competitive acquisitions.
- 8(a) firms are also able to form joint ventures and teams to bid on contracts. This enhances the ability of 8(a) firms to perform larger prime contracts and overcome the effects of contract bundling, the combining of two or more contracts together into one large contract. Also, see the Mentor-Protégé Program for more information on allowing starting 8(a) companies to learn the ropes from other more experienced businesses.

Requirements and Goals of the 8(a) Business Development Program

The overall program goal is to graduate 8(a) firms that will go on to thrive in a competitive business environment. There are some requirements in place to help achieve this goal. Program goals require 8(a) firms to:

- Maintain a balance between their commercial and government business.
- Limit on the total dollar value of sole-source contracts that an individual participant can receive while in the program: $100 million or five times the value of its primary NAICS code.
- To make sure 8(a) firms are on track to accomplish their goals and are following requirements, the SBA district offices monitor and measure the progress of participants through:
    - Annual reviews
    - Business planning
    - Systematic evaluations
- In addition, 8(a) participants may take advantage of specialized business training, counseling, marketing assistance, and high-level executive development provided by the SBA and our resource partners. You can also be eligible for assistance in obtaining access to surplus government property and supplies, SBA-guaranteed loans, and bonding assistance for being involved in the program.

It's worth mentioning that sometimes companies are owned and operated by individuals in name only and improperly take advantage of set-aside programs. For example, a company may be owned (on paper) by a female, minority, or disabled veteran, but others are actually running the show. Chapter 3 describes such schemes in more detail.

WAR STORY 1.10

During one large-scale fraud investigation, I found evidence that a government contracting office was abusing a contract award provision which allowed contracts to be awarded to Alaska Native Corporations (ANCs) without competition. I've been told that ANCs even have contract award priority over minority- and female-owned companies and others. After doing some research, I found that many of the ANCs were large corporations which have subsidiaries all over the United States and that the subsidiaries "fall under the corporate umbrella."

The subsidiaries were awarded lots of high-dollar government contracts. In one case, I found that the ANC was actually run by a man that was no more Alaskan or Indian than I am. But because the company fell under the corporate umbrella of an Alaska Native Corporation, it got awarded contracts without competition. This particular set-aside program has frequently been subject to media and political scrutiny.

Author's Note: *For more information on ANC set asides, visit the SBA website* (https://www.sba.gov/offices/headquarters/ogc_and_bd/resources/11498).

As stated, very often programs are established with good intentions but are exploited. However, it should be emphasized that many of these set-aside programs are legitimate and help provide assistance to the disadvantaged. You certainly can't fault people for legally taking advantage of opportunities. In fact, we should applaud their efforts.

HUBZone Set-Asides

Contracts are also set aside for businesses located in economically deprived areas or Historically Underutilized Business Zones (aka: HUBZones). The Government Services Administration (GSA) has a list of frequently asked questions on its website about small business set-asides (see: http://www.gsa.gov/portal/content/113371). The U.S. SBA also has much information about small business contracting opportunities on its website (see https://www.sba.gov/contracting/resources-small-businesses.)

WAR STORY 1.11

About HUBZone set-asides, the SBA's website reads: "(The) program helps small businesses in urban and rural communities gain preferential access to federal procurement opportunities."

I investigated an entity which was reportedly located in a mapped HUBZone. The company had been awarded several government contracts. Upon my arrival at the business address, I found a vacant building. The company's real office was located in the suburbs.

Contractual Modifications and Change Orders

It's worth mentioning that most contracts are not written in stone and can be modified and/or changed if one or both parties agree, as long as any applicable contracting rules and regulations are followed. We've all read in the newspapers about contract price overruns and we've all seen roads being worked on that never seem to get finished. I've seen some roads get worked on and completed, and then they seem to start the same work all over again. Of course, the more time it takes, the more money the contractors usually make.

Sometimes contracts are awarded for a certain number of widgets and then the buyer realizes that more widgets are needed, so the buyer and seller agree to modify the contract and add more quantity. Sometimes the seller realizes they need more time to complete a project and if both sides agree, the contract can be changed or modified. When big dollars are involved, it's especially important to ensure that the i's are dotted and the t's are crossed and all changes and modifications are documented. If not, there can be major problems if a dispute goes to court or mediation.

WAR STORY 1.12

During a review of one federal contract file, I found a change order was added to the contract to add work that was totally unrelated to the work described in the original contract. Both the buyer and seller were happy. The only problem was that it was illegal to add the unrelated work because it should have been awarded in a separate contract.

A separate contract would have required the need to be advertised and for the bids received to be evaluated. In other words, it would have taken much longer to get the work awarded in a new contract. Perhaps, more importantly, the price would probably have been different and the contract would probably have been awarded to a completely different vendor.

That's actually why the contracting officials tried to include the unrelated work in the existing contract. They wanted their buddy that already had the contract to do the work and they did not want anyone else competing for the job. At least in the U.S. federal government, that's illegal. I'll add that proving criminal intent is not always easy to do.

It's worth noting that buyers (and/or contracting officials) and those providing the services/goods sometimes conspire from the onset to commit fraud, eliminate competition, or both, because they all know in advance that what was advertised as being needed and what they know will be needed are two different things.

For example, they may all know from the onset that more work and/or other requirements will be added after the contract is awarded. The vendor with this inside information will intentionally submit a low bid to ensure it underbids its competition because that vendor knows it will more than make up for it financially with the additional work—which the competitors know nothing about.

Terminating Contracts

It's also worth mentioning that contracts can be terminated if either side fails to do things specified in the contract. Most, if not all, federal contracts have termination for default (sometimes called T4D) provisions and/or termination for convenience (T4C) provisions. The latter may be used just because the buyer changed its mind. The contractor might still be reimbursed for expenses and work performed to date, but that may depend on other factors. If it's written in the contract that both agreed to, it's hard for one side to complain if and when provisions are implemented.

Paper and Electronic Procurements

Although written paper contracts are most common, many utilize electronic procurements as a method of advertising, accepting bid proposals, and awarding contracts. The theory is that this process is quicker, less costly, and could more easily detect fraud. There are certainly many merits to using electronic procurements. But buyers should never assume that just because an electronic system is used it will prevent all forms of fraud, corruption, and collusion.

For example, you can just picture the tech-savvy business owner who owns two or more companies and submits separate bids from different e-mail addresses competing for the same contract award. On the buyer's end, corrupt employees will always find ways to favor certain vendors. For example, a short window of advertising a need may be used and only a select few contractors may be given advance notice. Just using your experience and imagination will identify plenty of possible schemes that could be incorporated.

WAR STORY 1.13

One of my favorite contracting stories is one provided by a contracting official to me during an interview. We were talking about how the government often wastes money purchasing unnecessary things toward the end of the year because "if they don't spend all the money this year, they won't get the same (or more) the next year." The federal government uses a fiscal year (FY), which starts on October 1 and ends on September 30.

The contracting official said that she worked in a contracting office that was tasked to award numerous contracts on September 30. Since it looked like they wouldn't be able to get all the contracts awarded quickly enough, her supervisor came up with a solution. He set the clock back several hours and ordered all of his employees to keep working until all the contracts were awarded.

WAR STORY 1.14

In a similar situation of trying to beat the clock before the FY ran out, one office on the East Coast had too much money left over as the year end approached. So, they transferred their excess funds to a subsidiary on the West Coast so that they would have an extra 3 hours to keep spending.

When Contract Fraud and Corruption Schemes Occur

Contract fraud schemes and related methods of collusion and corruption vary. They can occur during any and/or all of the following time frames:

- Before a contract is awarded;
- During a contract award process;
- After a contract is awarded.

Four Categories of Contract Fraud, Collusion, and Corruption

To best understand contract fraud and the related collusion and corruption schemes, this book breaks the types of schemes into four categories:

- Corruption;
- Source selection and competition;
- Contractor and vendor performance;
- Contractor and vendor payments.

These four categories are described separately in the next four chapters.

2 Corruption in Contracting

Although I had 10 years of previous experience investigating street crimes prior to investigating white-collar offenses, I learned very quickly that uncovering instances of contract fraud which also involve corruption is not easily accomplished. Proving it beyond the reasonable doubt is even more difficult. In fact, it can sometimes seem a bit overwhelming. Consequently, contract fraud and related corruption very often go undetected and therefore never prosecuted.

Author's Note: *Many contract fraud schemes also involve corruption. Factually, many honest employers and supervisors often ignore even the most obvious red flags just because the questionable activity is performed by employees that have long tenure or good reputations. In other words, too often, wrongdoers are given the benefit of the doubt. We should remember that the red flags are still red regardless of who is involved or how long they've been employed with the same entity.*

When first investigating contract fraud, to some degree I often relied on contracting and other officials to explain how a particular procurement and inspection process worked or how it was supposed to work. Thankfully, a few of them took the time to explain procedures. But some contracting officials left me more confused than when I started. Sometimes I think their misleading or vague replies were intentional.

Author's Note: *When investigating contract fraud, if you come across too many instances of what appears to be stupidity, start also thinking about corruption.*

> ### WAR STORY 2.1
>
> While investigating a vendor's false submission of test samples to a government laboratory, a government quality assurance inspector yelled at me. "You need to wake up and smell the coffee! That contractor is honest!"
>
> My first thoughts were, "Why is this lady being so protective of a government contractor and why the hell does she think she can yell at a federal agent?!"
>
> In the end, I proved that the government quality assurance inspector helped facilitate the vendor's repeated submission of false samples to a government laboratory for testing. She was supposed to personally obtain the

Corruption in Contracting 29

test samples, maintain their chain of custody, and ship the samples to a government laboratory for testing. Instead, she allowed the contractor to gather the samples unsupervised and to mail the samples to the laboratory for testing. She even provided the contractor with the government prepaid postage stamps! The government quality assurance inspector benefitted by being able to go home early (perhaps to smell some coffee).

WAR STORY 2.2

One time, I found that some U.S. military officers were actually doing work on a government contract for which a vendor was awarded a multimillion-dollar government contract to do. Predictably, some of the military service members were furious that they had to take time away from their own jobs to do work that the vendor was being paid millions of dollars to do. How could that happen? A high-ranking government officer in their chain of command instructed his subordinates to help the company get the job done. The high-ranking officer was pals with the owner of the company.

Players in Contract Fraud and Corruption Schemes

Anyone involved in the process of a contract award (directly or indirectly) can commit, or cause to be committed, contract fraud schemes and/or be involved in related corrupt practices. There are two sides of the fence: buyers and sellers. Buyers are responsible for the source selection and providing funds. Sellers provide (or sell) what the buyer wants and get paid. Regarding procurements and acquisitions, buyers and sellers are more or less supposed to be on opposite sides of the fence. But some people are improperly (or too frequently) on the other side. Sometimes they pivot between both sides. Contract fraud often involves corruption, but not always. However, the players' goal is always about obtaining money and/or something of value.

WAR STORY 2.3

During the later part of my federal law enforcement career, I was assigned to investigate a major contract fraud case along with a senior federal agent from another well-known federal investigative agency. That other agent, who I'll call Agent Cocky, had a great deal of experience conducting investigations but had never before investigated federal contracts. I think Agent Cocky thought the FAR (described in Chapter 1) was "a long, long way to run, that would lead us back to doh, oh, oh, oh..."

> Agent Cocky was assigned to his agency's public corruption squad and even though he didn't understand government contracting procedures, he insisted that our main focus must be on finding bribe money. In fact, the assigned federal criminal prosecutor, who I'll call Doc, also had never investigated a contract fraud case before and he agreed with Agent Cocky.
>
> Although there was apparent favoritism in the contract award process, Doc and Agent Cocky focused most of their efforts on finding bribe money. I agreed that we should search for bribe payments but I knew we also had to determine if any contract rules had been violated and by whom. Doc and Agent Cocky didn't want to invest any time into that. They wanted to look for money. Do you know why? Because looking for money is much easier than reviewing and dissecting the many documents associated with a major procurement. If they could prove that a government contracting official received funds from the contractor, that would pretty much end their investigation.
>
> But Doc and Agent Cocky never did find any money. Do you know why? Because no bribes, or anything else of value, were ever given to any contracting officials. So Doc and Agent Cocky closed their cases!
>
> There were still violations of federal law committed by several contracting and other high-ranking government officials, but none of those officials ever received a cent from the contractor.

Your takeaway points from that story are 1. Don't try to fit a square peg into a round hole. 2. Just because a particular crime did not occur does not mean that another crime didn't occur.

To successfully investigate and prosecute contract fraud, collusion, and related corruption, you must know and understand the schemes and how to investigate those types of offenses. By reading this book you are on your way to becoming familiar with both. Oh yeah, the trip to obtaining this knowledge will also be "a long, long way to run."

Author's Note: *This book does not include many legal definitions and/or list the many elements of crimes in all criminal statutes that might apply to contract fraud, collusion, and related corruption investigations. But some detailed descriptions are provided because of their importance. For legal definitions, please reference other sources which may expand upon and/or differ with the author's definitions and descriptions.*

Corruption

Corruption in contracting can take many forms. It always involves compromising one's integrity (*assuming one had integrity in the first place*) and acting in self-interest or in others' (not the buyers') interests. Most often, corruption involves an exchange, provision, and/or receipt of something of value from one person to another. The thing of value can take many forms, e.g. cash, cashier's checks, free use of condominiums, paid travel, tickets to sporting events, promises of future employment, etc. It involves at least one person doing something he or she is not supposed to do, or refraining from doing something he or she is supposed to do.

Author's Note: *Payments of bribes and gratuities are often disguised or laundered, making them difficult to trace. For example, in one of my cases, a corrupt contracting official confessed that a corrupt vendor paid for his daughter's wedding expenses. Investigators won't very often find checks payable directly from one bad guy to another—but sometimes they will.*

Author's Note: *When reviewing financial records, even-numbered dollar amounts such as $500.00, $1,000.00, $2,000.00, $2,500.00, $5,000.00, $10,000.00, etc. are red flags for bribes and kickbacks.*

Quid Pro Quo

Merriam-webster.com defines quid pro quo (a Latin phrase) as "something that is given to you or done for you in return for something you have given to or done for someone else." Other sources define it as "this for that" or "something for something." Quid pro quo is an important phrase for white-collar investigators to understand and remember when investigating corruption.

In War Story 2.3, I mentioned that Doc and Agent Cocky focused their limited investigative efforts on finding bribery payments. They didn't want to review contract files and they spent very little time reading the suspects' e-mails, even though we had legal possession of them. But let's say they found payments. True, that would be huge. But to prove the offense of bribery, they would still have to prove what was done in exchange for the money. If it could also be proven that the contracting officer intentionally avoided the required competition or tainted the bid evaluation process, that would certainly help establish what was done in exchange for any money received.

Perhaps Doc and Agent Cocky believed that if they couldn't find bribe money, the favoritism in the contract award process would not be worth pursuing. That might have been true for the criminal prosecutor. But my job as an investigator was not only to identify criminal wrongdoing, but also possible civil and administrative wrongdoing. If contracts were awarded with favoritism, that needed to be proven and stopped from reoccurring—even if nobody was charged with a criminal offense.

Author's Note: *To be thorough, those that investigate corruption in contracting and/or contract fraud must identify the corresponding scheme(s) that were performed. Only searching for bribe payments is not being thorough. In my opinion, that's being lazy and short sighted. Don't "think singular" by simply trying to solve or prove one case at a time. Instead, "think plural" and attempt to identify as much corruption, collusion, and/or contract fraud as possible. Very often this can be accomplished without much more work. By thinking plural, understanding the schemes, and utilizing the information and investigative guidance in this book, I believe you'll identify many more violations and catch more bad guys—sometimes like shooting fish in a barrel. Remember, always "think plural"!*

Although most of this chapter will provide interesting descriptions of the various contract fraud and collusion schemes, it is paramount that a better legal understanding of corruption is provided. The most common corruption offenses are described here.

Bribery

For the legal and probably most detailed description of the federal offense of bribery, please read U.S. Code (USC) 18 USC 201: Bribery of Public Officials and Witnesses (source: http://uscode.house.gov/browse/prelim@title18/part1&edition =prelim). A portion of the statute (minus the description relating to witnesses) is provided here.

Author's Note: *When reading the following description of bribery, notice the word "intent." It should also be noted that individual states also have their own laws for the offense of bribery and other corruption-related offenses.*

18 USC 201: Bribery of Public Officials and Witnesses

(b) Whoever-

(1) directly or indirectly, corruptly gives, offers or promises anything of value to any public official or person who has been selected to be a public official, or offers or promises any public official or any person who has been selected to be a public official to give anything of value to any other person or entity, with intent-
    (A) to influence any official act; or
    (B) to influence such public official or person who has been selected to be a public official to commit or aid in committing, or collude in, or allow, any fraud, or make opportunity for the commission of any fraud, on the United States; or
    (C) to induce such public official or such person who has been selected to be a public official to do or omit to do any act in violation of the lawful duty of such official or person;
(2) being a public official or person selected to be a public official, directly or indirectly, corruptly demands, seeks, receives, accepts, or agrees to receive or accept anything of value personally or for any other person or entity, in return for:
    (A) being influenced in the performance of any official act;
    (B) being influenced to commit or aid in committing, or to collude in, or allow, any fraud, or make opportunity for the commission of any fraud, on the United States; or
    (C) being induced to do or omit to do any act in violation of the official duty of such official or person;

... shall be fined under this title for not more than three times the monetary equivalent of the thing of value, whichever is greater, or imprisoned for not more than 15 years, or both, and may be disqualified from holding any office of honor, trust, or profit under the United States.

Gratuities

Illegal gratuities are essentially the same as bribery except that the element of intent does not have to be proven. Gratuities may be rewards for action already taken or to be taken in the future. *You probably thought of some politicians immediately after reading that.*

Kickbacks

Kickbacks are essentially provided by contractors or business owners and/or their employees or representatives in the form of money or other things of value, in exchange for referrals and/or business in which the payer of the kickback (or their entity) profits or will profit in the future.

Legal-dictionary.thefreedictionary.com provides the following description of kickbacks:

> The seller's return of part of the purchase price of an item to a buyer or buyer's representative for the purpose of inducing a purchase or improperly influencing future purchases.
>
> Under federal law kickbacks involving government officials or funds provided by the government are illegal.
>
> Kickbacks between a contractor and a contractor and a government official or government employee are prosecuted under the federal Bribery statute (18 USC 201).
>
> Kickbacks between private contractors working under a federal contract are prosecuted under 41 USC 51–58, otherwise known as the Anti Kickback Enforcement Act of 1986.
>
> Kickbacks to employees or officials of foreign governments are prohibited under the Foreign Corrupt Practices Act of 1977 (15 USC 78dd).
>
> Most states have commercial bribery statutes prohibiting various forms of kickbacks.

Conflicts of Interest

A conflict of interest might be described as "A situation in which a person is in a position to derive personal benefit from actions or decisions made in their official capacity" (source: http://www.oxforddictionaries.com/). For the federal law definition, see 18 USC 208.

Case Samples of Corruption in Contracting
OPERATION ILL WIND

Operation Ill Wind was a joint federal investigation conducted by the Federal Bureau of Investigation (FBI) and the Naval Criminal Investigative Service (NCIS). *(Actually, back then, the NCIS was called the Naval Investigative Service (NIS))*. The investigation started in 1986 and lasted for 3 years. In the end, forty-two Washington consultants, seven military contractors, and nine government employees were convicted.

Those convicted included the U.S. Assistant Secretary of the Navy (for receiving hundreds of thousands of dollars in bribes), the Deputy Assistant Secretary of the Navy (for accepting illegal gratuity and theft and conversion of government property), and the Deputy Assistant Secretary of the Air Force (for accepting bribes and conspiracy to defraud the government). This scandal led to the 1988 passage of the Procurement Integrity Act.

The Procurement Integrity Act

Prohibits the release of source selection and contractor bid or proposal information. Also, a former employee who has served in certain positions on a procurement action or contract in excess of $10 million is barred for 1 year from receiving compensation as an employee or consultant from that contractor (48 CFR 3.104-1-11). The post-employment restrictions on receiving compensation are in addition to the post-employment restrictions of 18 USC 207.

(Source: http://www.justice.gov/jmd/procurement-integrity.)

Author's Note: *The Procurement Integrity Act also regulates pay that contracting officials can receive for 1 year after they leave federal service and makes it illegal for them to provide bid and proposal information to their new employers. For additional information, see 41 U.S. Code 2101-2017 (penalties can be criminal and/or civil).*

WAR STORY 2.4

As a federal agent, I reviewed several government contracts which were hurriedly awarded. In one of the contracts, a high-ranking general (I'll call him General Ballsy) requested the need for a somewhat unique service while he was on active duty. A few months later, the general retired from federal service and became the co-owner of a new company.

Another co-owner of the new company then asked the government to award the new company a multimillion-dollar sole source contract (without competition) to provide the same service that General Ballsy (while on active duty) started the ball rolling on and obligated funds for while he was on active duty. Did General Ballsy get awarded the contract? As former Alaska Governor Sarah Palin would say, "You betcha!"

WAR STORY 2.5

While conducting a bribery investigation, I interviewed a recently retired government contracting official and his wife while sitting at their dining room table. He had been retired for slightly more than 1 year. Early in the interview, the wife took her high blood pressure medication. After the retired contracting official confessed to accepting the bribes that I already knew about, I asked if either of them received anything else of value from any other contractors. The wife said that one contractor still paid for her high blood pressure medication!

Vice President Spiro Agnew Accepted Bribes for Contracts

U.S. Vice President Spiro Agnew resigned on October 10, 1973, and then pled no contest to criminal charges of tax evasion. The plea was negotiated after a federal investigation found evidence that Agnew, while previously serving as an executive for the state of Maryland and as the Governor of Maryland, accepted over $100,000 in bribes in exchange for state contracts awarded. It was reported that the payments continued while Agnew served as vice president.

The Darleen Druyun and U.S. Air Force Contracting Scandal

In October 2004, Principal Deputy Undersecretary of the Air Force for Acquisition, Darleen Druyun, pled guilty to inflating the price of a U.S. Air Force aircraft contract to favor her future employer (Boeing). She reportedly later took a job with Boeing with an annual salary of $250,000 and a $50,000 signing bonus. Boeing reportedly paid a $615 million fine for its involvement.

The U.S. Air Force Thunderbirds $50 Million Contract Scandal

WAR STORY 2.6

On the heels of the Druyun Air Force contracting scandal, in 2006, while serving as a federal special agent for the DoD, I received a complaint from a losing bidder about favoritism in the contract award decision process used to award a multimillion-dollar Air Force contract to a recently retired four-star Air Force general's brand new company. I'll call him General Bly (a fictitious name).

After reviewing that and other Air Force contract files, along with other evidence obtained, it was obvious to me that many of the contract fraud schemes (described in this book) took place. The alleged wrongdoing involved several military and civilian contracting officials, some members of the U.S. Air Force Air Demonstration Team (the Thunderbirds), and several Air Force officers—including high ranking generals.

Early in the investigation, I was instructed by my superiors and the criminal prosecutor to stop conducting interviews and to stop reviewing other Air Force contracts. My first-line superior actually ordered me to close my case! But I refused to comply with those instructions. It would be an understatement to say that because of my persistence my life was made miserable.

During my 18-month investigation (while working about 70 hours a week), I obtained evidence indicating that the suspects who were employed by the government should have been considered for criminal prosecution and that the Air Force personnel listed as suspects (including several generals) should have been considered for military court martials. Needless to say, that would have resulted in more than a black eye for the Air Force.

In January 2008, after completing my final report (almost 275 pages, with supportive report documentation that filled a couple boxes), my report was whittled down by supervisory personnel to about 250 pages. And my report had critical information removed. Consequently, the full truth never became known. In fact, my original draft report emphasized that the investigation was not yet complete because additional interviews needed to be conducted and some people needed to be re-interviewed. That important piece of information was completely removed from my report. The deletion led readers to incorrectly conclude that the investigation was complete.

Even with the information that remained in my report, the case received national news media coverage and the Air Force still received a black eye of sorts. But in comparison, I received the equivalent of getting the crap kicked out of me.

My office was closed and the only official government place I had left to work from was my government car, and my bosses would not find or authorize any other place for me to work from. In contrast, many of my bosses got promotions and awards, and some got cash bonuses. In fact, a national newspaper reported that two of them received presidential awards for their job performance!

Author's Note: *The final January 2008 report (or what remained of it after the removal of information) was publically released in April 2008. A partially redacted version of the remaining 250-page report is available for review online, along with many related news articles.*

For more information on that case, search the internet using the key words "$50 million Thunderbirds Air Force Scandal." Just so you know, my name is not mentioned anywhere. If you do the research, you'll see reference to a second federal investigative agency participating in the investigation. Factually, they did little work and closed their case very early on. I continued investigating long after they quit and that's when most of the interviews were conducted and evidence

> compiled. This can be proven by checking the dates the activity was completed. While conducting the investigation, I didn't know that all the facts would never be known. Frankly, that would not have stopped me. As investigators, we only have control over what we do, not what others do. But it still irks me that those who hindered and/or impeded the investigation were actually rewarded. For a little more information about this case, see War Story 5.5. However, to CYA, it must be emphasized that all people are innocent unless proven guilty.

Thousands of other cases have been proven in which a contracting process was compromised due to corruption. In many countries outside the United States, payoffs and kickbacks are just the normal way of doing business. The Foreign Corrupt Trade Practices Act (FCPA) of 1977 describes the do's and don'ts about making and accepting things of value to assist in obtaining or retaining business. A description of the FCPA is provided here from the Department of Justice's website.

Foreign Corrupt Trade Practices Act

> The Foreign Corrupt Trade Practices Act (FCPA) of 1977, as amended, 15 USC 78dd-1, et seq (FCPA), was enacted for the purpose of making it unlawful for certain classes of persons and entities to make payments to foreign government officials to assist in obtaining or retaining business. Specifically, the anti-bribery provisions of the FCPA prohibit the willful use of mails or any means of instrumentally of interstate commerce corruptly in furtherance of any offer, payment, promise to pay, or authorization of the payment of money or anything of value to any person, while knowing that all or a portion of such money or thing of value will be offered, given or promised, directly or indirectly, to a foreign official to influence the foreign official in his or her official capacity, induce the foreign official to do or omit to do an act in violation of his or her lawful duty, or to secure any improper advantage in order to assist in obtaining or retaining business for or with, or directing business to, any person.
>
> Since 1977, the anti-bribery provisions of the FCPA have applied to all U.S. Persons and certain foreign issuers of securities. With the enactment of certain amendments in 1998, the anti-bribery provisions of the FCPA now also apply to foreign firms and persons who cause, directly or through agents, an act in furtherance of such a corrupt payment to take place within the territory of the United States.
>
> The FCPA also requires companies whose securities are listed in the United States to meet its accounting provisions. See 15 USC 78m. These accounting provisions, which were designed to operate in tandem with the anti-bribery provisions of the FCPA, require corporations covered by the provisions to (a) make and keep books and records that accurately and fairly

reflect the transactions of the corporation and (b) devise and maintain an adequate system of internal accounting controls...

(Source: https://www.justice.gov/criminal-fraud/statutes-regulations.)

Many companies and corporations take the FCPA very seriously and many provide periodic training for their employees to ensure they do not violate it.

You'll recall that during the recent financial crises, many financial institutions were considered "too big to fail" and many corporate leaders got off the hook for acting irresponsibly while the corporations paid hefty fines. In response, the Department of Justice (DoJ) took action in September 2015 to ensure that in future cases, corporate executives and others also be held responsible criminally and/or civilly for their actions.

The Yates Memo

On September 9, 2015, Deputy Attorney General Sally Q. Yates signed a seven-page memorandum that was sent to all U.S. Attorneys' offices nationwide (criminal and civil) and to the FBI and others with the subject "Individual Accountability for Corporate Wrongdoing."

The memorandum includes:

> One of the most effective ways to combat corporate misconduct is by seeking accountability from the individuals who perpetrated the wrongdoing. Such accountability is important for several reasons:
>
> - it deters future illegal activity,
> - it incentivizes changes in corporate behavior,
> - it ensures that the proper parties are held responsible for their actions,
> - and it promotes the public's confidence in our justice system.
>
> ... Six key steps to strengthen our pursuit of individual corporate wrongdoing...
>
> (1) in order to qualify for any cooperation credit, corporations must provide to the Department all relevant facts relating to the individuals responsible for the misconduct;
> (2) criminal and civil corporate investigations should focus on individuals from the inception of the investigation;
> (3) criminal and civil attorneys handling corporate investigations should be in routine communication with one another;
> (4) absent extraordinary circumstances or approved departmental policy, the Department will not release culpable individuals from civil or criminal liability when resolving a matter with a corporation;
> (5) department attorneys should not resolve matters with a corporation without a clear plan to resolve related individual cases, and should memorialize any declinations as to individuals in such cases; and

(6) civil attorneys should consistently focus on individuals as well as the company and evaluate whether to bring suit against an individual based on considerations beyond that individual's ability to pay…

… The guidance in this memo will apply to all future investigations of corporate wrongdoing. It will also apply to those matters pending as of the date of this memo, to the extent it is practicable to do so…

… We are making these changes because we believe they will maximize our ability to deter misconduct and to hold those who engage in it accountable…

(Source: https://www.justice.gov/dag/file/769036/download.)

In short, at least as far as corporate investigations go, the DoJ is now required to conduct thorough and complete criminal and civil investigations—simultaneously—from the onset to identify all wrongdoers and hold all of them accountable (even if they have no money). That guidance is certainly an improvement. However, you will see that this book teaches how to conduct much more thorough and complete investigations.

The next chapter describes source selection and competition schemes.

3 Source Selection and Competition Schemes

This chapter describes schemes that often determine which vendors are selected by buyers and contracting officials; the services, goods, supplies, or other needs that the vendors will often be responsible for providing; and ultimately the money which the selected vendors will receive in return for providing what was required by the contract(s).

Author's Note: *In the following descriptions, I'll often use the words vendor and contractor interchangeably, which also mean sellers, suppliers, and others that submit bids/proposals and/or are awarded contracts or other orders.*

Author's Note: *Keep in mind that many investigations in which the following schemes are utilized may also involve corruption and other schemes described in this chapter and other chapters. You don't want to have tunnel vision when investigating contract fraud. Many different schemes may have been utilized by the "bad guys," and initially you might only be scratching the surface. It's been my experience that contracting officials are often very protective of each other. Sometimes it's simply because they've developed close friendships. Sometimes it's because they too are involved in wrongdoing and of course many share the opinion of "Nobody likes a rat." It's worth noting (especially for any contracting officials reading this book) that most contracting officials are honest.*

The source selection and competition schemes listed as follows are divided into two categories: Contractor and Vendor Schemes and Buyer Schemes.

Contractor and Vendor Schemes

Bid-Rigging

Bid Rotation

Bid rotation takes place when two or more vendors discuss and agree with each other in advance on the dollar amounts they will offer on bids or proposals for the same contract(s), and then actually submit those agreed-upon bids or proposals.

By submitting previously agreed-upon bid prices, the vendors increase the likelihood that a particular participating vendor will be selected (usually because their price is the lowest). Typically, the conspiring bidders alternate or rotate being the low bidder. Alternating which vendor bids the lowest reduces the chance of detection over time. After all, if the same vendor kept getting awarded all the contracts, that might raise some red flags.

Another benefit for those that participate in these schemes on a regular basis (unless they get caught) is that all of the participants will have steady work. It's not uncommon for the winning bidders to subcontract with or split awarded contracts with one or more of the other bid riggers. Also, by ensuring that the offered prices are similar, the buyer or contracting official is more likely to deem their prices to be "reasonable" because the buyer will often assume the vendors' proposals were compiled independently of each other.

In federal contracting, another (improper) advantage for the vendors involved in the bid rigging is that having several vendors bidding similar prices may negate the requirement for the winning bidder to have to certify to their cost and pricing data. As described earlier, contract awarding rules often dictate that if there is adequate competition and price comparability, the certification of cost and pricing data may not be required. Not requiring the vendor to certify to their pricing allows the vendor to not have to provide documentation to support their prices and costs.

In such cases, it's possible that the bid prices offered are all artificially inflated to begin with. But because two or more vendors offered similar prices, many buyers and contracting officials will assume the vendors' prices are the marketplace norm for such services, supplies, or goods.

WAR STORY 3.1

In the early 1980s, several vendors across the United States in the clothing and textile industry conspired to submit mutually agreed-upon bid prices for several U.S. military contracts worth hundreds of thousands of dollars each (and sometimes worth millions).

To ensure all the vendors got steady work, the corrupt vendors alternated which vendors would submit the lowest bids. To guarantee that the scheme worked, they also paid bribes to the contracting officers that received their bids and awarded the contracts. Taking it a step further, the vendors sometimes paid bribes or gave gratuities to the government quality assurance inspectors after the contracts were awarded. They all won—until they got caught.

Complementary Bidding

Complementary bidding is similar to and often the same as collusive bidding. Perhaps the main difference is that sometimes a vendor convinces a second vendor to submit a "complementary bid" for a contract that the second bidder doesn't actually want to be awarded. The second bid just gives a better appearance of adequate competition and, usually, price comparability. For example, if an item actually only costs $50, but Vendor A wants to greatly increase its profit, it may submit a bid price of $100 per item. That bid price might seem way out of line. But if a second vendor submits a bid for $101 per item, then the price might appear to be reasonable.

> ## WAR STORY 3.2
>
> During an investigation, I reviewed a bid abstract which listed all the bidders and the bid prices they offered for a specific government contract. In that case, Vendor Shirty (a fictitious name) had been awarded the government contract and was suspected of providing inferior products. The products were military shirts. I noticed that Vendor Shirty did not offer the lowest but offered the second lowest bid price.
>
> While interviewing Vendor Shirty's president about the defective products, I asked him why his company was awarded the contract since it was not the lowest bidder. His response did not make sense to me. He said something like, "Vendor A was the low bidder. But they got awarded a different multimillion-dollar contract so they backed out of this one. After Vendor A declined the contract, we had no choice and had to go through with it."
>
> I thought his choice of words didn't fit a typical reaction by someone that had won a high-dollar contract. He said he "had no choice" and "had to go through with it." I thought a more typical choice of words would have been "We were ecstatic! We were so happy that we got awarded the contract!"
>
> I contacted a fellow federal agent (who I'll call Agent Greg) that I knew had previously investigated and arrested several vendors in the same industry. Agent Greg told me that he had previously charged Vendor A with bid rigging and for paying bribes. He said one of Vendor A's executives shot himself after being confronted by the investigators!
>
> Come to find out, Vendor A was charged with bid rigging and bribery immediately after Vendor Shirty got awarded the multimillion-dollar shirt contract that I was investigating.
>
> So in my opinion, it all fit like a glove. The president of Vendor Shirty had "no choice but to go through with" the contract after submitting a complementary bid, because Vendor A backed out and Vendor Shirty's president knew the feds were investigating bid riggers. Vendor Shirty not only provided inferior products on the shirt contract but it appeared that the company also submitted a complementary bid which resulted in Vendor Shirty being awarded the contract.
>
> What I needed to determine next was: How many other times did Vendor Shirty submit bids on government contracts? What other vendors bid on those same contracts? What other government contracts had Vendor Shirty been awarded? What other vendors bid on those contracts? Have there been any complaints received about Vendor Shirty's performance on

any of their other contracts? Who were the contracting officers on those other contracts? Have those contracting officers ever been investigated for (or later convicted of) accepting bribes?

Fictitious Vendors

Fictitious vendors are often used during the pre-award process to submit bids under the names of entities that don't actually exist. Some vendors have been known to submit bids under fake company names for the same reasons previously described for collusive bidding and/or complementary bidding.

Red flags for detecting fictitious vendors and some bid riggers include:

- The mailing address is the same (or similar) as that of another vendor that also submitted a bid
- Postmarks on mailed bids are from the same city and state, even though the bidders are not located near each other
- The fax number is the same as that of another vendor that also submitted a bid
- The telephone number is the same (or the last digit is the only difference) as that of another vendor that also submitted a bid
- The point of contact's name is the same as that of another vendor that also submitted a bid
- The point of contact's voice is the same as that of another vendor that also submitted a bid
- The tax ID number is the same as that of another vendor that also submitted a bid
- The e-mail address is the same or similar as that of another vendor that also submitted a bid
- Signatures appear similar to those of another vendor that also submitted a bid
- The vendor bid has the same misspellings or the same exact wording as another vendor that also submitted a bid
- Bids are printed on the same type of (unique) paper
- The bidder has no website, physical structure, or verifiable information

WAR STORY 3.3

The owner of one vendor I investigated for submitting inferior products and shorting shipments on government contracts also owned a second company which was awarded government contracts from the same government agency. The owner used a storage room in the building next door as a business address for the second company. I learned that the second company was also providing inferior products and shorting shipments on government orders.

44   Chapter 3

Bid Suppression

In bid suppression schemes, one or more vendors that usually submit bids for certain types of contracts intentionally refrain from submitting bids so that another known vendor(s) will most likely get awarded the contract(s). Along those same lines, as described in War Story 3.2, sometimes a low bidder that would have won the contract will suddenly back out or refuse to accept the contract, which assures that the next low bidder gets awarded it. The new low bidder could then split the higher-priced contract work with the bidder that backed out, or just pay a kickback to the vendor that backed out.

Market Division

Some contractors that sell the same type of products or goods or provide the same type of services will conspire to split specified markets among themselves by not competing against each other—even though they could. For example, one vendor might only sell to companies or individuals east of the Mississippi River and the other vendor only sell to companies and individuals west of the Mississippi. They may both artificially inflate their prices and if asked to provide quotes in the other's area, they will either refuse to provide a quote or provide a ridiculously high price quote. This assures that both participating vendors will always get the highest prices.

Price Fixing

Price fixing occurs when vendors intentionally maintain, raise, or fix the prices of their goods and services at artificially inflated prices. For example, once while driving from Las Vegas to California, I stopped to get gasoline at a gas station just off the interstate. The two gas stations on the north side of the interstate (which most people saw first when traveling westbound on the interstate) sold gas for the same exact high price per gallon. However, a gas station on the south side of the interstate (slightly out of view of the other two) sold its gas for about 40 cents less per gallon. I made that trip to and from California dozens of times over the years and the gas price pattern always remained the same.

Author's Note: *The brightest red flag for detecting bid rigging is finding that each or many of the vendors that are awarded contracts split or subcontract the work with vendors that also submitted bids for the same contracts. I think you'll agree that shows that the vendors have close business ties and relationships.*

Author's Note: *To prove most bid rigging cases, you will need to review and analyze historic bids and proposals that were submitted and the awarded contracts which followed. Bid evaluations and ratings and other contract file documents will also have to be reviewed. Other investigative tools and techniques will need to be utilized as well. But interviews will often provide some of the most informative results. Federal investigators have been known to legally intercept and/or record phone and other conversations to* obtain evidence. In addition, legally obtained e-mail exchanges and/or telephone text messages often provide incredibly useful information and evidence. Planning such investigations is described in more detail in Chapter 11.

The Sherman Antitrust Act

Ohio Senator John Sherman was the principal author of the Sherman Antitrust Act, which was signed into law in 1890 under President Benjamin Harrison. The intent of the Act was/is to maintain fair and open competition in the marketplace and to help protect consumers. The Act's scope was subsequently expanded under The Clayton Antitrust Act, passed in 1914. The Robinson-Patman Act of 1936 amended the Clayton Act.

According to the Federal Trade Commission's website:

> The penalties for violating the Sherman Act can be severe. Although most enforcement actions are civil, the Sherman Act is also a criminal law, and individuals and businesses that violate it may be prosecuted by the Department of Justice. Criminal prosecutions are typically limited to intentional and clear violations such as when competitors fix prices or rig bids. The Sherman Act imposes criminal penalties of up to $100 million for a corporation and $1 million for an individual, along with up to 10 years in prison. Under federal law, the maximum fine may be increased to twice the amount the conspirators gained from the illegal acts or twice the money lost by the victims of the crime, if either of those amounts is over $100 million.
> (Source: https://www.ftc.gov/tips-advice/competition-guidance/guide-antitrust-laws/antitrust-laws.)

At the federal level, vendors involved in collusion and rigging bids are usually charged criminally under the Sherman Antitrust Act and very often with some additional offenses such as conspiracy, false statements, false claims, wire fraud, and/or mail fraud.

Consultants, Middlemen, and "10 Percenters"

While serving as a federal agent investigating several contracts that possibly involved corruption, I learned that sometimes vendors hire contractors and middlemen (sometimes called "10 percenters") that provide services to assist vendors to get awarded government contracts. The contracting facility I was investigating actually had a separate room designated for the middlemen to hang out in. The consultants got paid a percentage (usually 10 percent) of the total dollar amount of any contracts they helped get awarded to their vendors.

To my knowledge, there was/is no law that said the consultants couldn't represent more than one vendor at a time. In fact, they could very well have represented several vendors that were competing for the same contracts. The consultants' names usually won't appear on any of the bids or contracts but they certainly can play a big role in the process.

In fact, there are some legitimate (well-paid) consultants and companies that assist vendors put together their bids and proposals just because the government's procurement system is so complex.

These consultants have lots of "contacts" in the industry. Since they are not actual vendors, many buyers and contracting officials might rationalize accepting things of value (especially free lunches) from the consultants.

WAR STORY 3.4

I investigated one vendor (whom I'll call Queen, Inc.) for submitting false claims and paying bribes on government small purchase orders (under $25,000) for medical supplies. I learned that Queen had also recently been awarded a multimillion-dollar contract by the same government contracting directorate to supply hospital field beds.

Since I always try to find dots to connect, I suspected that the government contracting officer who awarded the multimillion-dollar contract probably also accepted bribes.

I checked Queen's business telephone records because I wanted to see if the vendor ever telephoned the contracting officer's home. I found no evidence of that but I did learn that Queen had hired a consultant (*a 10 percenter*) to assist in securing the hospital field bed contract.

I later checked the consultant's phone records and found that he telephoned the contracting officer's home early in the morning before the bids were to be opened for the multimillion field bed contract. Based on the number of minutes listed on the phone bill for that call, it appeared that the consultant and the contracting officer spoke for about 15 minutes.

It wasn't a crime for the consultant to speak to the contracting officer just before the bids were unsealed, but I thought of it as a bright red flag. It was also interesting that that one call was the only time the phone records showed that the consultant called the contracting officer's home. Yes, I checked the contracting officer's home phone records, but found no suspicious calls. I should note that this was before the existence of throw-away cell phones.

Curious about the background of this consultant, I asked others about him. One vendor said something like, "Oh yeah I know that guy! He was an all-star college basketball player destined to play for the NBA but he got caught accepting illegal payments after shaving points off one of his college games so gamblers could win their bets. His basketball career ended after that."

The takeaway from that story is that as a contract fraud investigator you should keep in mind that there may be "middlemen" that are directly and indirectly involved in the contract process before and after the contracts are awarded. Some of them might be legitimate business persons.

WAR STORY 3.5

A fellow federal agent that I often worked with (whom I'll call Agent Bub) worked a high-profile corruption-in-contracting case. Bub told me that while executing a search warrant on one of the facilities, he found stacks of hundred dollar bills. When he interviewed the contracting officer who had control of the area about the source of the cash, the contracting officer said something like, "I got the cash from my mother. She's a prostitute."

I guess the idiot assumed the experienced federal agents would just take his word for it and never interview the guy's mother, who just happened to be about 70 years old.

Agent Bub told me that the contracting officer later asked to call his own wife so he could tell her that he would be home late. The agent allowed the contracting officer to make the call while Bub openly listened to one side of the conversation. Toward the end of the call, the contracting officer said to his wife, "Don't forget to feed the bird."

After the call, Agent Bub said to the contracting official something like, "Hey wait a minute. What was that about feeding the bird?" When the agents later searched the contracting officer's house for bribe payments, there wasn't any bird. They later learned that "feed the bird" was the contracting officer's signal to his wife to start getting rid of evidence.

False Surety Bonds

Some contracts require vendors to be bonded to cover possible losses in the event that the vendor cannot complete the work or the contractor runs into financial or other difficulties which prevent the vendor from completing the project/work. Prior to the award of the contract(s), the vendor may have been required to provide proof of being bonded in the form of surety bonds. My research has found that such bonds may cost the vendor 3 to 5 percent of the total contract dollar amount. Incurring this expense will usually require the vendor's bid price to be higher because of having to pay for the bonding.

An unscrupulous vendor may provide false surety bonds and/or falsely certify that they are bonded. This generally only presents a problem for the buyer (and/or the vendor's suppliers or subcontractors) if the vendor can't complete the contract or experiences financial difficulties during the contract's performance. However, providing false surety bonds and/or certifications may allow a vendor to bid lower and get awarded contracts which they would not have otherwise received, causing honest competitors to potentially lose business they submitted bid proposals for. Contracting officers and/or buyers should do their own due diligence and ensure surety bonds are legitimate.

Red Flags for False Surety Bonds:

- The bond has no corporate seal;
- The bonding date does not correspond with the solicitation/contract date;
- The bond is handwritten;
- The bond is for less than the contract amount;
- Only a photocopy of the bond is available;
- The photocopy appears to have been altered.

False Ownership

As described in Chapter 1, very often percentages of contracts are set aside for small businesses and businesses owned by minorities, women, disabled veterans, and others. However, sometimes businesses list owners that fall into the set-aside categories but, in reality, those "owners" have little or nothing to do with running the company. By lying or misleading others about true ownership and/or who actually runs the company, some entities are awarded contracts they should not be.

False Location

As described in Chapter 1 and War Story 1.11, some federal contracts are set-aside for Historically Underutilized Business Zones (HUBZones). The Small Business Association (SBA) reports that "the program helps small businesses in urban and rural communities gain preferential access to federal procurement opportunities."

But sometimes the business addresses provided are false or misleading, allowing the entity(s) to get awarded contracts they would not have otherwise received. For more information on HubZones, visit the SBA website: https://www.sba.gov/contracting/government-contracting-programs/hubzone-program.

For more information about federal small business set-asides, visit the Government Service Administration website's frequently asked questions, http://www.gsa.gov/portal/content/113371, and the SBA's website, https://www.sba.gov/contracting/government-contracting-programs/8a-business-development-program.

Defective Pricing

In negotiated contracts with the federal government, the contractor may be required to provide their cost and pricing data. In other words, the contractor will be asked to provide proof or supportive documentation regarding their prices. For example, if the contractor is required to certify to their cost and pricing data, the contractor can't tell the government that their costs for material will be $100 per yard and then, after the contract is awarded, only pay the contractor $50 per yard. Well, perhaps they could, but the contract price would have to be modified to lower the dollar amount of the contract so the government wouldn't lose money. A successful criminal act of defective pricing could cause the customer/buyer to make more profit than they should have.

Buyer Schemes

Contracts Awarded without Required SBA Certificate of Competency

Contracting officials are responsible for ensuring that all requirements, including applicable clauses, are included in the final contracts signed by both parties. Sometimes, the solicitation requirements are incorporated into the contract. In those instances, the investigator will not only need to review the contract, but also the solicitation which preceded the contract (which is normally a good idea to review anyway). If a required clause is not included or, for the purpose of this discussion, intentionally excluded by the contracting officer, the contractor awarded the contract can't be required to abide by it.

As previously mentioned, the federal government requires that a certain percentage of contracts be set aside for small and disadvantaged businesses. To be considered eligible to participate in the program, a small business must be determined to be "competent" by the SBA. Once found to meet the requirements, the SBA will issue the company a "Certificate of Competency," commonly referred to as a CoC, which will allow the contractor to be considered eligible to be awarded a specific government contract.

One of the requirements is that the contractor must abide by the "limitations on subcontracting" requirements (described in detail in Chapter 1), which essentially require the contractor to incur at least a specified percentage of cost in performance of the contract. In short, the contractor can't just immediately subcontract out 100 percent of the work.

For more information about SBA CoCs, visit https://www.sba.gov/content/certificate-competency-program-0.

> **WAR STORY 3.6**
>
> While reviewing a federal contract file, I found that a contract was awarded to a small business that I'll call Company A. This was the first federal contract that Company A had ever been awarded. In fact, the contract file included printed e-mails which indicated that the contracting officer just about held the company owner's hand through the complex process of becoming approved by the SBA to be awarded federal contracts.
>
> But other witnesses told me that Company A didn't actually perform any of the work on the contract. Instead, the company just subcontracted out 100 percent of the job to another company that was not an approved government contractor.
>
> While reviewing the file, I learned that prior to the contract's award, the contracting officer's supervisor requested that the SBA issue a CoC on Company A, so the contract could be awarded to Company A.
>
> Although the contract was subsequently awarded to Company A, the contract file did not contain a copy of the CoC. I also noticed that the contract did not include the limitations on the subcontracting clause (FAR 52.219-14).

I knew that several contracting officials in that particular contracting office had a habit of intentionally not following contract award procedures, which enabled them to award contracts to favored vendors. So I went to the local SBA Office and inquired if a CoC had ever been issued on Company A for that contract. The SBA said that they did issue the COC, but that it wasn't issued until several months after the contract had already been awarded. The SBA corroborated that the limitations on the subcontracting clause was required to be in the contract if it was awarded as a small business set-aside.

Armed with a copy of the SBA's issued CoC, dated after the contract had been awarded, I went back to the contracting office to interview the contracting officer's supervisor.

I chose my series of questions carefully to "box-in" the supervisor with his own responses. The interview went something like this:

Me: Let me make sure I got this straight. A CoC was required to be issued on this small business set-aside before that contract could be awarded to Company A, correct?

Supervisor: *That's correct.*

Me: And when a small business set-aside contract is awarded, the company must complete a certain percentage of the work, is that correct?

Supervisor: *That's correct.*

Me: How does the contractor know that they can't just subcontract out 100 percent of the work? Is it because you include the "Limitations on Subcontracting" FAR clause (52.219-14) in the contract?

Supervisor: *That's correct.*

Me: Is that clause required to be in the contract?

Supervisor: *Yes, it is.*

Me: And a CoC must be approved by the SBA before the contract can be awarded, is that correct?

Supervisor: *That's correct.*

Me: Was it your job as a supervisor to review this contract before it was awarded?

Supervisor: *Yes, I reviewed this contract before it was awarded.*

Me: So why was this contract awarded, before a CoC was obtained from the SBA?

Supervisor: *Ahhh. Ahhh. I don't know.*

Me: Well here, let me show you the dates on the documents (*CoC and contract document dates shown*). See how the CoC is dated several months after the contract had already been awarded?

Supervisor: *I'll be darned.*
Me: And why did this contract not include the Limitations on Subcontracting clause?
Supervisor: *Ahhh. Ahhh. I don't know.*
Me: Take a look at the contract yourself. I don't see that required clause in there. Do you? (*Contract handed to supervisor to review*).
Supervisor: (*after reviewing contract*) *No, it's not in there, but it should have been. But the contractors know the rules. They know what they can and can't do.*
Me: Seriously? Company A never had a federal contract before and you're telling me that Company A knew all the rules?
Supervisor: *Listen, the requestor was in a hurry to get this contract awarded fast and we strive to keep the requestors happy.*
Me: So you don't follow the contract rules so you can make the requestors happy. Is that what you are telling me?
Supervisor: *We don't do it like this all the time.*

I later interviewed the contracting officer who actually awarded the contract and asked him similar questions. That interview went something like this:

Me: I noticed that this contract was awarded to Company A who never before had a federal contract and your e-mails reflect that you basically held their hand to show them how to become an approved contractor. After Company A got the contract, they subcontracted out all of the work to Company B. Can you explain why you awarded this contract to Company A?
Contracting Officer: *This whole contract was reverse engineered. I wanted to award the contract to a reputable company. But then a four-star general told me that I had to award the contract to Company B. Company B didn't want to be a government contractor so I asked Company A if they would accept the government contract and then subcontract the work to Company B. Company A said they wanted 10 percent of the contract price so I bumped up the price 10 percent to accommodate it.*
Me: But the Limitations on Subcontracting clause would prevent Company A from subcontracting the work to Company B, wouldn't it?
Contracting Officer: *I had to do what I was told to do. I've never done anything like this before. I was just following orders. That clause was intentionally not included in the contract.*

> **Me:** Did your supervisor know about all this?
> **Contracting Officer:** *He knew and he approved the contract award....*

The takeaway point from this story is that contracting officials can easily manipulate the contract award process in less traditional ways than are described in most contract fraud seminars.

After finding numerous other contracts in that same contracting office that were awarded with favoritism and failure to follow contracting rules, that same contracting supervisor said to me something like, "Those leaders have always been pushing their weight around here and telling us how to do our jobs. They never expected someone like you would come in here and piece everything together." I took that as a compliment.

It takes some time, but if you get really good at investigating contract fraud and corruption, you can really shock some people and uncover some big-time historical wrongdoing. Generally speaking (pun intended), the bad guys can't undo the paper trail they leave behind (especially contract documents and notes, as well as e-mails). But it will be your combined knowledge of contracting procedures and schemes, your interview skills, and your persistence that will pay the highest dividends.

Splitting Purchases

Splitting purchases is a scheme completed by the buyer's purchasing representative (usually an employee), who intentionally splits what could be one order into two or more orders. The reasons for doing this may vary.

One reason a buyer might corruptly split an order is to keep the total order's dollar amount under a certain dollar threshold which would have required either more formal competition (like having to award a contract instead of a simple purchase order). For example, the rules may allow a buyer to award small purchase orders for under $2,500 by just obtaining one telephone price quote. But if the orders are over $2,500, they may be required to obtain three price quotes (see War Story 1.6).

Another reason to (wrongfully) split orders might be to allow a certain buyer (contracting official) to continue to have authorization to make the award. For example, a particular buyer (or representative) may only be allowed to award orders/contracts under $100,001. So rather than pass a $300,000 need up the chain through proper channels for someone else to award a single contract, the buyer may split the order into three separate orders for $100,000 each. (*See paragraph early in Chapter 1 about the county mayor.*)

Another reason to split orders might be to award line items (or portions) on an individual order to a certain vendor and other line items (or portions) to another vendor.

Source Selection and Competition Schemes

Sometimes splitting orders can actually save the buyer time and/or allow the order to get awarded more quickly because the procedures to award smaller dollar orders may take less time to complete than higher dollar contracts. However, it may violate the buyer's contracting rules to split such orders. If nothing else, splitting orders is generally considered a red flag. An investigator should look for patterns of abuse with the same buyers repeatedly placing orders to the same vendors (perhaps at inflated prices) or making an obvious attempt to favor certain vendors over other qualified (and perhaps less expensive) vendors.

There is a strong possibility that the buyer who repeatedly splits orders is receiving or has received bribes, gratuities, or something else of value from the vendor(s) that they awarded the contracts/orders to. Sometimes it actually takes buyers more time and effort to split orders than to have placed one large order. If that's the case, you have to wonder why the heck they would waste their own time. My first guess is because they are receiving something illegal in return.

Release of Bid Information

A buyer's purchasing representative (usually an employee) could release bid information to a bidder before the bid closing time/date so that the favored bidder can underbid others' proposals.

In high-dollar procurements, sometimes "sealed bids" are required to be mailed in to the contracting office and the bids are supposed to all be opened at the same time in a controlled setting. But corrupt buyers have been known to secretly unseal bids received before the official bid opening and then share the inside information with favored bidders.

WAR STORY 3.7

While reviewing a buyer's small purchase order files, I analyzed the contracting official's method of documenting the three telephonic quotes he obtained to determine the low bidder. After reviewing about 50 files, I thought it odd that the third caller was always the low bidder. You would think that, once in a while, the first or second bidder would provide the lowest price quote. But that was never the case.

In my opinion, this indicated that the contracting official had provided the third vendor with the other vendors' price quotes, which allowed the third vendor to always underbid, sometimes by as little as 50 cents per item.

I later found evidence of the quid pro quo in the form of cash payments and cashier's checks paid by the third vendor to the contracting official.

I confronted the contracting official with the evidence of what he did in exchange for the bribe money. During the interview, I was adamant that he told the third vendor the prices that other vendors provided. The contracting official said he never once told the third vendor what the other vendors bid. I asked him to explain why that particular vendor was always called last and how the third vendor always managed to slightly underbid the competition.

The contracting official said something like, "After I got the first two price quotes, I called the third vendor and asked him to provide his quote. His quote was often higher than the competitors so I told him that if he really wanted the order, he'd have to lower his price. We continued this exchange until eventually his price beat the competition. But I never once told him what the other vendors bid."

In the contracting official's own mind, what he did made perfect sense. The only problem was that his actions were illegal.

Accepting Late Bid Proposals

A buyer's purchasing representative (usually an employee) might accept bids later than authorized and still consider the late bids for the contract award. That's a red flag but does not in and of itself prove a crime has been committed. Obviously, it's an indicator that perhaps the late bidder received inside information about the other bidders' prices. If the late bidder won the award, then you'd certainly have another red flag.

Changing of Bid Prices and Blank Bids

The use of white liquid correction fluid and inked cross-out marks and corrections on bid prices are both considered red flags. Historic cases have shown that sometimes corrupt bidders send in bids with no dollar amount listed in the bid price because they know the buyer (who they paid off) will fill it in with the winning bid price. Another red flag would be the bid price being written in a different color ink than the rest of the proposal, or everything being typed except the bid price, which is written in ink. That would indicate that perhaps the buyer may have filled in the price or provided the inside information to the winning bidder.

Reposting the Same Need

A buyer's purchasing representative (usually an employee) could cancel a request for a bid proposal after many bidders had provided their bids and then shortly afterward repost a second request for bids for the same need. Obviously, this would trouble the honest bidders that had already provided their best offers because the cancellation and reposting would be a red flag that their bid proposal information might have been shared with one or more other vendors.

Making Unnecessary Purchases

If a buyer or customer is receiving bribes/kickbacks or gratuities, they may place orders for goods or supplies that are not even necessary. It might be difficult to prove beyond a reasonable doubt that a buyer or contracting official is knowingly and intentionally placing unnecessary orders. When confronted, they'll probably provide seemingly valid excuses. But once you prove they illegally received something in return for the orders, it makes it a bit easier to prove other wrongdoing.

> ### WAR STORY 3.8
>
> In the case that I previously mentioned involving my buddy Agent Bub (War Story 3.5), a contracting officer (the one that told his wife to "feed the bird") continually ordered excessive amounts of wooden pallets for the government storage facility. The contracting officer had also received bribes from the vendor that supplied the pallets. Agent Bub later learned that the procuring activity was actual burning excess pallets so they could justify re-ordering more.

> ### WAR STORY 3.9
>
> In a nationwide scam, a vendor that supplied printer ink cartridges and toner to military bases regularly shipped double quantities of the ink and toner ordered. Sometimes they shipped toner that was never ordered at all. After each shipment, the vendor submitted invoices and received payments. One government employee told me that they seldom placed orders with the vendor but that the vendor kept on shipping (and billing for) more ink and toner. While in his office building, the employee showed me an entire room full of unopened boxes of toner which would have lasted a couple of decades. As I conducted more interviews, I learned that the vendor always sent the purchasing office large bags of chocolate candy with every order. The bags were huge, like the ones sold at discount warehouses.
>
> I mention this story under the category of *Competition and Source Selection* because I'm of the opinion that the bags of candy swayed the employees to make payment for the orders that were never made. The employees knew they had an entire room full of toner cartridges that would never be used, but they kept paying for them anyway—most probably because they kept receiving the huge bags of chocolate candy.

Excluding Qualified Bidders

Many of us have worked for supervisors or had school teachers that just nitpicked our writing over inconsequential details. Similarly, honest and good vendors sometimes have their bids *kicked to the curb* just because they didn't follow instructions to the tee. But in the fraud and corruption arena, a buyer's purchasing representative (usually an employee) could intentionally (and often unjustly) exclude a qualified bidder for the purpose of intentionally favoring another.

The bid evaluator(s) might even be able to justify providing poor ratings to exclude a particular vendor(s). The misdeeds can often only be detected by carefully examining and comparing all of the bids received and their evaluations and ratings.

As described in War Story 1.5, a fair evaluation of bids should not allow one vendor to be excluded for one fault and then allow another vendor to still be considered for the same fault. From experience, I learned that proving favoritism can sometimes only be done by identifying a series of inconsistencies in the evaluation process. The proof you obtain might be more along the lines of "death by a thousand cuts" rather than just one blow. Investigators, examiners, and auditors should make the time to carefully dissect the documentation of the bid evaluation process. It can be time-consuming, but very revealing.

Vague Specifications or Contract Requirements

War Story 1.3 illustrates how vague (or incorrect) specifications listed in an advertisement for a contractual need can affect which vendor gets awarded a contract. In that case, the most recent military specification was not listed in the advertisement (or the contract), which allowed a vendor to underbid its competition and provide a less expensive and inferior product.

In the buyer schemes previously described, the focus was most often on the buyer's purchasing representative (usually an employee). However, in large organizations, the purchasing representatives (contracting officials) are not usually the same individuals that generate or request the original need for the goods, supplies, or services. Someone else specified and requested that they wanted something. I'll call that original requesting person "the customer." Often the customer and the contracting official that eventually awards the order are located in two different offices or buildings (maybe even in different states or countries).

Sometimes the customer might request to purchase something that is vaguely described (not specific). This vague description may later be provided when the buyer advertises the need and requests bid proposals. But when the bids come in, the prices may vary greatly. If there is collusion or corruption involved, the intentionally vague description may allow a favored vendor that possesses inside information to underbid the competition and get awarded the contract because the favored vendor knows exactly what's wanted.

WAR STORY 3.10

A military general told a contracting officer that he wanted a vendor to provide a long-term service that would educate, entertain, and inspire people at military air shows. That's pretty darn vague. In response, the assigned contracting officer advertised a request for information (RFI). The RFI allowed possible interested vendors to provide descriptions of what they thought would accomplish the objectives. The vendors presented ideas that varied greatly. During my post-contract award investigation, I opined that some responses to the RFI were simply amazing and some were downright stupid (*not that my opinion mattered*).

After the contracting officer received and reviewed the responses, he conducted market research to determine if the prices were reasonable. He identified one similar service that was provided years before by another branch of military service. Based on his findings, the contracting officer advertised a formal request for bid proposals (RFP). The same vendors responded.

Evidence was later obtained that before the general even made his request known, he knew which vendor he wanted to provide the service. In fact, the general previously tried to have the contract awarded to that particular vendor without competition.

But the contracting office told the general that awarding such a high-dollar contract without competition would be illegal and that they were required by law to advertise the need so that there would be full and open competition. Needless to say, neither the general nor that favored vendor were very happy. Because of the required competition, that favored vendor was required to submit a detailed bid proposal for the contract, just like other vendors.

After the bids were received, many of the bid evaluators seemingly went through the motions and pretended they were being objective when deciding which vendor would get awarded the contract. A $50 million contract was subsequently awarded to the favored vendor, which the general wanted all along. Was that a coincidence? I don't think so, and the evidence obtained indicated it was not a coincidence.

Because the description of the service needed was vague, there was a great disparity between the vendors' proposed ideas and their prices. One capable vendor bid half as much (about $25 million) as the vendor that was awarded the contract (for $50 million). But the bid evaluators seemingly didn't seem to care about keeping costs down. (After all, it was only U.S. taxpayer money being spent, not their own.)

You may recall from Chapter 1 that FAR 15.402 requires that government contracting officers must ensure that contracts only be awarded if the prices are determined to be *fair and reasonable*. Because there was not "price comparability" in the bid submissions and the ideas and services proposed were completely different, I asked the contracting officer why he did not require the vendor to certify to its cost and pricing data.

I emphasized to the contracting officer that since the vendors' proposed concepts were so different, he was not comparing apples with apples in terms of the reasonableness of their prices. For example, if one contractor proposed flying a plane and one proposed people jumping on pogosticks, he couldn't compare their prices and determine they were similar.

> The contracting officer admitted that he had dropped the ball and should have required the vendor to certify to its cost and pricing data.
>
> This failure to ensure the contract award price was fair and reasonable and the failure to require that the awarded vendor certify to the accuracy of its costs had implications. It allowed the vendor to get paid whatever it wanted for anything billed for, just as long as the vendor didn't exceed the total cost of the contract. So why did the contracting officer drop the ball and award the contract to this more expensive vendor and not require the vendor to certify to its costs? He said that's what his superiors wanted him to do.

As you can see, many contract fraud schemes are caused or permitted to occur because other contract fraud schemes were first committed and/or because of corruption and even supervisory pressures. Sometimes, one scheme must occur before another one can.

To be most effective, a contract fraud investigator needs to know, understand, and/or at least be willing to research contract rules and regulations so that the investigator can detect and identify violations (or potential violations) and spot patterns. This knowledge and those findings will also allow the investigator to know what questions to ask during interviews. The most successful contract fraud investigators want to see the full picture and be willing to locate and put together all or most of the pieces of the puzzle.

Author's Note: *When one or a few of these schemes are found to have occurred, it's very often just the tip of the iceberg. Many will try to downplay findings and perhaps deem them to be isolated incidents. They are usually dead wrong, don't know what they are talking about, and/or may be involved in some illegal scheme(s) themselves.*

WAR STORY 3.11

Regarding War Story 3.10, as my investigation began to focus on some additional high-ranking generals, I started asking who the original customer was. I wanted to know who was responsible for making the very first request to obtain the services which would educate, entertain, and inspire people at military air shows.

Nobody I asked, including generals at the Pentagon, knew the answer to that question. They were spending $50 million of taxpayers' money and nobody knew who ordered it!

In fact, many people involved in the process said they didn't even like the idea and thought it was a complete waste of money! Some said the military branch actually had its own internal capabilities and resources to provide the service and could do it at much less cost than any of the bidders.

Even though I was ordered by my immediate supervisor to stop investigating this case, I persisted. (*Don't ya' love it?!*) The ensuing interviews I conducted, along with e-mails and other contract documentation reviewed, found evidence that the person who originally requested this service was a four-star general. A witness said that same general even allocated funds to start the process while he was on active duty. Less than 1 year after he retired from military service, that same general became part owner of the company that was awarded the $50 million contract to provide the same service.

In short: The evidence and witness statements indicated that a four-star general started the ball rolling that later led to the high-dollar contract while he was on active duty. Less than 1 year later, his new company got awarded a $50 million contract to provide the same service he initiated the process for while he was on active duty. Many people would call that a major conflict of interest.

Overly Specific Specifications or Contract Requirements

Sometimes the customer or buyer knows in advance which vendor they want to be awarded the contract, but are required to solicit competition. To ensure the favored vendor will get awarded the contract, the specifications or requirements will be written (tailored) so that only that particular vendor will be able to complete the requirements.

WAR STORY 3.12

When analyzing one U.S. military contract's requirements, I learned that the most important evaluating factor was called "strategic insight." I noticed that all but one of the bidders got terrible ratings for strategic insight. Frankly, I didn't know what the heck strategic insight meant, so I asked the contracting officer. He said it meant "knowledge of the U.S. military."

Well, it just so happened that the co-owner of the company that received high ratings for strategic insight was a retired four-star U.S. military general. None of the other vendors had retired military generals on their staff.

It did not seem to me that it was a coincidence that knowledge of the U.S. military was the most important factor and was given the most weight when determining which vendor would be awarded the contract. This vendor was the same one that U.S. military leaders previously wanted to award the contract to without competition. After they were forced to advertise the need, they wrote the requirements in such a way that they very much favored this particular vendor.

Surprisingly, while bids were being evaluated, a U.S. military unit volunteered that they could provide the service and save millions of tax dollars! The unit's leader suggested they be allowed to provide the service. But rather than cancel the solicitation and let that U.S. military unit do the work, the contracting officials made that military unit submit a bid! Never before in my life had I seen a government unit or organization submit a formal bid proposal to do work!

If that wasn't bad enough—guess what kind of rating the bid evaluators gave the U.S. military unit on their strategic insight? They gave the military unit lower ratings for their knowledge of the military than they gave the company that had a retired general on their staff. That stank to high heaven!

I even asked the contracting officer, "You mean to tell me that you thought the retired four-star general knew more about the U.S. military than an entire U.S. military unit?" I guess the bid evaluators just assumed that nobody would ever examine how they came up with their rating scores.

Overly Broad Specifications or Contract Requirements

Some vendors may not be qualified or have the capability to provide a specified service. But if the buyer or customer still wants that particular vendor to be considered for and/or get awarded the contract, they might intentionally write the specifications or requirements vaguely or overly broad so that the favored vendor will still qualify.

Unjustified Sole Source

Sometimes customers or buyers will require that only a certain brand name or manufacturer's part/items can be provided. That usually limits the pool of potential bidders. In some cases, especially with machinery and electronics, only a specific company's parts or related items will suffice. But if the order is for office supplies, it usually really doesn't matter which company manufactured them.

WAR STORY 3.13

While reviewing one contract file, I noticed that the contract was awarded without competition. I asked the contracting officer why she did not obtain more than one quote. She said that she determined that only one vendor could provide the service. When I flipped through her corresponding work papers inside the contract file, I found she had previously printed pages from several competitors' websites showing they could have also provided the service. The dates she printed the pages were printed on the bottom right corner of the papers.

> I told the contracting official that I found those competitors' printed pages in her file and asked why she didn't get quotes from them. She replied that she didn't learn about those other vendors until after the contract had already been awarded. I showed her the dates on the bottom of the printed pages, which indicated she knew about the other vendors before she awarded the contract. She then confessed that her supervisor ordered her to award the contract to that particular vendor and that the only way she could justify making the award to that company was by saying that the vendor was the sole source.

Change Order and Modification Manipulation

This was described in Chapter 1 (see War Story 1.12). In such a corrupt procurement, the buyer and/or contracting official, along with a conspiring vendor, will know in advance that the contract will be changed and/or modified after it's awarded to favor that particular vendor. In that case, additional products or services might be added or the time to complete the schedule extended, or other deviations added so the vendor benefits. Because all of this information is not provided in advance, many vendors may not compete, and those that do may bid higher because they don't have access to all of the information.

Author's Note: *Occasionally, vendors in the same industry that compete for similar contract awards monitor contracts that are awarded to others and changes to other vendors' contracts. Sometimes they make complaints and/or file official protests about contracts awarded to others. It's suggested that investigators carefully review and consider those complaints because many of them have merit. Each complaint may only seem like one red flag. But if you expand your investigative search based on the information provided, you might identify a pattern that even the original complainant was not fully aware of. Take all complaints seriously. Generally, there are not any central databases for all complaints made by competitors. Consequently, each complaint or protest is typically evaluated on its own merit. But if you knew of all or most complaints and evaluated them collectively, you'd probably identify many more instances of corruption and wrongfully awarded contracts and other purchases.*

The next chapter describes schemes used to commit fraud during contractor and vendor performance.

4 Contractor and Vendor Performance Schemes

This chapter describes many of the schemes utilized by contractors and vendors to commit fraud after they are awarded contracts. As previously stated, when investigating one type of offense, investigators should be cognizant of possible other offenses that may have also occurred and/or are still occurring. Those other offenses may be related or unrelated to what you started out investigating.

> ### WAR STORY 4.1
>
> I investigated a contractor for repeatedly supplying less than what was ordered on many of his shipments. I learned that the contractor's profit margin per item was very small. In fact, the contractor's bid prices were sometimes lower than the market average. The investigation later proved that this contractor also paid bribes to the contracting officer who awarded the contracts.

If a contractor has numerous complaints against him or her for short-shipping or other contract performance issues, you have to wonder why the wrongdoing has occurred. It's possible that what you are investigating is the only issue. But think about it. How could a contractor afford to offer bid prices that are below market price and still make a profit? In this case, you'd also have to ask how the contractor could afford to bid so low, pay bribes, and still expect to make a profit. Those facts will certainly help when you later interview such contractors because it's apparent that they intended from the onset not to provide what was ordered when submitting the bid proposals. They are most probably crooks! In this case, the contractor initially denied any intent. But he eventually told the truth and even provided incriminating evidence against himself and the contracting officer.

Author's Note: *Your case will certainly be easier to prove beyond reasonable doubt if you also obtain a lawful confession from the contractor or another criminal(s). That said, you should be thinking about and preparing for your future interviews while conducting other parts of your investigation.*

Listed next are some of the schemes utilized by contractors and vendors to commit fraud after they are awarded contracts.

Short Shipments

Some vendors intentionally ship less than what the customers order with the hope that the shortages won't be detected. When investigating such offenses, beware that some vendors will first test the water to see what they can get away with. If the customer has weak internal controls to detect such shortages, the vendor can continue and/or gradually increase the shortages in each shipment until they get caught. If and when they do get caught, they may correct the deficiency and then wait a while before continuing the scheme.

Investigators should attempt to determine if the shortage(s) being investigated are isolated incidents or if similar instances have previously occurred. Don't assume that this was/is the first time it's happened or the last time it will happen. If it's been a reoccurring problem, you may be able to strengthen your case by monitoring, documenting, and photographing future shipments received so that you have stronger evidence of the misdeeds.

Ghost Shipments

Worse than short shipments are "ghost shipments," in which vendors don't ship anything at all to the customer except an invoice indicating that they did ship the ordered items. Once again, if the customer has weak internal controls to detect such shortages, the vendor can continue this scheme indefinitely. In fact, it's not unusual to find that the same vendor that submits invoices for goods never shipped has also submitted invoices for short shipments (and vice-versa). It could be that because the customer's internal controls are so weak the vendor just gradually took their scheme to the next level.

WAR STORY 4.2

One contractor had numerous complaints made against him for invoicing for items that were never received. When confronted about the complaints, the contractor said that he did ship each order and blamed the customer's receiving department for being unorganized. The contractor even provided proof that he shipped each order through the U.S. Postal Service. Initially, it appeared that the contractor might be telling the truth. With proof that he shipped the items, it was hard to argue that he didn't.

But after reviewing hundreds of the postal receipts, I noticed some anomalies. Some of the postal receipts were photocopied and the contractor had provided them as proof of delivery for more than one shipment on different days. Some of the same named signatures on certified mail receipts appeared different on other copies.

I took some of the questionable postal receipts to the post office where the shipments were allegedly made from. The postmaster said that most of the receipts were bogus and that some receipts applied to one shipment but not all the other shipments.

> The vendor, who was a very successful businessman, was also very organized. He was very believable during his initial interview. In that regard, I guess you'd say he was a very good actor. But the facts don't lie. So he ended up also being a very good federal penitentiary prisoner.

Author's Note: *Always be mindful that there's a chance that someone in the customer's receiving department and/or the buyer or contracting officer that placed the order or awarded the contract could be part of the scheme. If you suspect that's the case, take it into consideration when conducting interviews at the buyer's facility. You don't want to unnecessarily alert co-conspirators about your investigation because they could screw up your case.*

Author's Note: *In these scenarios, there's also a possibility that the employee for the vendor that submitted the false invoices could be the sole person responsible for the scheme and may have embezzled ill-gotten gains. The vendor may not even have known anything about the false invoices. You should find out either way if you conduct a thorough investigation.*

Shipment of Wrong Items

Some vendors may intentionally ship the wrong items to customers knowing that if they get caught they will have a plausible explanation. Like many of the schemes described, depending on the customer's dollar loss, you're usually looking for a pattern of wrongdoing. Honest mistakes are going to happen.

Shipment of Items Never Ordered

As described in War Story 3.9, some vendors might ship and invoice for items that the customer never ordered. Large organizations that have separate people or sections responsible for ordering, receiving, and making payments may not know or have much interaction with each other. Many will just assume that if goods were received and invoices received, then the goods must have been ordered. In fact, many will assume that if an invoice was received, the goods must have also been received and ordered. It's difficult to prove that a vendor was trying to commit fraud if they actually shipped what they invoiced for.

Product Substitution

Some vendors will provide items that may appear to be what was ordered but not be of the quality requested and paid for. Two examples are listed here:

Products Not Meeting Specifications

The U.S. military is known for requiring that contractors provide items that meet stringent and detailed specifications. Providing materials and goods that do not meet the required specifications can result in the product or goods being totally useless (and perhaps dangerous) to the customer. Very often, contractors can unlawfully increase their profits by intentionally providing a product of lesser quality.

> ## WAR STORY 4.3
>
> One vendor was awarded government contracts to provide meat and fish to several different government agencies. The government specified the grade of meat to provide and items were usually paid for by the pound. The vendor used several different schemes to defraud the government.
>
> One scheme was to repackage expired meat and put new dates on the packages. Another scheme was to mix meat with other products like soybeans. Another scheme was to let shrimp sit in saltwater for extended periods so that the saltwater would be retained in the shrimp and show higher weights per pound.
>
> A team of federal agents executed search warrants on the large refrigerated facility and obtained evidence of the wrongdoing. National media coverage had a field day with the part about the vendor selling expired meat to schools. The same day that the warrant was executed, one of the vendor's executives committed suicide.

Defective Products

Some vendors may cut corners and/or use lesser grade materials in an effort to save money. An example could be when a vendor waters down mixtures of cement, or just about any other product, to make more with less, affecting the quality and/or safety of the items.

> ## WAR STORY 4.4
>
> One company provided sealants (like glue) on government contracts. The sealants were used on just about anything and everything to help hold items in place—including aircraft windows. That contractor was found to have placed new expiration dates on packages of expired sealant. They also intentionally provided less expensive and less effective adhesives on some contracts.
>
> While executing a search warrant on the facility, I found a logbook in an employee's desk drawer which had columns listing specific government contract numbers, the type of adhesive requested, and a separate column listing the adhesive substituted. The column heading actually read, "Item Substituted." After finding the logbook, it was kind of humorous that none of the employees wanted to claim ownership of that desk.

WAR STORY 4.5

In a similar case, a company provided adhesive tape on government contracts. I never knew there were so many different kinds of tape until assisting on that case. We loaded a couple of trucks full of evidence from that facility, including uncut rolls of tape that were almost as long as streetlight poles.

Buy American Act Violations

In federal procurements, some contracts require items, or a high percentage of the items and/or components, to be made in America. To save money, some contractors intentionally violate this requirement by using non-approved foreign-made goods or components. One of the reasons for this law/requirement is to protect American jobs. Another is to ensure high quality of the products or items and another is environmental concerns because some foreign countries improperly dispose of hazardous waste (which is another reason they can provide less expensive items).

WAR STORY 4.6

One company in Florida was providing circuit boards on federal contracts and we learned that the circuit boards were actually imported from China, which was in violation of the terms of the contracts. While executing a search warrant on the facility, we found boxes of circuit boards that had labels marked "Made in China." But when the labels were removed, the circuit boards were permanently imprinted with "Made in the USA."

By having the outside stickers marked "Made in China," the items passed inspection when coming into America through U.S. Customs. But once delivered, the company employees removed the stickers from each circuit board before shipping the circuit boards to customers. The customers were deceived into believing the boards were made in America.

By importing the circuit boards from China, the contractor was able to underbid competitors that submitted higher bid prices for the boards made in America that had to be manufactured in compliance with more stringent environmental laws. In addition to finding the circuit boards with labels still attached, we found many removed stickers in the company's trash cans.

Author's Note: *Buy American Act requirements and prohibitions are described in Federal Acquisition Regulation (FAR) 52.225-1 through 52.225-26. Contractors that are required to abide by this requirement must also provide Buy American Certificates, as described in FAR 52.225-1. For information, view all 26 sections of FAR 52.225:* http://farsite.hill.af.mil/reghtml/regs/far2afmcfars/fardfars/far/52_220.htm

Contractor and Vendor Performance Schemes 67

Author's Note: *Many states, counties, and municipalities also have requirements that a certain percentage of contracts and/or subcontracts (and/or percentage of total contract dollar amounts) be awarded to or performed by vendors that are located within their geographical boundaries.*

Chapter 1 described a high-profile city contract in Memphis, TN that came under scrutiny because it appeared that a prime contractor located outside of Memphis may have created unnecessary work to pay a Memphis contractor just to comply with the contract terms. Many speculated that the city would actually be paying for unnecessary work to be performed by the Memphis contractor.

Many assume that they are doing their communities a favor and keeping jobs in their area by contracting and/or subcontracting with local vendors and contractors. But sometimes the only thing that's local is the street address of the company. Sometimes, most of the funds paid are actually going to subcontractors located elsewhere and/or benefitting other geographical areas.

Performing Unnecessary Services

Some vendors deceive customers into believing that work is needed that actually is not needed. Very often, buyers rely on the expertise of the vendor to determine what work is needed. A fraudster can take full advantage of the buyer's ignorance, busy schedule, and/or reliance on the integrity of the contractor. That's why the best advice is often to get three or more opinions or price quotations.

Providing Fewer Materials than Invoiced

Similar to short shipments, some vendors reported that they used more materials than they actually did or that they paid more for materials than they actually did. In one case I worked, a contractor was supposed to provide a large quantity of "rip-rock" stones for erosion control at a specified location along the Mississippi River. It was alleged that the contractor billed for more stone than was actually delivered. I had to get assistance from the Army Corps of Engineers to help determine the validity of the complaint because many of the stones were under water.

False Certifications or Test Results

Many contracts require vendors to provide one or more certifications in which the vendor and/or its supplier or subcontractor must certify that contractual requirements were met during performance. For example, a vendor might be required to perform various testing during performance and/or after assembly to ensure that the end items are safe and/or meet all requirements. Sometimes the certifications provided are knowingly false. In all of the product substitution cases I've worked that were successfully adjudicated, one of the most important pieces of evidence used against the contractors was the false certification they provided indicating they did something that they didn't or that the item provided or work accomplished met some requirement which they knew, or had reason to know, it did not.

> **WAR STORY 4.7**
>
> One contractor certified that electrical items they had provided passed the required testing. But when tested by the buyer, the same items failed testing. During interviews with some of the contractor's employees, I was told that the calibration of the testing equipment was rigged so that all items would pass testing, no matter what. The contractor convinced himself that he could say items passed testing when he knew that the testing method had been manipulated.

Consumer Scams

There are countless consumer scams and schemes that may or may not involve contracts in which unscrupulous vendors or contractors deceive customers into believing they will obtain a service or product, but where they actually receive another service or product or nothing at all. One of the most common schemes is to have a buyer pay in advance for repair services, and then the contractor/vendor never returns.

The Federal Trade Commission has a list of consumer scams and scam alerts on their website.

For more details, visit https://www.consumer.ftc.gov/scam-alerts.

Another informative website that describes common scams and frauds is https://www.usa.gov/common-scams-frauds.

The next chapter describes the payment schemes used by many vendors and contractors.

5 Contractor and Vendor Payment Schemes

This chapter details many of the schemes contractors and vendors are known to commit after they are awarded contracts to get paid money they are not entitled to from buyers. In some shape or form, the below schemes require the submission of and/or request for payment—usually by submitting an invoice or claim document. Contract and related fraud have probably been going on since the time contracts were first written.

The Lincoln Law (The False Claims Act)

During the American Civil War, some contractors on the Union side (and probably on the Confederate side too) were involved in price-gouging (charging excessively high prices) and supplied defective bullets, guns, supplies, and even horses. This fraud led to the passing of what became known as *The Lincoln Law*, which is now more commonly known as *The False Claims Act*. Essentially, anyone who submits a false claim to defraud the U.S. government can be found liable for a civil penalty of not less than $5,000 and not more than $10,000, plus three times the amount of damages which the Government sustains because of the act of that person. The Act also has *qui tam* provisions which allow whistleblowers the opportunity to file suit on behalf of the government and then profit from the judgments.

The False Claims statute is especially popular and useful in health-care fraud investigations as well as false claims submitted by contractors to the Department of Defense (DoD). Many states also have their own False Claims statutes.

Author's Note: *For more information on the federal statute, see the Federal Civil False Claims Act: 31 U.S. Code 3729-3733:*
https://www.justice.gov/sites/default/files/civil/legacy/2011/04/22/C-FRAUDS_FCA_Primer.pdf.

Listed next are some of the schemes utilized by contractors and vendors to receive payments they are not entitled to.

Author's Note: *In this writing, the words contractor and vendor are often used interchangeably.*

Duplicate Invoices

Some vendors submit two or more invoices for the same services or goods provided. It's not unusual for an unscrupulous vendor to test the water first to see if they will get paid twice. If it works, they'll do it again and again. If they are caught, they will likely blame it on a faulty billing system or human error with no intent to deceive.

Duplicate invoices are submitted with the same or different invoice numbers. Sometimes the description of costs will be comingled with other costs in an effort to confuse the payers into paying twice for the same goods or services. Some smaller companies—especially sole proprietors—may not have the best record-keeping systems and may never include invoice numbers when submitting requests for payment. In my opinion, a vendor that frequently submits duplicate payment requests is most probably doing it on purpose.

Inflated Hours

Vendors can inflate the number of hours spent working on projects or assignment(s). It's been established that sometimes such vendors charge for work that was never performed or charge several different clients for the exact same hours (the same work). For example, an attorney could spend time working on one project but rationalizes charging two or more clients for the very same time. Along those lines, I once investigated a university for billing two different government agencies for the same research and development efforts.

Some contracts allow contractors to be reimbursed based on the hours that employees spend working on those specified contracts. Unscrupulous contractors find creative ways to inflate hours and costs as described next.

Cost Mischarging

In some schemes, contractors log labor hours for employees that never worked at the facility, no longer work at the facility, or are on vacation. Sometimes false time cards are created to support the false billings. Sometimes contractors charge for materials and time used on one contract to another contract.

Cost-mischarging schemes are some of the most difficult white-collar investigations to prove. Typically, these cases involve the manipulation of lots of numbers, lots of documents (and/or data), and often lots of different high-dollar contracts (always at least two contracts).

Chapter 1 described some of the different types of contracts awarded—including Cost-Plus contracts. Cost mischarging occurs when reimbursable expenses, costs, and/or time are improperly charged (often with criminal intent) from one or more contracts to one or more other contracts. Listed here are three examples of typical mischarging cases.

Example #1: Cost-Plus-Labor Mischarging

To illustrate how this scheme can be executed, let's say that there is a large corporation that manufactures aircraft and aircraft parts. We'll call that entity Big Buck Aircraft, Inc. (a fictional name), hereafter referred to as BBA.

BBA also has lots of political connections and is responsible for the gainful employment of many people across the country. BBA has numerous contracts with several different federal government agencies including the DoD—specifically, the U.S. Air Force, Navy, and Army.

BBA has ten cost-plus-labor contracts and 100 firm-fixed-price contracts. On the cost-plus-labor contracts, BBA will be paid an agreed-upon amount plus the cost of the labor they use on those specific contracts. For the firm-fixed-price contracts, BBA will be paid a specific amount on each of those contracts regardless of how many labor hours are utilized on those contracts.

In this scenario, cost mischarging will have occurred if BBA charges labor hours that were used on the firm-fixed-price contract(s) to a cost-plus-labor contract(s).

Example #2: Cost-Plus-Materials Mischarging

Similarly, let's say BBA was also awarded a couple of cost-plus-materials contracts wherein the government would reimburse BBA for the materials they utilized on those specific contracts. If BBA purchased and billed the government for materials from the cost-plus-materials contracts, but actually used the materials on the firm-fixed-price contracts or the cost-plus-labor contracts, that would be fraud.

Example #3: Government Furnished Materials Fraud

Sometimes, the government actually provides the contractor with the materials to be used on specific contracts. (Those materials are actually called "Government Furnished Materials" [GFM].) Sometimes the government already has the materials in storage or can acquire the materials at less cost than contractors can. If BBA uses the GFM on some other contracts, that would be fraud. BBA would have, in effect, stolen or misappropriated the GFM and unjustly increased their profits on the other contracts by using GFM that they did not own.

In some ways, cost mischarging is like a shell game where there are usually three shells and a pea and you have to try to guess which shell the pea is under after the shells are shuffled around on a table. Except in cost mischarging cases, there are a million shells and a few peas. Frankly, cost mischarging cases make my head hurt. When investigating cost mischarging cases, try to gain assistance from one or more competent auditors.

WAR STORY 5.1

In an investigation of a large corporation, it was found that several employees' labor hours were charged to a DoD cost-plus-labor contract. This type of contract allowed the contractor to get reimbursed for agreed-upon costs plus all labor assigned to that specific contract. Some employees' hourly wages or salaries were higher than others.

> The same contractor had several additional DoD contracts, including several fixed-price contracts. The fixed-price contracts paid the contractor the same dollar amount regardless of the number of labor hours assigned to them.
>
> A DoD auditor reviewed and analyzed the contractor's time cards and documented their findings. But determining whether there was criminal intent to commit fraud could only be accomplished by conducting interviews.
>
> Both the joint agent assigned to the case and I were conscious of the fact that current employees are often reluctant to provide damaging information about their employers due to concern that their employers might retaliate and fire them.
>
> We interviewed employees at their homes during the early evening hours and asked what projects they were working on during specific time frames and how they documented their work time. The employees were forthright about which projects they worked on and said they never listed the project (contract) numbers they worked on when logging their time. Instead, personnel in the corporate administrative office determined which contracts to assign their time to. The employees opined that their only concern was that they'd get paid for the hours they put in, not what their bosses did with their time cards.
>
> Word got back to the contractor's corporate attorney that we were conducting interviews and the attorney advised that we could not interview any more employees without the attorney's approval. In that particular case, we could not prove intent to commit fraud beyond a reasonable doubt. However, we still had a strong civil case where we only had to prove wrongdoing by the preponderance of evidence. In the end, the DoD got their money back.

Fictitious Vendor Fraud

Fictitious vendor fraud can occur in many ways. The simple version occurs when a shell company submits false invoices directly to the buyer for payment. In high-dollar contracts, a prime contractor could create a shell company or simply generate some invoices with a fake company name(s), reflecting that funds were paid to the fake vendor, and then the prime contractor submits an inflated invoice (which includes the fake company's costs) to the buyer for payment.

Employees for the buyer or the contractor could also commit fraud by generating false invoices with fictitious vendors' names on them and have payments mailed to addresses which the employee has control over. In those instances, the employer may have absolutely no involvement in or knowledge about the fraud scheme. If that's the case, the employer should be very helpful in your investigation.

Defective Pricing

As described in Chapter 3, in negotiated contracts with the federal government, the contractor may be required to provide their cost and pricing data. In other words, the contractor will be asked to provide proof or supportive documentation regarding their prices. For example, if the contractor is required to certify to their cost and pricing data, the contractor can't tell the government their costs for material will be $100 per yard and then after the contract award only pay the supplier $50 per yard. Well, perhaps they could, but the contract price would have to be modified to lower the dollar amount of the contract so the government wouldn't lose money.

After a negotiated contract is awarded that required the contractor to certify to cost and pricing data, the awarded contractor could (illegally) submit inflated invoices/claims for payment by either falsifying invoices or conspiring with suppliers and/or subcontractors to have them submit inflated invoices, with kickbacks paid in return.

For example, let's say a contractor certified to the government they would pay a supplier $100 per yard for material. But in reality, the contractor conspired with the supplier to provide an artificially inflated quote at $100, knowing that the supplier would actually charge the contractor $50 per yard. The supplier could even provide the contractor with a fabricated invoice for $100 per yard in case the government asked for proof. But after the contractor is paid, they may actually pay the supplier $75 per yard and both the contractor and supplier would illegally profit by an additional $25 per yard each. Actually, a contractor wouldn't even need to conspire with a supplier to pull off a similar scheme. Instead, the contractor could just create some false and inflated invoices for their proof. Of course, they might get caught if the invoices are audited.

WAR STORY 5.2

While investigating *Contractor* A for providing defective products, I learned that after being awarded a multimillion-dollar government contract, *Contractor* A decided to use a different supplier of materials (called Supplier #2). Supplier #2 sold the goods at half the price that Supplier #1 did. In other words, before the contract was awarded, *Contractor* A said they would use Supplier #1, who quoted the price for their material at $100 per yard. The government knew Supplier #1 had a good reputation of providing excellent quality material.

But after the contract was awarded, *Contractor* A switched suppliers to Supplier #2, who sold the material to *Contractor* A for $50 per yard. This material was in terrible shape and the samples sent to the government for testing failed at a high rate.

I was a rookie federal agent when working that case. When I learned that *Contractor* A switched suppliers and was going to make an extra million dollars profit, I told the contracting officer that the government needed to recoup the cost difference. The contracting officer looked at me like I was stupid (which maybe I was). She said something like, "The contractor is allowed to switch suppliers because he didn't have to certify to cost and pricing data. The contractor said he would use Supplier #1 but after the contract was awarded, he could switch to any supplier he wanted to as long as he provided good final products."

I asked the contracting officer why she didn't make the contractor certify to their cost and pricing data. She told me that the FAR rules stated that if there was adequate competition and price comparability, no certification of cost and pricing data was required and in this case, two or more bidders bid similar prices.

I said something like, "Wait a minute. The government is going to spend a million dollars more than it needs to. Why is that okay?" The contracting officer got frustrated with me because I didn't understand the contracting rules. But I understood the rules just fine. I just thought the rules were stupid because they let contractors take advantage of the government and taxpayers' money.

In the end, I proved that the contractor submitted false samples of material to the government for testing. Guess how he did it? Late in contract performance, he purchased some good material from Supplier #1 and sent a bunch of Supplier #1's material for government testing, falsely indicating that the samples came from Supplier #2's material.

WAR STORY 5.3

I investigated another contractor for providing defective products to the government. I learned that he too obtained a high price quote for components from a supplier. But after the contract was awarded, the contractor "negotiated" a reduced price for the components with the same supplier and was legally allowed to keep the extra profit. However, the contractor's greedy plan failed because I later proved he sent the government defective products.

Expense Reimbursement Fraud

Almost all companies, corporations, and government agencies reimburse employees and contractors for authorized expenses incurred—especially when traveling. It's not uncommon to find that false expense reimbursement claims have been submitted by personnel from the lowest levels to the highest levels. Examples include false or inflated hotel bills, inflated number of days in travel status, inflated meal costs, false or inflated rental car costs, and inflated mileage claims. In fact, some will claim they drove their own cars when they actually carpooled with another employee. Because the costs are usually low as compared with other costs, the information is seldom verified before being paid. Most consider copies of receipts as sufficient proof. But sometimes the receipts have been altered or are completely bogus.

Credit Card Fraud

Some contractors are reimbursed for their credit card expenses. As you know, many office supply stores and other establishments sell gift cards for restaurants, for downloadable music and movies, and for dozens of other business establishments. Some vendors might charge things on their credit cards that are for personal use and are totally unrelated to their job performance. When purchasing gasoline, some vendors have been known to fill up their own personal gas tanks and even fill gas cans that are not affiliated with their job(s).

Progress Payment Fraud

Some high-dollar contracts allow vendors to submit invoices for costs incurred as they progress. It's arranged so that the contractor won't have to go into debt waiting for payment for expenses they've already incurred. Progress payment fraud occurs (even on fixed-price contracts) when contractors submit inflated claims for payment reflecting that they incurred greater costs in the production process than they actually did. Some vendors unjustly submit such false claims to get paid in advance (which equates to interest-free loans). The danger comes when a contractor receives large payments in advance and then can't complete the contract. If that happens, the buyer loses out.

Some vendors have been known to have two or more contracts that they submit progress payment claims on and they use those funds to keep their company afloat. It's kind of like borrowing from Peter to pay Paul. At some point, the money might run out and not only might the contracts with progress payments be defaulted on, but so will the company's other contracts.

WAR STORY 5.4

A reputable contractor had been awarded a several hundred thousand-dollar DoD contract to provide gun mounts for Navy ships. No complaints had ever been received about the quality of any of the contractor's products. The contractor received progress payments on the gun mount contract over a period of several months. At some point, the contractor certified that they had completed about 90 percent of the contract and therefore received almost 90 percent of the funds through progress payments. But in reality, the contractor had only completed about 20 percent of the contract. The owners were using the funds received through progress payments to pay for costs associated with other contracts.

> One morning, the Naval Criminal Investigative Service (NCIS) agent, that was working the case jointly, and I knocked on the front door of the president of the company's house. Needless to say, he was surprised to see us. Quite honestly, we were kind of surprised he invited us inside. At first, the president denied submitting the false progress payment requests. But when we showed him the evidence, he swallowed hard and admitted he did submit the false claims. The president said he needed the money to keep his business afloat but that he hoped to finish the gun mount contract with progress payments received from future contracts he anticipated getting.

WAR STORY 5.5

This War Story is a spin-off of the same case that was briefly described in War Story 2.6. A contractor submitted a progress payment request for about $2 million the day after his company was awarded a multimillion-dollar contract. A company executive certified that his company had already incurred those costs immediately after being awarded the contract. I also found an e-mail from the contracting officer telling the company to submit the claim for payment. Initially, everyone thought that the executive submitted a textbook example of a false progress payment request.

But it was later established that several months before the contractor was ever awarded the contract, a senior four-star military general told the contractor to start doing the work. For some reason, the general apparently decided he didn't need to follow federal contracting rules (or he forgot about them) and that he could get contracts awarded to whomever he wanted to—without competition.

Legally, the general did not have the authority to tell the contractor to do work if there was no contract. Because this was a multimillion-dollar service request, the general was supposed to first ensure funding was available and set aside (obligated) for the project. Next, the need for the service was required to be advertised for competition and then a responsible bidder would be selected and a contract awarded.

Well, I guess the contractor liked what the general told him to do and he apparently liked the price the general agreed to pay. I guess the contractor knew he was going to make a lot of money and just assumed the four-star general had the authority to commit government funds to him, so he started the work without a contract.

It really blew up in the four-star general's face when he learned he could face criminal charges and possibly be forced to pay the funds himself for telling the contractor to do work—especially millions of dollars' worth of work—without a contract first being awarded.

Making it worse for the general and the contractor, the military later told that same contractor that he had to submit a bid to compete with other vendors to do the work that the general had previously promised the favored contractor he could do. With favored bid proposal ratings given to his company, the same contractor was later awarded a multimillion-dollar contract to provide the service.

But the contractor got ticked off when the government refused to pay the $2 million claim. In fact, the contractor got so angry that he filed a lawsuit against the U.S. Government!

To my surprise, the agents I worked with and the prosecutor focused mostly on the civilian contractor, not the four-star general. Everyone around me wanted to pursue charges against the civilian contractor for submitting a false claim. I concurred that there was a possibility that the contractor's $2 million claim might be inflated, but the contractor did what the general (perhaps illegally and certainly improperly) told him to do. Plus, the contracting officer told the civilian contractor (via e-mail) to submit the claim. Just the same, the crosshairs seemed set on the civilian contractor. I wondered why everyone wanted to charge the civilian instead of the four-star general. In fact, I argued against it. That was my wake-up call. I learned firsthand that power rules.

Just as I thought the four-star general had learned his lesson, I learned that he had instructed his own active duty service members to do work on the contract that the contractor was supposed to do! The general even added work to the same contract without first getting the contract modified.

During the investigation, I reviewed several other related government contracts and found similar instances of apparent abuse of power (improper influence) in the contracting award process. You've read some generic versions of those instances in this and previous chapters. Contracts were improperly awarded to companies because that's what the high-ranking military officers wanted done.

As previously stated, the criminal prosecutor told me to stop looking at those other contracts. Then he told me to stop conducting interviews. Then he told me to stop writing reports. He told me I couldn't do anything! I told my own supervisors what was going on and they told me to stop making waves and to do what the prosecutor told me. Next, my immediate supervisor ordered me to close the entire case!

When I argued and persisted, everyone (including the alleged good guys) made me out to be the bad guy. But I kept on investigating anyway.

I met with the contracting officer (who was a captain) and asked him why he had told the contractor to submit the $2 million claim so quickly after the contract was awarded. The captain said that he had received a phone call from a two-star general who told the captain not to delay payment to the contractor. The contracting officer told me something like, "I never received a phone call from a general before in my life!"

By now, you're probably wondering what the end result was. Well, I uncovered evidence of wrongdoing by some of the highest-ranking U.S.

military generals, and many others. Witnesses and suspects even told me what had transpired, and I documented everything. In my opinion, the case could have gone down as one of the biggest military fraud scandals ever exposed. But my final report was drastically changed which, in the end, had the effect of a whitewash. A couple of suspects got the equivalent of slaps on the hand and the generals were allowed to retire and collect their pensions. Make no mistake about it, all too often, power rules. Factually, that one case had examples of many of the contract fraud schemes described in this book.

Author's Note: *Odds are you will never experience anything as unjust as I did on that case. If you do, you'll have to do some deep soul-searching to decide if you want to risk your career and perhaps your livelihood by being honest and doing "the right thing." I paid a huge price for doing the right thing. But ya' know what? I'd do it again. As far as I'm concerned, if I had closed my case and looked the other way, I would have been just as guilty as the people I uncovered evidence against.*

Having read that last War Story, you are either fired up to investigate contract fraud, collusion, and corruption or you're backpeddling, wondering if you really want to get involved in this arena. My guess is that you want to investigate this stuff even more. So read on!

The next chapter details investigators, enforcers, and statutes.

6 Investigators, Enforcers, and Statutes

Contract and procurement fraud, collusion, and corruption are investigated worldwide by individuals, companies, corporations, and government agencies. Although all deserve credit for their efforts, contributions, and accomplishments, it would be a herculean task to attempt to list them all in this writing.

This chapter highlights a few U.S. federal agencies, task forces, and others that regularly investigate and/or enforce the laws which involve such wrongdoing on a frequent basis or on a large scale. This chapter also includes a listing of federal statutes often considered and/or used in such cases.

Department of Defense Contracting

The Department of Defense (DoD) probably awards the highest dollar amount of contracts in the United States each year. In 2015, the Government Accountability Office (GAO) reported that the DoD obligates more than $300 billion annually on contracts for goods and services, including major weapon systems, support for military bases, information technology, consulting services, and commercial items (source: http://www.gao.gov/highrisk/dod_contract_management/why_did_study).

Federal Investigative Agencies

Offices of Inspector General

Many federal organizations have oversight and/or investigative responsibility of their own agencies' contracts, procurements, and acquisitions. Since the passing of the Office of Inspector General (OIG) Act in 1978, over 70 federal OIGs have been created that investigate fraud, waste, and abuse involving their own agencies. Most (if not all) employ federal special agents, auditors, and other specialists to assist in their efforts.

Defense Criminal Investigative Service

The Defense Criminal Investigative Service (DCIS) is the investigative arm of the DoD-OIG. Among other investigative responsibilities, the DCIS investigates fraud, waste, and abuse involving the DoD. Many of the retired and current senior DCIS Special Agents are the best trained, skilled, and experienced agents at investigating contract and procurement fraud schemes as well as collusion and corruption.

Military Criminal Investigative Organizations (MCIOs)

The U.S. military's own branches also have special agents that investigate fraud, waste, and abuse as well as other criminal offenses. Although most agents investigate base-level activity, some are also assigned to focus their efforts on fraud—including contract and procurement fraud, collusion, and corruption. Those military investigative agencies include:

- U.S. Air Force Office of Special Investigations (AFOSI);
- U.S. Army Criminal Investigation Division (Army CID);
- U.S. Navy Criminal Investigative Service (NCIS).

The Federal Bureau of Investigation (FBI)

The FBI, which is part of the Department of Justice, works public corruption cases and often works jointly with other agencies investigating contract and procurement fraud and/or collusion.

The Government Accountability Office (GAO)

The following is from the GAO's website (http://www.gao.gov/about/index.html):

> The U.S. Government Accountability Office (GAO) is an independent, nonpartisan agency that works for Congress. Often called the "congressional watchdog," GAO investigates how the federal government spends taxpayer dollars. The head of GAO, the Comptroller General of the United States, is appointed to a 15-year term by the President from a slate of candidates Congress proposes.
>
> The GAO's work is done at the request of congressional committees or subcommittees or is mandated by public laws or committee reports. The GAO also undertakes research under the authority of the Comptroller General. We support congressional oversight by:
>
> - auditing agency operations to determine whether federal funds are being spent efficiently and effectively;
> - investigating allegations of illegal and improper activities;
> - reporting on how well government programs and policies are meeting their objectives;
> - performing policy analyses and outlining options for congressional consideration; and

- issuing legal decisions and opinions, such as bid protest rulings and reports on agency rules.

The GAO advises Congress and the heads of executive agencies about ways to make government more efficient, effective, ethical, equitable and responsive. Our work leads to laws and acts that improve government operations, saving the government and taxpayers billions of dollars.

Other Federal Investigative Agencies

Many other federal investigative agencies investigate and/or assist in investigations involving contract and procurement fraud, collusion, and/or corruption. Some of those agencies are the U.S. Postal Inspections Services, U.S. Customs and Border Protection, U.S. Environmental Protection Agency–Criminal Enforcement, Internal Revenue Service–Criminal Enforcement, and others.

Task Forces

The Department of Justice (DoJ) has formed task forces so that investigative agencies can share information and work together to investigate contract and procurement fraud, collusion, and corruption, nationally and internationally. The task forces are composed of members from many agencies including OIGs, MCIOs, and other federal investigative agencies including the U.S. Postal Inspection Service and the FBI, as well as attorneys from the DoJ—including the U.S. Attorney's offices around the country. Two such task forces are:

- The National Procurement Fraud Task Force;
- The International Contract Corruption Task Force.

Enforcement

Department of Justice: Antitrust Division

The source for the following is https://www.justice.gov/about.

> The mission of the Antitrust Division is to promote competition through enforcing and providing guidance on antitrust laws and principles. The Division prosecutes certain violations of the antitrust laws by filing criminal suits that can lead to large fines and jail sentences. In other cases, the Division instates civil action seeking a court order forbidding future violations of the law and requiring steps to remedy the anticompetitive effects of past violations. Many of the Division's accomplishments on these fronts are made possible by unprecedented level of cooperation and coordination with foreign antitrust agencies and with state attorneys general.

The U.S. Federal Trade Commission

The source for the following is https://www.ftc.gov/about-ftc/bureaus-offices/bureau-competition.

> U.S. antitrust laws are enforced by both the FTC's Bureau of Competition and the Antitrust Division of the Department of Justice. The agencies consult before opening any investigation. The Antitrust Division handles all criminal antitrust enforcement.
>
> Bureau of Competition
>
> The FTC's Bureau of Competition enforces the nation's antitrust laws, which form the foundation of our free market economy. The antitrust laws promote the interests of consumers; they support unfettered markets and result in lower prices and more choices.
>
> The Federal Trade Commission Act and the Clayton Act, both passed by Congress in 1914, give the Commission authority to enforce the antitrust laws. These laws prohibit anticompetitive mergers and business practices that seek to prevent hard-driving competition, such as monopolistic conduct, attempts to monopolize, and conspiracies in restraint of trade. The Bureau of Competition investigates potential law violations and seeks legal remedies in federal court or before the FTC's administrative law judges. The Bureau also serves as a resource for policy makers on competition issues, and works closely with foreign competition agencies to promote sound and consistent outcomes in the international arena.

U.S. Attorneys' Offices

In addition to the DoJ's Antitrust Division, there are U.S. Attorneys' offices around the country that play a huge part in bringing to justice those involved in contract and procurement fraud, collusion, and corruption.

The source for the following is https://www.justice.gov/usao/mission.

> The U.S. Attorneys serve as the nation's principal litigators under the direction of the Attorney General. There are 93 U.S. Attorneys stationed throughout the United States, Puerto Rico, the Virgin Islands, Guam, and the Northern Mariana Islands. U.S. Attorneys are appointed by, and serve at the discretion of, the President of the United States, with the advice and consent of the U.S. Senate. One U.S. Attorney is assigned to each of the 94 judicial districts, with the exception of Guam and the Northern Mariana Islands where a single U.S. Attorney serves in both districts. Each U.S. Attorney is the chief federal law enforcement officer of the United States within his or her particular jurisdiction.

U.S. Attorneys conduct most of the trial work in which the United States is a party. The U.S. Attorneys have three statutory responsibilities under Title 28, Section 547 of the U.S. Code:

- the prosecution of criminal cases brought by the Federal Government;
- the prosecution and defense of civil cases in which the United States is a party; and
- the collection of debts owed the Federal Government which are administratively uncollectible.

Although the distribution of caseload varies between districts, each U.S. Attorney's Office deals with every category of cases and handles a mixture of simple and complex litigation. Each U.S. Attorney exercises wide discretion in the use of his/her resources to further the priorities of the local jurisdictions and needs of their communities.

Project on Government Oversight

I first learned about the Project on Government Oversight (POGO) in 2006 while serving as a federal agent after I initiated a corrupt procurement investigation, involving some of the highest-ranking U.S. military officers, into the awarding of a $50 million government contract. While watching the national news, I saw a POGO investigator telling a news reporter all about my new case. Apparently, POGO had received information about the matter and dug into it long before I received any information about the wrongdoing. I'll add that everything POGO related was right on the money.

POGO was founded in 1981, and is famous for exposing overpriced military spending on items such as a $7,600 coffee maker and a $436 hammer. It is a nonpartisan, independent watchdog that champions good government reforms.

POGO's website reads: "POGO investigators and journalists take leads and information from insiders and verify the information through investigations using the Freedom of Information Act, interviews, and other fact-finding strategies ..." For additional information, visit POGO's website at www.pogo.org.

Federal Statutes to Consider

Listed here are many federal criminal and civil statutes that might be considered when investigating/prosecuting contract and procurement fraud, collusion, and corruption. The list is not all-inclusive. Individual states will have similar or other statutes to consider. Please consult and review the actual statutes and sources.

Chapter 6

Federal Criminal Statutes

18 USC 2:	Aiding and Abetting
18 USC 4:	Misprision of a Felony
18 USC 201:	Bribery of Public Officials and Witnesses (NOTE: also see 18 USC 201-209, re: Conflicts/Restrictions)
18 USC 207:	Federal Employee Post Employment Restrictions (NOTE: also see 5 USC 3110: Restrictions on Employment of Relatives)
18 USC 208:	Acts Affecting a Personal Financial Interest (Conflict of Interest)
18 USC 209:	Federal Employee Dual Compensation Restrictions
18 USC 286:	Conspiracy: Claims
18 USC 287:	False Claim (does not have to be paid)
18 USC 371:	Conspiracy
18 USC 548:	Removing or Repacking Goods in Warehouses
18 USC 623:	False Declarations Before Grand Jury or Court
18 USC 641:	Theft of Public Money, Property or Records
18 USC 643:	Embezzlement of Public Money
18 USC 798:	Disclosure of Classified Information
18 USC 842:	Unlawful Acts Re: Explosives
18 USC 922:	Unlawful Acts Re: Firearms or Ammunition
18 USC 1001:	False Statement (Oral, Written)
18 USC 1002:	False Papers
18 USC 1028:	False Identification
18 USC 1030:	Computer Fraud
18 USC 1031:	Major Fraud Against the United States (involving $1,000,000 or more: contract, subcontract, subsidy, loan, guarantee, grant, insurance, or other form of Federal assistance, or any constituent part thereof)
18 USC 1341:	Mail Fraud
18 USC 1342:	Fictitious Name or Address
18 USC 1343:	Wire Fraud
18 USC 1344:	Bank Fraud
18 USC 1361:	Destruction of Government Property
18 USC 1365:	Tampering with Consumer Products
18 USC 1382:	Entering Military, Naval, or Coast Guard Property for Any Purpose Prohibited by Law or Lawful Regulation
18 USC 1510:	Obstruction of Criminal Investigation
18 USC 1512:	Tampering with Witness, Victim or Informant
18 USC 1516:	Obstruction of a Federal Audit
18 USC 1621:	Perjury
18 USC 1831:	Economic Espionage
18 USC 1832:	Theft of Trade Secrets
18 USC 1905:	Disclosure of Confidential Information
18 USC 1956:	Money Laundering

18 USC 1961-1968:	RICO (Racketeer Influenced and Corrupt Organizations) Statute
18 USC 2326:	Senior Citizen Marketing Scams
15 USC 1-7:	Sherman Antitrust Act (amended by the Clayton Act in 1914 [15 USC 12-27]).

Prohibits activities that restrict interstate commerce and competition in the marketplace. Prosecuted by U.S. Department of Justice's Antitrust Division, Washington, D.C.

15 USC 78dd-1:	Foreign Corrupt Trade Practices Act
15 USC 1644:	False Credit Card
22 USC 2778:	Control of Arms, Exports and Imports
31 USC 1341-1342:	Antideficiency Act (also see 31 USC 1517 if in excess of specified dollars), re: federal employees that involve the government in any obligation to pay money before funds have been appropriated for that purpose, or in excess of amount available; accepting voluntary services for the United States, or employing personal services not authorized by law etc. (possible administrative discipline and/or criminal penalties)
41 USC 2101-2107:	Procurement Integrity Act (Restrictions on Obtaining and Disclosing Certain Information—Also re: Employment, Post Employment, and Offers)
41 USC 8701-8707:	Anti-Kickback Act (applies to prime contractors and their subcontractors)

The Park Doctrine: Individuals and executives of corporations can be held liable for first-time misdemeanor and possible subsequent felony under the Park Doctrine.

For additional information, visit http://www.fda.gov/ICECI/ComplianceManuals/ RegulatoryProceduresManual/ucm176738.htm.

Author's Note: *The following provide for both criminal and civil remedies:*

- The False Claims Act;
- RICO;
- The Procurement Integrity Act;
- The Anti-Kickback Act.

Author's Note: *"A corporation or individual convicted of a Sherman Anti-Trust Act violation may be ordered to make restitution to the victims for all overcharges. Victims of bid-rigging and price-fixing conspiracies also may seek civil recovery of up to three times the amount of damages suffered."* Source: https://www.justice.gov/atr/ price-fixing-bid-rigging-and-market-allocation-schemes.

Federal Civil Statutes

10 US Code 2306a: Truth In Negotiations Act (cost or pricing data). NOTE: If a false statement/certification was provided with the intent to defraud, this could also be a criminal case—consider 18 USC 1001 (False Statement) and/or 18 USC 287 (False Claim).
15 USC 1125: False designations of origin, false descriptions, and dilution (including trademarks).
31 USC 3729–3733: Civil False Claims Act: This statute also allows private parties to prosecute civil action against perpetrators(s) on behalf of the government.
31 USC 3801–3812: Program Fraud Civil Remedies Act: Includes False Claims and the collection of civil penalties and assessments.

Other Titles and U.S. Codes of Interest

The Title 5 U.S. Code describes government organizations and employees. The Ethics in Government Act is also included, of which Title 1 describes the federal employees' financial disclosure requirements. The Inspector General Act of 1978 is included in Title 5.

Common U.S. Customs Violations

18 USC 545: Smuggling Goods into the U.S.

> "Whoever knowingly and willfully, with intent to defraud the United States, smuggles, or clandestinely introduces or attempts to smuggle or clandestinely introduce into the United States any merchandise which should have been invoiced, or makes out or passes, or attempts to pass, through the customhouse any false, forged, or fraudulent invoice, or other document or paper; or
> Whoever fraudulently or knowingly imports or brings into the United States, any merchandise contrary to law, or receives, conceals, buys, sells, or in any manner facilitates the transportation, concealment, or sale of such merchandise after importation, knowing the same to have been imported or brought into the United States contrary to law
> Shall be fined under this title or imprisoned not more than 20 years, or both. Proof of defendant's possession of such goods, unless explained to the satisfaction of the jury, shall be deemed evidence sufficient to authorize conviction for violation of this section.
> Merchandise introduced into the United States in violation of this section, or the value thereof, to be recovered from any person described in the first or second paragraph of this section, shall be forfeited to the United States. The term 'United States', as used in this section, shall not include the Virgin Islands, American Samoa, Wake Island, Midway Islands, Kingman Reef, Johnston Island, or Guam."

19 USC 1304: Marking of Imported Articles and Containers. In the United States, the marking statute, Section 304, Tariff Act of 1930, as amended (19 USC. 1304) requires that, unless excepted, every article of foreign origin (or its container) imported into the U.S. shall be marked with its country of origin. For more information, visit http://www.cbp.gov/trade/nafta/guide-customs-procedures/country-origin-marking.

Common U.S. Environmental Law Violations

15 USC 2601-2692: Toxic Substance Control Act.
For information on criminal provisions, visit https://www.epa.gov/enforcement/criminal-provisions-toxic-substances-control-act-tsca.
33 USC 1251-1387: Clean Water Act.
For information on criminal provisions, visit https://www.epa.gov/enforcement/criminal-provisions-clean-water-act.
42 USC 6901-6991: Resource Conservation and Recovery Act (re: hazardous waste).
   For information about the act and its enforcement, visit https://www.epa.gov/laws-regulations/summary-resource-conservation-and-recovery-act.

NOTE: For additional information on the U.S. Environmental Protection Agency Enforcement Actions, visit https://www.epa.gov/enforcement.
   The next chapter describes investigative sources and resources to consider when conducting investigations of contract and procurement fraud, collusion, and corruption.

7 Investigative Sources and Resources

Much of the information and documentation needed to gain knowledge about your case and assist in proving contract and procurement fraud, collusion, and/or corruption can be obtained from many sources, including:

- the customer that originated and requested the need for services, supplies, etc.;
- the contracting official that awarded the contract and the inspectors and auditors;
- the vendors that submitted bids for the contract;
- the awarded vendors' suppliers and subcontractors;
- other sources.

Information, documentation, and proof of illegal payments, gifts and/or gratuities may be available at these locations but will more often be located elsewhere, e.g. banks and financial institutions, etc.

Sometimes the information you need is or was once available from more than one source. E-mails are a good example. If someone sent an e-mail, their computer, e-mail service provider, server, and/or cloud service provider should have copies, and the same is true for whoever received the e-mail. Sometimes courtesy copies (cc) and even blind copies (bcc) of the same e-mail were intentionally sent to others. Also, the receiver or cc recipient may have forwarded the e-mail to others. Some e-mails might have been deleted from one source but not from another. Therefore, you should often consider requesting (or otherwise legally obtaining) the same information from more than once source—perhaps simultaneously.

Also, because many of these offenses involve two or more partners in crime, the information you want to obtain may be time sensitive. For example, in a bid-rigging case, once you execute a search warrant or issue a subpoena at one vendor's location, other partners in crime might be informed about your investigation. In fact, sometimes the news media is at the scene when warrants are executed. If the word gets out about the investigation, it's highly probable that the other criminally involved bidders will start removing and/or destroying evidence. And they'll probably also be getting their stories straight, which could hamper your future interviewing efforts. (For more information on investigative planning, see Chapter 11.)

Investigative Sources and Resources 89

This chapter describes many sources of information and resources to obtain information that may assist in your investigations.

Author's Note: *A business entity that wants to receive contracts from the federal government must first request and obtain a "Cage Code" (described below), which is a unique number assigned to that entity. Many queries conducted within federal systems may require searches by the entity's Cage Code, not their business name. Some searches can also be performed by the entity's DUNS Number (also described below).*

Commercial and Government Entity Code

Cage Code stands for Commercial and Government Entity Code.

It is a five-character ID number used extensively within the federal government, assigned by the Department of Defense (DoD)'s Defense Logistics Agency (DLA). The CAGE code is used to support a variety of mechanized systems throughout the government and provides a standardized method of identifying a given legal entity at a specific location. The code may be used for a facility clearance, or a pre-award survey.

(Source: https://www.fsd.gov/fsd-gov/answer.do?sysparm_number=KB0011119.)

NATO Commercial and Government Entity Codes (NCAGE Codes)

CAGE codes for entities located outside the United States and its territories are called NATO Commercial and Government Entity (NCAGE) codes. NCAGE codes are assigned internationally as part of the NATO Codification System (NCS), and are required for all foreign entities or the registration will be considered incomplete.

(Source: https://www.fsd.gov/fsd-gov/answer.do?sysparm_number=KB0011119.)

Data Universal Numbering System Number (DUNS NUMBER)

Created in 1962, the Data Universal Numbering System or D-U-N-S® Number is Dun & Bradstreet's (D&B) copyrighted, proprietary means of identifying business entities on a location-specific basis.

Assigned and maintained solely by D&B, this unique nine-digit identification number has been assigned to over 100 million businesses worldwide. A D-U-N-S® Number remains with the company location to which it has been assigned even if it closes or goes out-of-business.

The D-U-N-S® Number also "unlocks" a wealth of value-added data associated with that entity, including the business name, physical and mailing addresses, tradestyles ("doing business as"), principal names, financial, payment experiences, industry classifications (SICs and NAICS), socio-economic status, government data and more. The D-U-N-S® Number also links members of corporate family trees worldwide.

(Source: https://fedgov.dnb.com/webform/pages/dunsnumber.jsp.)

The D-U-N-S® Number is widely used by both commercial and federal entities and was adopted as the standard business identifier for federal electronic commerce in October 1994. The D-U-N-S Number® was also incorporated into the Federal Acquisition Regulation (FAR) in April 1998 as the Federal Government's contractor identification code for all procurement-related activities.

(Source: https://fedgov.dnb.com/webform/pages/dunsnumber.jsp.)

Investigative Sources and Resources

Sources and Resources in Contract and Procurement Fraud and Collusion Investigations

The type and volume of information that might be available on a contract and procurement fraud or collusion case depends on the type of contract awarded and dollar amount. If you are only investigating a simple violation like a short shipment, you are probably not going to need every single document involved in the contract award process. But if you are investigating collusion, questionable sole source awards, or high dollar contracts awarded with no competition, you should review everything you can legally get your hands on concerning the contract's award. Information that can be obtained from several sources is listed here.

From the Requestor, Customer, or Buyer

Documentation of the Request for Need

Someone made a request for goods, services, supplies, construction, or whatever. Depending on the complexity and/or the dollar amount involved, a paper trail should exist, reflecting that someone communicated that they had a need. This documentation could be in the form of an e-mail sent, minutes from a meeting, hand-written notes, or perhaps just a requisition or order placed.

If there was a meeting and/or discussions with several individuals about the need, the names of those individuals might be documented. (If not, during your interviews you can inquire about or corroborate who was present.) There may be documentation that others agreed or disagreed with the idea, concept, or need. For example, it might be a red flag if the customer requested or demanded that a specific vendor be used when other capable vendors could have filled the need just as easily. Depending on the type of case you are investigating, anyone present during such meetings could possess valuable information or insight.

Author's Note: *What was said or communicated before, during, and even after a contract is awarded can be very valuable to your investigation.*

Funding Requests and Approval

If the contract was for a large-dollar amount, there should be documentation showing that funding was (1) requested, (2) approved, and (3) allocated. Sometimes this is done before the need is even requested. For example, before expressing the need to others, the requestor might have ascertained if funding (or a certain dollar amount) was available and could be allocated to a certain project. Sometimes the requests and approvals are communicated by internal e-mails.

From the Contracting Office

*Documentation of Receipt of Request for Need
(and Related Communication)*

In large organizations, contracting and order placements are handled by designated individuals and/or offices. Regardless, the expressed need (and perhaps funding approval) will be communicated or provided by the customer or buyer to the contracting/ordering office or personnel. In other words, there should be some form of documentation showing that someone specifically asked for something to be ordered or acquired. This request is usually communicated in person, by e-mail, or by phone.

After the request is received, there will usually be some form of confirmation of receipt that is communicated and perhaps follow-up questions asked and answered. Records or notes about that communication are usually kept or maintained by the contracting officer or ordering official. You'll need to determine who communicated and how they communicated. Next, you'll need to ascertain where records of that communication are maintained.

Contract File

The contract file will usually be of tremendous value during your investigation. Some contract files are not just one file. I've obtained contract files on multimillion-dollar contracts that required a small SUV to load all of the boxes of documents!

Author's Note: *If you intend to remove the original contract file documents from the contracting office, sometimes the contracting officials will still need copies. If you are working a possible corruption case, it would probably be unwise to just let the contracting office copy the files unsupervised because documents could be intentionally removed. To avoid others tampering with potential evidence, you or your office might be on the hook to copy every single document inside the file(s). That could result in major downtime and expense, so keep this in mind when planning your investigation.*

Contract File Contents

The contract file should contain documentation from the inception until the completion of the order. Documentation included in the contract file may include the following:

- Customer's request;
- Market research and/or price history search results;
- Requests for information (RFI) (seeking information from vendors);
- Request for bids (RFB) (or solicitations or advertisements) that solicit bids/proposals;
- Records of vendors' price quotations received (telephonic or otherwise);
- Bid proposals received from bidders;
- Bid abstract (or similar listing of all vendors that submitted bids and their price quotes);
- Statement of value and/or cost and pricing data (pre-award) provided by vendor(s) with their proposals or soon thereafter;
- Contracting official's request for additional information and/or supportive documentation;
- Vendor responses to the requests for additional information and/or supportive documentation;
- Bid proposal evaluations and ratings;
- Conflict of interest certifications (contracting officials, bid evaluators, and/or vendors);
- Buyer's pre-award surveys and/or inspection of bidder's premises, first articles, demonstrations, internal and external testing, and test results;
- Small Business Administration (SBA) requests for Certificates of Competency (CoC);
- SBA response approval/disapproval and/or issuance of CoC;
- If sole-source or set-aside—supportive documentation justifying the selection;
- Records of all pre-award conferences, meetings, source selection recommendations, and source selection decisions;
- Record and/or certification of price *reasonableness* and/or determination of best value;
- Contracting officer's certification that the selected vendor was deemed "responsible" and/or financially stable/sound;
- Signed contract;
- Protests and/or complaints from vendor(s) not awarded the contract;
- Results and/or responses to protests and/or complaints from vendors not awarded the contract;
- Signed amendments, modifications, and change orders;
- Documentation supporting the request/need for amendments, modifications, and change orders;
- Records of requests for inspection and requests for testing;
- Records of inspection and test results;
- Records of acceptance (and/or refusal to accept);
- Customer (or end user) complaints;
- Resolution of customer (or end user) complaints;
- Vendor claims for payment (and supportive documentation if required);
- Statement of value and/or cost and pricing data (post award);

- Approvals and/or disapprovals of payments;
- Records of payment;
- Records of communication for any and all of the above;
- If contract was terminated before completion—supportive documentation justifying the termination, notice to contractor, response(s) from contractor; and official contract termination.

Author's Note: *The contract file could contain more or less of these documents and/ or additional documents. Typically, only a few e-mail exchanges will have been printed and included in the contract file.*

Other Customer-Related Files (Including Payments and Complaints)

Large organizations may have separate offices or departments that handle inspections, acceptance, payments, and reports of discrepancies (RODS) or complaints, etc. Unfortunately, sometimes the contracting officer, contracting office, and/ or person that placed the order or awarded the contract may be totally unaware of any problems that occurred after the contract was awarded. Because some or many post-award complaints are assigned or delegated elsewhere, the investigator may have to contact many others to fully investigate some wrongdoing. The contracting officer that awarded the contract should be able to provide points of contact for all officials involved before, during, and after the contract was awarded.

Prime Contractors' Files

Vendors that have been awarded contracts are often referred to as prime contractors and they may utilize subcontractors. The prime contractor will likely have all documents (or copies) they provided to and received from the buyer or contracting officers prior to, during, and after the contract was awarded. They will also have documents pertaining to their use of suppliers, vendors, shippers, trucking companies, and others used to assist or complete the contract. These documents may include the prime contractor's search for, selection, and use of suppliers, vendors, and subcontractors, as well as records of communication with them. The prime contractor may also have copies of test results, certifications, proofs of shipping and delivery, invoices, and payments made and received, etc.

Subcontractors' Files

The prime contactor's suppliers, vendors, shippers, trucking companies, and others used to assist or complete their contract(s) (often referred to as subcontractors) may also have similar documentation to the prime contractor. However, the subcontractors usually won't have any interaction with the original buyer or documents pertaining to the original buyer's contract. Subcontractors can often provide useful information to your investigation, but because of their close relationship with the prime contractor, don't assume your inquiries will always be held confidential.

Chapter 7

Third-Tier Contractors' Files

The subcontractors, suppliers, vendors, shippers, trucking companies, and others may have also used others to assist or complete their contract(s). Ordinarily, they won't have any interaction with the original buyer or documents pertaining to the original buyer's contract. Third-tier contractors can often provide useful information to your investigation but because of their close relationship with the subcontractor and perhaps the prime contractor, don't assume your inquiries will always be held confidential.

Losing Bidders' Files

If you are conducting an investigation with concerns about favoritism in the source selection process, at some point you probably should contact some or all of the vendors that submitted bids or proposals and/or provided price quotes and were not awarded the contract(s) in question. These vendors will probably possess documents and records of communication pertaining to the contract(s) in question. Very often, competitive vendors can provide useful information and incredible insight into the contract selection and award processes used on the contract(s). They can sometimes shed light on other possible improprieties on previous contracts awarded.

Author's Note: *Keep in mind that if you suspect that any of the losing bidders participated in collusion and/or bid rigging, you'll have to plan accordingly so as to not jeopardize the success of your investigation. You could opt to interview the least likely involved losing bidders first. Conversely, you could opt to interview the most likely involved first. Draft your plan and then consider the possible repercussions and benefits concerning your timing and the tools and techniques you're considering. Like playing chess, think about your moves in advance because whatever you do will usually result in some type of reaction.*

U.S. Mail and Overnight Delivery Services

In corruption investigations, sometimes vendors ship goods and money to contracting officials' home addresses. The shipments may be addressed to the individual, the spouse, or even a company name. Unrelated to corruption investigations, goods or supplies may have also been shipped (or reportedly shipped) through the U.S. Postal Service or an overnight delivery service. Proof of shipment and delivery can often be obtained from the U.S. Postal Service or the overnight delivery service.

Trucking Companies

If goods were shipped (or reportedly shipped), proof of shipment and delivery can often be obtained from the trucking companies. Trucking companies will more likely have listings of quantities and perhaps weight. Very often they can also provide the names and signatures of people who released and signed for deliveries.

E-mails

Legally obtained e-mails with communication about illegal or prohibited activity can make your case even easier to prove. E-mails are especially useful in collusion and corruption investigations. At a minimum, they will probably greatly assist in your preparation for future interviews.

Text Messages

Like e-mails, lawfully obtained and reviewed text messages can result in great evidence—especially in collusion and corruption investigations.

Telephone Records

Telephone records can be helpful as they will show whose number was called, the dates and times of calls, duration of calls, frequency of calls, etc. Sometimes it's interesting to learn who someone called immediately before or after a specific event. Although you won't know what was said during the calls (unless you are law enforcement and had approval to monitor), the information obtained can be of great investigative value and/or assist in planning for your future interviews.

Public Records

There are numerous public records and other databases that may provide useful information during contract and procurement fraud, collusion, and corruption investigations. Some are listed here:

- Secretary of State business records;
- Judgments and uniform commercial code filings;
- County tax assessor records;
- Federal bankruptcies;
- Marriage and divorce filings;
- Department of vital statistics (birth and death records);
- Internet and news media.

Federal Government's Exclusion List

To help determine if a contractor has been debarred from federal government contracting, visit the U.S. Department of Labor's website dealing with Office of Federal Contract Compliance Programs (https://www.dol.gov/ofccp/regs/compliance/preaward/debarlst.htm).

The following was copied and pasted from the website on June 7, 2016:

Office of Federal Contract Compliance Programs (OFCCP)

OFCCP Debarred Companies

To find a list of current companies (Entity) or individuals that have been declared ineligible to receive Federal contracts due to a violation of Executive Order 11246, as amended; Section 503 of the Rehabilitation Act of 1973, as amended 29 U.S.C. Section 793; and/or the Vietnam Era Veterans' Readjustment Assistance Act of 1974, as amended, 38 U.S.C. Section 4212, follow the instructions below to access the System for Award Management (SAM). SAM contains the electronic roster of debarred companies excluded from Federal procurement and non-procurement programs throughout the U.S. Government (unless otherwise noted) and from receiving Federal contracts or certain subcontracts and from certain types of Federal financial and nonfinancial assistance and benefits. The SAM system combines data from the Central Contractor Registration, Federal Register, Online Representations and Certification Applications, and the Excluded Parties List System.

Author's Note: *The website includes a link to SAM (www.sam.gov), where anyone can search by terms (including entity name), DUNS number, or Cage Code. (The CAGE Code is a five-character ID number used extensively within the federal government, assigned by the DLA). The website also has an advanced search option.*

Social Media

Individual's as well as entity's social media profiles and their photos and videos publically shared on the internet can sometimes be of tremendous value to many types of investigations—including collusion and corruption investigations. If you found photos of a contracting officer with a contractor in a social setting away from work, that could be of evidentiary value and certainly helpful when planning your future interviews. Sometimes people say they don't know someone but their social media's "friends" or "connections" lists may indicate otherwise.

Author's Note: *After searching the internet by one name, you could also include a second person's name in the same search to see if you get any results. For example, in the same search, you could list the contracting officer's name and the awarded vendor's owner's name.*

Dun and Bradstreet (Comprehensive Report)

Dun and Bradstreet (D&B) allow their subscribers to obtain comprehensive reports on entities that can be very useful in contract and procurement fraud and collusion investigations. The information, available for a fee, includes but is not limited to:

- Company size;
- Years in business;
- Financial solvency;
- Payments and histories;
- Bankruptcy proceedings;

- Liens;
- Suits;
- Uniform Commercial Code (UCC) filings;
- Officer and director identification;
- Officer and director stocks;
- Corporate affiliations;
- General banking and financial information;
- Total assets and liabilities;
- And much more.

Author's Note: *To view an overview and sample comprehensive report visit* https://www.dnb.com/product/comsampl.htm.

Other Investigative and Law Enforcement Agencies and Units

There are many international, federal, state and local investigative agencies that investigate contract and procurement fraud, collusion and/or related corruption. Investigators will do well to have professional contacts with other agencies that investigate such offenses because the fraudsters and bribe payers harming your agency may very well also be harming other federal, state, and local agencies. Combining your intelligence and investigative resources could "blow the roof off" the bad guys' ploys.

Sources and Resources in Corruption Investigations

If conducting a corruption in contracting investigation, you'll still need information about contracts awarded and bids/proposals, as described above. All or most of the above will also be important to your investigation. But to prove corruption, you'll need to look for and find proof that something of value was provided and received. There are many sources where those items can be found, including those listed below. This chapter highlights a few possible sources to assist in identifying payments made.

Author's Note: *Illegal payoffs can take many forms, including cash, checks, wire transfers, debit cards, gifts, stays at condos, jobs or job offers, etc. Investigators would do well to become knowledgeable about money-laundering methods. The Association of Certified Fraud Examiners (ACFE) provides an online self-study course titled Investigating Money Laundering.* (For more information, visit: http://www.acfe.com/products.aspx?id=2838.)

Finding Evidence of Bribery Payments from Contractors/Vendors Illegal Payments

A vendor that has made illegal payments to a buyer or contracting official must have obtained those funds from somewhere. The illegal payments could have been made by the company's owner, executives, or even sales personnel. The funds could have originated from the vendor's business accounts or even personal accounts. You'll need lawful authority to search bank records. Very often, law enforcement and criminal prosecutors utilize grand jury subpoenas to obtain bank records.

Sometimes (but not too often) a vendor's bribe payments are made in the form of checks that are payable directly to the buyer or contracting officer. Sometimes vendor checks are made payable to someone in the same company who will actually make the bribe payment. Such checks would be a red flag if they are not for salary or reimbursement for travel or expenses. Similarly, checks payable to cash could also be a red flag. For additional information, see the section in this chapter titled *Requesting and Reviewing Bank Statements*.

Author's Note: *Even-numbered dollar amounts are always red flags (for example, checks payable to anybody for $500, $1,000, $2,500, $5,000, or $10,000, etc.).*

Finding Evidence of Bribery Payments Paid to Contracting Officials and Buyers

The brightest red flag indicating that contracting officials or buyers have received bribes is when they live beyond their means. Examples include driving a very expensive vehicle, exotic vacations, frequent attendance at sporting events which require highly price tickets, or being able to send their kids to private or highly priced schools (not on scholarships) when peer employees can't afford to. Finding the source of the bribe money is not always easy. Sometimes contracting official's spouses (or former spouses) know what's going on and even assist in hiding and/or laundering ill-gotten gains. For additional information, see the following section.

Requesting and Reviewing Bank Statements

Unless someone voluntarily and lawfully provides you with monthly bank statements, or you obtain them through some other lawful manner, searching for bribe payments through financial institutions (usually by using grand jury subpoenas) can be time-consuming and expensive.

Keep in mind that people may have accounts held individually and/or jointly. Individuals might even have companies on the side that are not directly related to the contracts of interest. So, when trying to identify bribes from bank accounts, you may also want to ask for accounts "held individually and/or jointly and/or any and all other accounts with signature authority." You could consider also requesting information about Certificates of Deposit (CDs), Individual Retirement Accounts (IRAs), safety deposit boxes, and everything else (*the kitchen sink*). (Please check with your attorney or legal counsel before requesting/enacting.)

Regarding bank statements, you'll get results back faster and at less cost if you first request, receive, and analyze the monthly bank statements before asking for copies of any checks, withdrawal slips, wire transfers, etc.

For example, if you immediately request copies of all checks above a certain dollar amount, it will take the bank longer to comply and it will cost you more in labor and copying costs. I've found it's better to first request and review the bank statements. After that, make a second request for copies of specific check numbers, money transfers, withdrawal slips, etc. that you are interested in. You may need to make three or four follow-up requests after each review.

I've found it unwise to ask for copies of *all checks* because the bank will provide copies of small-dollar checks that had nothing to do with bribe payments. Asking for copies of all checks (especially of a business) will seriously delay getting the results and the bill for labor and copying will be unnecessarily high. Plus, your boss, prosecutor, or client won't be very pleased if they get a lot of expensive invoices from the banks. Depending on the case, the suspects may have several different accounts at several different financial institutions, so being cost-conscious is usually in everyone's interest. An exception to this may be if you are relatively certain that a specific account has what you are looking for or if time is of the essence. As previously stated, high-dollar, even-numbered dollar amounts are always of special interest when investigating corruption cases.

Additional Sources and Resources in Contract and Procurement Fraud, Collusion, and Corruption Investigations

Previous Investigation Checks

Law enforcement agencies have the ability to check if the suspects (including suspect entities) of your investigation were ever investigated by law enforcement before. Even if they were not charged in a criminal or civil court, the information and intelligence gained from previous investigations could prove very valuable to your current investigation. You may be able to solve/prove an old case(s) based on information developed in your new case.

Criminal History Checks

Running criminal history checks on your suspects certainly can shed some light as to their past involvement with wrongdoing. But, factually, many white-collar suspects' backgrounds are free from previous arrests. Conducting a criminal history check is still worthwhile.

Author's Note: *Although law enforcement can run criminal histories through the FBI's National Crime Information Center (NCIS), others (including members of the general public) can still check federal, state, county, and local publically available court records, but it is much more time consuming. Also, many states allow anyone to check names for arrest and/or convictions for a fee. Usually you will need to provide your suspects' dates of birth and social security numbers when making such requests. The specific details about arrests will often have to be obtained from the arresting agency(s) and/or courthouses. Many state's websites also have the corresponding court records available for download and purchase for an additional fee. As a private investigator and* *consultant, I've often conducted searches and obtained details about arrests and court cases from many official state's websites without ever leaving my office. Don't confuse the state websites with other non-government websites that claim to conduct criminal history checks for a fee.*

The Government Accountability Office (GAO)

The GAO is responsible for receiving, reviewing, and determining the merit of official protests made by bidders who were not awarded contracts for which they submitted bid proposals regarding the awarding of any federal contract. The GAO's website provides details about bid protests, including how to file an official protest. Investigators and members of the general public can conduct searches on the GAO's website to learn facts about many protests filed.

Searches can be queried by agency, solicitation number (this is the contract's solicitation advertisement number which precedes the actual contract number; a federal contract will usually include the solicitation number on its first page), protestor's name, or GAO protest number. You can also search for protest decisions by using key words. For more information, visit http://www.gao.gov/legal/bid-protests/search.

Other Useful Government Public Websites

Although federal, state, and local government investigative agencies have legal access to many different agencies and sites to query and search for useful contractor and contract information, the general public can also access many websites to conduct searches. Just a few are listed here.

- https://www.sam.gov: To search for an entity and their Cage Code, visit the federal government's SAM website. You can search for entities doing business with the federal government by name, cage code, and/or DUNS number. The site may also provide information about entities' exclusion status. Visit the site for additional information and information about its limitations.
- https://www.usaspending.gov/Pages/Default.aspx: USAspending.gov is a publicly accessible, searchable website mandated by the Federal Funding Accountability and Transparency Act of 2006 to give the American public access to information on how their tax dollars are spent. You can search this website by name, state, and/or zip code to identify prime federal contracts awarded, grants, loans, and other financial assistance. After identifying the entity/person, it will usually provide their address, award number, dollar amount awarded, and more.
- http://www.defense.gov/News/Contracts: DoD contracts awarded for $7 million and over are announced daily (archived records may also be viewed).
- https://www.FedBizOpps.gov: This site lists federal government contract opportunities. The system can be searched by opportunities posted by interval, including just in the past day or all the way up to the past 365 days. This is the go-to website for contractors to search for federal contract opportunities.

Investigative Sources and Resources   101

Non-Government Websites

There are many non-government websites that have useful information about federal contracts (especially DoD contracts) won and awarded, and they provide information about the contractors, dollar amounts of awards, and dates of awards, etc. Searches can even be performed by name, city, county, state, etc. Some charge a fee to download specific information, but some websites provide incredible amounts of potentially useful information at no cost. Although not endorsed by the author, the publisher, or anyone affiliated with this book, you could search the internet entering key words, "government contracts won" or "government contracts awarded."

Additional Sources and Resources

The Defense Contract Audit Agency (DCAA)

The DCAA is not an investigative agency; however, it often provides investigative assistance and referrals for the DoD and other federal investigations.

> The Defense Contract Audit Agency (DCAA) provides audit and financial advisory services to DoD and other federal entities responsible for acquisition and contract administration. DCAA operates under the authority, direction, and control of the Under Secretary of Defense (Comptroller)/ Chief Financial Officer.
> (Source: http://www.dcaa.mil/about_dcaa.html.)

The Association of Certified Fraud Examiners (ACFE)

The ACFE provides antifraud training on numerous antifraud subjects including contract fraud and corruption. The ACFE also sells helpful books and its bimonthly *Fraud Magazine* helps keep fraud fighters up to date with some of the latest fraud schemes, fraud-fighting tools, tactics, and stories. The ACFE's annual *Report to the Nations on Occupational Fraud and Abuse* provides an analysis of thousands of cases of occupational fraud that occurred in over 100 countries throughout the world. The networking opportunities with other antifraud professionals are plentiful, including the ACFE's annual Global Fraud Conferences held in the United States and other locations across the globe. Individuals may also pursue and obtain the professional Certified Fraud Examiner (CFE) credential, which is internationally recognized as the gold standard for a fraud fighter. For additional information, visit www.acfe.com.

The Internet, Websites, and Social Media Sites

Last, and by no means least, the internet is a useful source and resource for obtaining information or leads to assist in contract and procurement fraud, collusion, and corruption investigations. Investigators should search the internet by entering the suspects' names (along with some other related key words). The amount of publically available information (including photographs) on the internet about people and companies is staggering. Sometimes, suspects post useful information about themselves, their activities, and their associates for the whole world to see on social media sites (e.g. Facebook, Twitter, Pinterest, and LinkedIn). In addition, company websites often have a great deal of current and historic information about the company, their executives and employees, and other useful information.

The next chapter describes investigative tools and techniques to consider utilizing when conducting investigations of contract and procurement fraud, collusion, and corruption.

8   Investigative Tools and Techniques

Investigative tools are things you'll use to legally access and/or obtain information and/or evidence to assist in your investigation. I personally think of techniques as how you apply or use the tools. Chapter 11 details investigative case planning, but before you can plan you must know what investigative tools are available and how to best use them.

As previously related, law enforcement investigators have access to more tools than do non-law enforcement investigators and/or members of the general public. The results can be incredible when all are working as a team. Of course, it's worth reminding ourselves that we are only trying to establish and prove the truth.

Tools and Techniques

The following is a list of tools and techniques commonly used when conducting investigations involving contract and procurement fraud, collusion, and/or related corruption.

Hotlines

Hotlines are one of the best tools used to identify fraud and possible collusion and corruption. Most hotlines allow callers the option of providing their names or remaining anonymous. For an investigator, it's always better when the caller leaves his or her name and contact information so that he or she can be re-interviewed in more detail.

Informants

Informants can be very valuable to investigators investigating contract and procurement fraud, collusion, and corruption.

Author's Note: *Unfortunately, some investigative agencies "put the cart in front of the horse" and excessively push investigators to develop "confidential informants." To comply, some investigators unnecessarily turn witnesses, who never sought confidentiality in the first place, into confidential informants. Don't unnecessarily make a potential* witness a confidential informant just to impress or comply with your agency's requirement or desire to increase the number of informants. In the end, it will be much better (or easier) if your witnesses do not require that their identities be protected.

Computers, Hardware, and Software

Probably the most frequently used tools when conducting white-collar investigations are computers and their related hardware and software. Many useful books and articles have been written about the use of analytics, data mining, data mapping, and so forth to detect fraud and/or assist in investigations. This chapter only includes general descriptions of each.

- **Analytics:** The process of collecting, organizing, and analyzing large sets of data to discover patterns, anomalies, and other useful information.
- **Data mining:** The process of turning raw data into useful information by identifying patterns, trends, and/or relationships.
- **Data mapping:** The process of creating data element mappings between two distinct data models.

Search Warrants

A legally executed search warrant(s) can be the most effective tool to obtain evidence of wrongdoing in contract and procurement fraud, collusion, and/or corruption investigations. Requesting, planning, and executing search warrants can take extra time and manpower. Depending on the type of case being investigated, large amounts of documents and electronic data may be seized from the premises. Arrangements will then have to be made to transport the seized items as well as secure them. The chain of custody of items seized must also remain intact. The investigator(s) must later review and examine the items that were seized.

During or immediately after the execution of a search warrant on a business, the company's owner, executive, and/or attorney may say that they need copies of many or most of the documents seized in order to continue operating their business. Unless there is a legal reason not to comply, you and/or your agency will be on the hook to provide the copies. And when the investigation is complete, you'll be required to return, properly dispose of, and/or release most of the stuff you seized.

Author's Note: *Experienced law enforcement officers understand to "dot the i's and cross the t's" because the suspect's attorney(s) will most probably attempt to find fault with everything the cops did during their investigation—especially regarding the search warrant and/or the affidavit used to obtain the search warrant. While at the warrant scene, the police will often shoot video after entering, before searching, and immediately prior to departure. The person using the video camera usually knows to not include audio to avoid "unnecessary" verbiage from being recorded. However, many facilities also have their own internal security cameras which are capable of filming the police performing their duties during the execution of search warrants. They might also have* the ability to record audio. In short, when executing search warrants, be conscious of others' possible use of cameras and recorders.

Subpoenas

Criminal case and/or civil case subpoenas are often used to obtain documents and records or other tangible items (*subpoena duces tecum*). Some subpoenas can be used to compel testimony (*subpoena ad testificandum*). It's been my experience that documents, information, and testimony obtained by the use of grand jury subpoenas cannot be used in any civil case. That problem does not exist if the documents were obtained from a search warrant or from the use of administrative or non–grand jury subpoenas. The information a person provides during an interview without a grand jury subpoena can also be used in both criminal and civil cases. Sometimes witnesses are reluctant to be interviewed, but serving them with a grand jury subpoena for testimony can make the investigator's job a bit easier.

Authorized and Civil Investigative Demands

Authorized Civil Investigative Demands (often referred to as AIDs) can be issued by the Department of Justice (DoJ) for records when investigating healthcare offenses and False Claims Act cases. These are more commonly known now as Civil Investigative Demands (CIDs). They are essentially the same as civil subpoenas and are often used by the FBI, which is part of the DoJ.

Subpoena Log

I've personally conducted investigations in which many grand jury and administrative subpoenas were utilized on the same case. In one case, over 60 subpoenas were utilized. I've found that creating a log using Microsoft Excel helps keep track of the serving and compliance of each subpoena. It's not unusual for a bank or other entity to request additional time to gather and sometimes copy documents before providing them. Some provide their responses piecemeal.

For example, in one subpoena, a bank was required to provide several years' worth of copies of an entity's cashed checks, deposits and withdrawal slips, and cashier's checks and money orders purchased with proceeds of some of the entity's cashed checks. The bank did a good job of complying, but they provided results piecemeal. Sometimes they provided copies of 1 year's worth of checks and other times they'd provide months' worth. Because I had also served several other subpoenas to other banks on the same case while simultaneously conducting other unrelated investigations, it could have been difficult to remember who was complying and what they provided. But I kept track of the subpoena compliance progress by maintaining an up-to-date subpoena log which kept track of the documents provided by each bank. You must document the progress or risk losing track and perhaps wrongly assume that the recipients fully complied when in fact they did not.

Contractual Right to Review

Many or most government contracts (and perhaps business and/or private contracts) include provisions or an "inspections clause" which allows the buyer (or government program) that awarded the contract(s) the right to review and/or audit any claims and related information possessed by the awarded party to support the accuracy and authenticity of claims, costs, products, inspection and testing process, and results etc. What that could mean for an investigator is that some documents and other items can be legally reviewed, copied, and perhaps obtained by the authorized investigator(s) without the use of subpoenas or other investigative tools.

One of the advantages of using subpoenas, AIDs, and CIDs, and/or allowing the subpoenaed party to furnish the requested records to comply with contractual agreements, is that the subpoenaed/requested party must provide what you asked for and that they usually make copies of everything before they provide the materials. It's been my experience that most of the time they provide all documents in an organized manner. The disadvantage of using subpoenas, AIDs, CIDs, and/or allowing the subpoenaed party to furnish the requested documents in compliance with contractual requirements (while you are not present) is that they have the opportunity to alter or destroy documents and/or provide less than what was requested.

WAR STORY 8.1

While serving as a rookie federal agent, I attempted to review and make sense of a bunch of documents inside several boxes that were provided by a business owner in response to a subpoena. (The case was reassigned to me after another agent was transferred.) The suspect owned a medical supply company and was suspected of short-shipping orders to increase his (illegal) profits. The boxes included invoices, shipping documents, bills of lading, payment records, and all kinds of stuff. Every time I looked through the boxes, I got more confused and disillusioned about my ability to serve as a fraud investigator. I later interviewed the company's office manager who told me that after receiving the subpoena, employees worked together to gather all of the requested documents and stapled each order's paperwork together separately.

The office manager added that the day before they were to provide the subpoenaed documents to my office, the company owner announced "Un-staple everything and mix up all the documents! My attorney just told me we are required to provide the Feds what they asked for but there is no requirement to keep it organized." The employees reluctantly did what their boss told them to do.

Well, at least I learned why I was having such a difficult time when trying to review those documents. To make a long story short, with the help of witnesses, the company owner was later sentenced to prison for submitting false claims for payment to the government.

Analysis and Audits

Many government agencies and private entities employ their own compliance, risk management, security, and/or antifraud personnel or staff that routinely audit or analyze data, expenses, and/or costs to determine if fraud may have occurred. Although those audits and analysis are usually performed before making referrals for official investigations, they are still valuable tools when it comes to investigating contract and procurement fraud. Sometimes the same personnel can run additional queries to assist in an investigation after it's been initiated. The same personnel do not typically search for or try to identify red flags involving possible collusion or corruption. An investigator should not totally rely on others to identify potential instances of these often-overlooked crimes.

Trash Covers

Trash covers is the name for when law enforcement searches through and/or takes the trash that their suspect puts to the curb for trash pickup. Investigators should check their state's and local laws regarding the taking of or looking through other people's trash cans. But when legally performed, sometimes strong evidence can be obtained simply by looking through a suspect's trash. Many people (including business owners) think that once they put documents or other items in the trash that the documents no longer exist. But as identity thieves have proven, the documents still exist and may contain valuable information.

Mail Covers

As a federal agent, I often used mail covers in my white-collar crime investigations. Essentially, the law enforcement investigator prepares and submits an official request that meets the U.S. Postal Services' guidelines. If approved, the post office will provide a written description of the information listed on the outside of the envelopes/packages delivered to the address (or specified name(s) at the address) to the investigator in 30-day increments for a specified time period (usually up to 90 days). The information provided only includes things like the addressed-to name, the return address, and the postmark date, city, and state. The results provided to the investigator cannot be copied and must actually be returned to designated U.S. Postal Service officials.

Mail covers are an especially valuable tool in collusion and corruption investigations. The information obtained often helps identify the suspect's alias names, other business names used, and affiliated financial institutions. In contract and procurement fraud investigations, mail covers can assist in identifying other customers that an entity is doing business with. This is a nice way to identify potential victim entities.

If you are a federal agent investigating major contract and procurement fraud, collusion, or corruption, I highly recommend you request long-term mail covers on all suspects' addresses and ensure that your request includes mail addressed to all persons and all businesses. *(Author's Note: You will have to provide justification for the additional names in your request.*) If your request only includes your suspect's name, you will not receive results for mailings to other names used at the same address. I must emphasize that the envelopes are never opened by postal employees and the contents of the mailings are never known by the investigator.

Surveillance

Surveillance of a suspect can often result in useful information, good insight, and/or solid evidence being obtained. The evidence will normally be in the form of photographs and/or video. Long-term surveillance on most contract fraud schemes is not usually necessary. However, timely and well-planned surveillance in corruption investigations can be very beneficial.

Author's Note: *Some (perhaps all) high-definition video cameras might display the date and time when played on your video camera but may not show the date and time after you download the video to your computer. I contacted other private investigators across the United States, and many have experienced the same problem. Some investigators found solutions by first recording the video directly to a DVD recorder (not to their computer) and then copying the DVD to their computer. As a private investigator, I purchased some hardware that comes with its own software that allows me to download the video to a computer with the date and time stamp. It's called "Dazzle DVD Recorder HD," and comes with a CD (software) with Pinnacle Studio for Dazzle. I also had to separately purchase a Sony Handycam AV cable (# VMC-15MR2). This combination works for me when using my Sony HD video camera. Please do your own research before making any purchases.*

Undercovers

Approved and legally performed undercovers often result in undisputable proof of illegal acts. Having audio and/or video proof is very difficult for the suspect or their attorney to overcome. The most obvious defense attempt will be to suggest entrapment by the person(s) working undercover. Depending on the type of case, it's sometimes good to get more than one day of evidence to show a clear pattern of illegal activity.

Consensual Monitored Recordings

Witnesses, and sometimes suspects, can be asked to voluntarily (without coercion) meet with and/or telephone select other individuals who are believed to have knowledge (and/or be involved in criminal activity) and to converse with and record those conversations in an attempt to obtain evidence which may assist in proving or disproving criminal activity or other wrongdoing. Approval is normally granted by the law enforcement agency's high ranking superiors—often preceded by internal counsel's legal review.

Investigative Tools and Techniques   109

Author's Note: *Law enforcement and others considering the use of recording devices should ensure that they are following the letter of the law(s). Non–law enforcement personnel should ensure they follow the laws of the states that both the callers and receivers are in.*

Polygraphs and Deception Detectors

Investigators should know and abide by any applicable laws before even asking anyone if they would take or consider taking a polygraph (commonly referred to as a lie detector) or participate in any other deception-detecting examination. That said, such tools, when used by trained professionals, have been found useful to not only identify liars but also identify truth-tellers, which can eliminate some people from further suspicion.

Websites and Social Media

Websites

Although also listed as a source and resource, viewing websites is a great tool. Most businesses have their own websites which often provide incredible amounts of useful information for investigators. Websites may include the names and photographs of owners, executives, and employees. The company's services, products offered for sale, and other potentially useful information will probably also be listed along with their hours of operation and so forth.

Author's Note: *A sometimes useful website to view historic website screenshots from a known website is called "The Wayback Machine," and can be found at https://archive.org/web/. The historic captured screenshots can provide useful background information. Sometimes the names (and photographs) of previous employees and/or executives can be found.*

Social Media

Many people and businesses publically post useful information and photographs on social media sites like Facebook, Twitter, Pinterest, and LinkedIn. Some also create and post YouTube videos. Because LinkedIn is intended for professional profiles, people often list their current and former employers, where and when they went to school, and sometimes their e-mail addresses and telephone numbers.

It should be noted that, at the time of this writing, those with LinkedIn accounts have the ability to see who has viewed their profile unless the person viewing chose to be anonymous. Check your own settings before viewing others' LinkedIn profiles if that is a concern.

Author's Note: *An attorney once informed me that, while attending a training conference, the instructor said that if an investigator checks/views a represented party's LinkedIn profile, it could be considered unlawful communication (because they are* represented by an attorney). The instructor reasoned that the represented party could see who checked their profile and therefore it was a "communication." Based on that information, you should check with your own legal counsel before making such searches or clicking on someone else's profile (that's my CYA note), and it's probably another reason to make sure your own profile search settings are listed as anonymous.

The Internet

In addition to being a source and resource, searching the internet is also a great investigative tool. In addition to searching for and checking website and social media sites, court cases, news reports, obituaries, and tons of other information can often be found to assist in your investigation.

Ask

During my 30-plus years as an investigator, I've received some of the best information and evidence just by asking for it. People I've interviewed sometimes bring evidence with them and even glance at it during the interview. When the interview is completed, I ask if I can make copies (of the originals) of those documents. Sometimes former and even current employees bring home physical proof of wrongdoing because they didn't like what was going on at work. Even business owners and company executives will sometimes give you documents just because you asked for them. Remember that people have the right to refuse, so don't do or say anything that could be perceived as coercion. Some might suggest that it would also be smart to get them to sign something (perhaps a consent form) saying that they provided the documents freely and without coercion. You might want to have them initial and date each page that they give you.

WAR STORY 8.2

While conducting a bribery investigation, I interviewed a business owner and asked him about illegal payments that I knew he had previously made to a government contracting officer. I had possession of about two dozen cashier's checks that the business owner paid to the contracting officer and which had been deposited into the contracting officer's bank account. My case was pretty solid. Although the business owner initially denied paying the bribes, once I showed him copies of a couple of the cashier's checks, he realized I wasn't bluffing. After that, the business owner said he wanted to cooperate. I told him that I believed he had copies of all the cashier's checks he gave to the contracting officer. He nodded affirmatively. I then asked the business owner if he was willing to give those to me. The business owner later provided me with copies of many more cashier checks than I even knew about. (It never hurts to ask.)

Other

The above listing is not inclusive of all possible investigative tools and techniques available when investigating contract and procurement fraud, collusion, and corruption. You can make any pen and ink entries here if you so desire.

Author's Note: *You can use as many or few investigative tools and techniques as needed to get the job done, and you can use two or more simultaneously when you think the timing is right. It doesn't always have to be "one or the other." Sometimes it can be some or all of the above.*

Author's Note: *It's a good idea to have handy a list of all investigative tools at your disposal. You may want to also include the tools that others who often work with you have at their disposal. I've been known to tack a list of investigative tools on my wall which I reference when creating and updating investigative plans. Sometimes it's easy to forget you have a useful tool in your toolbox. Don't use a hammer when you could use a screwdriver.*

The next chapter details my favorite investigative tool: interviews and interrogations. Along with computers, interviews are probably the most frequent and useful tool to utilize when investigating contract and procurement fraud, collusion, and corruption.

Author's Note: Portions of this chapter were derived, copied, and/or modified from Chapter 7 (Investigative Tools and Techniques) of *Healthcare Fraud Investigation Guidebook*, by Charles E. Piper, copyright 2016 by Taylor & Francis Group, LLC. CRC Press is an imprint of Taylor & Francis Group, an Informa Business.

9 Interviews and Interrogations

It's important to understand the difference between an interview and an interrogation. An interview is non-accusatory. An interrogation is accusatory (directly or indirectly). An example of a direct accusation to a suspect after he/she denies committing a fraud might be "The investigative facts show that you did commit this fraud." An example of an indirect accusation under the same scenario might be "Because we conduct extremely thorough investigations, we know the facts before conducting our interviews. I think there's more that you'd like to tell me."

Interviews (not interrogations) are conducted with witnesses, complainants, and others who may have information which will assist in the investigation. Ideally, suspects are initially interviewed before being interrogated. Well-planned and thoroughly conducted interviews are often the key to the success of many investigations. The same is true of interrogations, if they are needed and actually conducted. Therefore, investigators should continually strive to improve their interview and interrogation (I&I) skills. Many seasoned investigators mistakenly assume that they know all they need to know about interviewing because they've done it for so many years. That's kind of like a Major League baseball outfielder saying they don't need to take batting practice or shag some fly balls before a game. Why wouldn't you want to perform at your absolute best?

In my opinion, all investigators should spend as much time training on their I&I skills as they do with any other tools/skills they use—including firearms and arrest technique training. However, I&I training does not always have to be conducted formally in a classroom. There are many books and courses available to public and private-sector investigators and others that will complement classroom training previously completed.

Two great sources for I&I classroom training are available through the following:

- John E. Reid & Associates (for more information, visit: www.reid.com)
- Wicklander-Zulawski & Associates, Inc. (for more information visit: www.w-z.com)

Both also offer I&I certification opportunities and their websites have online stores where helpful books and other training materials (including audio CDs and videos) are available for purchase. I suggest studying both of these methodologies and others. To best improve, you should continually broaden your skills and understand that there may be pros and cons to using any professional interviewing method.

Author's Note: *When making lengthy road trips in my car while alone (and sometimes when I'm on long-term surveillances), I often listen to I&I training CDs to brush up on my skills. You might want to give that a try, too. (Yes, I also listen to rock and roll—I'm not completely obsessed with the job or training.)*

I also recommend that you read my book, *Investigator and Fraud Fighter Guidebook: Operation War Stories*,* which has a chapter titled "Interviewing." The chapter also includes 15 of my own personal I&I "War Stories," some of which are humorous.

The topics included in that chapter on interviewing include:

Interview and interrogation;
Rapport;
Listen and then talk;
Note-taking;
Corroboration;
Word choice;
Planning;
Body language;
Props;
Finish the job;
Empathy;
Statement analysis:
- Pronouns
- Partial truths equal deception
- Specificity
- Minimizing
- Can't recall

Think plural;
Interview notes;
Interview room sketches and photographs.

Rather than repeating everything on the subject of interviewing that I wrote in *Investigator and Fraud Fighter Guidebook: Operation War Stories*,* the information which follows will pertain to interviews and/or interrogations involving contract and procurement fraud, collusion, and corruption investigations.

The importance of developing rapport before conducting interviews cannot be overemphasized. Also, most professional investigative interviewers will probably agree that, before conducting an interrogation, the suspect should be interviewed. In other words, don't start off directly or indirectly accusing a suspect

---

*Piper, Charles E., *Investigator and Fraud Fighter Guidebook: Operation War Stories*, John Wiley & Sons, Hoboken, NJ, 2014. (Copyright 2014, Wiley-VCH Verlag GmbH & Co. KGaA. Reproduced with permission.)

of wrongdoing. Instead, interview them in a non-accusatory manner first. Also, remember that the interviewee is probably watching and studying you just as closely as you are watching and studying them. Chapter 11, "Investigative Case Planning, Goals, and Strategies," provides guidance on how to strategically plan the order of interviews during the course of your investigations to increase the likelihood of successful conclusions.

Contact and Procurement Fraud, Collusion, and Corruption Interviews and Interrogations

Interviewing Complainants and Whistleblowers

One of the first steps to complete during contract and procurement fraud, collusion, and corruption investigations (on cases that were initiated from a source other than yourself) is to interview whoever initially made the complaint or provided the information or tip.

In street crime investigations, the first interview is most often the victim. In white-collar investigations, the "victim" might be "the government" or a business entity that suffered a loss. You really can't interview the government or a company, but you should be able to interview those entities' representatives that have knowledge of or made the complaint. In short, unless you generated the case yourself or it stemmed from a proactive investigative effort, what you'll want to know is, "What's this all about?"

If you received a written referral of any type, even if it's a written summary from someone that took an anonymous hotline complaint, study the heck out of it. If it was an anonymous hotline complaint, interview the person who took the call because they often only fill in the blanks or use template forms to complete their reports. Their reports might not include other tidbits of information that you'd find useful. Make sure you actually understand what is being alleged and who it is being alleged against.

Author's Note: *Usually I make a copy of the written referral (and sometimes the attachments) and use a highlighter and make notes on my copy. Sometimes I write questions on my copy and/or a separate sheet of paper. Factually, some initial referrals in white-collar cases are very difficult to understand because of the complexity—especially during the first read.*

After reading the referral/complaint, do as much preliminary research as necessary to be confident enough to ask somewhat intelligent questions about the subject matter. Early in my white-collar investigative career, I learned to throw my ego aside and to flaunt my ignorance when trying to learn about the losses, schemes, applicable policies and procedures, and so forth from others (especially from complainants and victims) who want to help me succeed during the investigation. I try not to flaunt my ignorance to suspects (unless it's a ploy). But I've found it's counterproductive to act like you know it all, when you in fact don't, around people that can help educate you if you just ask them to.

My best advice when conducting an interview is: After you ask a question—remain silent and listen to the answer. It's surprising how many "interviewers" are too busy thinking of their next question instead of listening. Sometimes interviewers actually cut off or interrupt others who are still providing information. If you want to learn, then you must listen.

When planning your investigations, you should also be thinking about who your potential witnesses are going to be if your case goes to trial. You can't testify to everything. Find out who has the knowledge that can help your case and listen to them.

Author's Note: *Although investigators are usually taught to first obtain the non-suspect interviewee's name, position, employer address, telephone number, and perhaps date of birth and social security number, I've found it best to instead obtain the contact and identifying information at the conclusion of the interview. In my opinion, asking for all of that typical police report–type information at the beginning of an interview puts the friendly witness/complainant on edge. I find it's better to learn their name, position, and employer's name at the onset and then develop some rapport before asking case-related questions. Just make sure you don't forget to obtain the other identifying information before concluding the interview.*

Time Duration and Interview Settings

High-dollar, white-collar crime interviews can often last between 1 and 3 hours, or more. Therefore, they should be scheduled at times and places where the interviews can best be accomplished. Privacy is paramount and interruptions should be avoided.

Recordings

If you plan on electronically recording interviews, ensure you follow all applicable laws. Some states require both (all) people's consent before recording conversations. You should also obtain written and/or recorded verbal consent from the interviewee to have the interview recorded. Keep in mind that, with today's technology, the interviewee may actually be secretly recording the interview. Because recording devices or apps are so readily available, don't be surprised if the interviewee asks you if he or she too can record the interview after you ask him or her for permission to record.

Many states require law enforcement officers to electronically record interviews conducted with people in custody and states and other agencies may have additional policies concerning the electronic recordings of interviews.

On May 12, 2014, the Department of Justice (DoJ) distributed a memorandum to all U.S. attorneys, the director of the FBI, and other DoJ law enforcement leaders from the Drug Enforcement Administration (DEA), U.S. Marshals Service, and the Bureau of Alcohol, Tobacco, Firearms and Explosives (ATF). The memorandum described the DoJ's new policy concerning electronic recording of statements. Although some exemptions were outlined in the memorandum, it required those DoJ members to electronically record in-custody interviews. The policy took effect on July 11, 2014. For additional information, search the internet or visit https://www.justice.gov/opa/pr/attorney-general-holder-announces-significant-policy-shift-concerning-electronic-recording. Investigators (especially law enforcement) should stay abreast of all policy changes which may affect them and their investigative efforts.

Preparing for the Interview

Most often, I type my interview questions in advance. After putting the questions in the order I want them, I number them. One reason that I do this is because it makes it easier to take notes. For example, my notes to interviewee responses might just read: *1. The contractor's office in Memphis, TN*; and if I look at my questions sheet, I'll see that the first question I asked was: Where did the fraud take place? My list of questions is basically just a guide. I often stray from my list and also ask additional questions that are not on the list. But prior to the conclusion of the interview, I'll look at my list of questions to ensure I asked the ones I intended to and/or obtained all the information I needed.

Author's Note: *Do not leave your list of questions out in the open for the interviewee to read. Some people are pretty good at reading when the papers are upside down too. You don't want the interviewee knowing what the questions will be before you ask them.*

When asking questions, do not ask follow-up questions at the same time. Let the interviewee answer each question separately and then ask a follow-up question. It's suggested that you first let a complainant or whistleblower provide a short overview of his or her allegations. If you've read their complaint in advance, you might just want to verbally summarize it and ask if that information is correct. An alternative is to let the interviewee present his or her case in its entirety and then ask questions as the interview progresses.

For contract and procurement fraud complainant and whistleblowers interviews (especially in product substation or defective product cases), I try to structure my questions so that they help me understand the complaint. Very often, the interviewee will have professional knowledge about his or her products and complex specifications and a vocabulary to match it. But I need to understand this information for my future interviews. It's better to flaunt your ignorance to him or her instead of flaunting it later when interviewing others. Future interviewees are likely to form an opinion about your grasp of the subject matter and if you don't understand the case, they may take advantage of that and provide you with less information.

I'm conscious that this structured interviewing approach could limit the responses to what the complainant or whistleblower wants to tell me. So after I have a grasp of the subject matter and allegations from his or her responses, I'll follow up with a question like "What else have we not discussed that you need to or want to tell me about?" Sometimes this question *opens a can of worms*, so do not close your notebook and assume that the interview is almost complete when you ask that question—what you've discussed thus far may have only been the tip of the iceberg.

Seven General Questions to Ask During an Interview

As you probably know, when conducting investigations and interviews, you are seeking answers to the questions:

Who?
What?
When?
Where?
Why?
How? and
How much?

Additional Questions to Ask a Complainant or Whistleblower

The following is a list of questions that will normally need to be asked of a complainant or whistleblower at some point during the interview. It's not an all-inclusive list. The order of the questions can be rearranged as the interviewer deems appropriate. Before asking the questions, make sure you have properly identified the interviewee. Also, introduce yourself (and your position). Prior to asking these questions, the interviewee should have provided at least a basic description of the wrongdoing. In the following scenario, it's assumed this is a contract and procurement fraud or perhaps collusion case. Many of the same or similar questions can also be utilized when interviewing someone about corruption.

Author's Note: *You can tailor your questions to the specific schemes being alleged. For example, you may decide to change the word "fraud" to "scheme." If investigating collusion or corruption, some of the questions will not apply. (See Chapters 3, 4, and 5 for descriptions of contract and procurement fraud, collusion, and corruption schemes.)*

Author's Note: *Remember not to ask the follow-up questions until the interviewee finishes answering your first question. Ask one question at a time.*

Forty Specific Questions to Ask a Complainant or Whistleblower

A.

1 How do you know about this fraud?
2 When did you first learn about the fraud or possible fraud?
3 How long has it been going on?
4 Is it still going on?
5 Who are the victims?
6 Who suffered the greatest financial loss?
7 What's the estimated dollar loss?

8   Are there any accomplices or others who helped facilitate the fraud? If so, name them and their positions.
9   Did they assist reluctantly, unknowingly, or did they intentionally assist in known fraud? 9B. Did you participate in any way? If so, explain.
10 (*Ask if the investigation concerns a defective product*) Is the product defective or is there a safety issue involving this product? If so, describe?

B.

11 Do you have proof of the wrongdoing? If so, what is it, where is it, and how did you get it?
12 Can you get proof? If so, where from and how?

C.

13 Who else knows about the fraud and how do you know?
14 Who else has proof? What proof do they have and how do you know this?
15 Who else can get proof?
16 Where else can proof be obtained?

D.

17 Who else do you think will cooperate in this investigation and why?
18 Who else do you think will not cooperate in this investigation and why?
19 Who else have you discussed this fraud with and when?

E.

20 Have you ever discussed this fraud with the suspect(s)? If so, when and what was said? Was anyone else present during this discussion? (Elaborate on all.)
21 Do you know if the suspect(s) knows what he/she did (or is doing) is illegal or wrong? If so, elaborate.

F.

22 Do current or former employees know about the fraud? If so, what are their names and how do you know that they know about the fraud?
23 Do you have contact with any of the current or former employees outside the office?
24 Do you have or can you get their contact information?

G.

25 Other than what you've already mentioned, how can your complaint be proven?
26 What other evidence exists that can prove the fraud and who committed it?
27 Why (for what reason) do you suspect the fraud was committed?

H.

28 Tell me how the system is supposed to work and how it was compromised so the fraud could be committed.
29 How could this fraud have been prevented?
30 How can this type of fraud be prevented in the future?

I.

31 What happened to the money that was received as a result of the fraud?
32 What type of assets does the suspect own?

J.

33 Why are you providing this information?
34 Why did you not provide this information earlier?
35 Who did you tell about this interview?
36 Who do you plan on telling about this interview?

K.

37 What else have we not discussed that you need to or want to tell me about?

L.

38 What is the best telephone number to reach you at?
39 Is it okay if I contact you in the future if I have some additional questions?
40 Do you have anything to add?

Toward the conclusion of the interview, ask the interviewee if he or she has any documents or other proof that he or she wants to provide you with or they said would be provided during the interview. Also, make sure you provide your business card and ask the interviewee to contact you if he or she thinks of anything else or becomes aware of any activity that might be of interest to the investigation—including any attempts to obstruct or impede it.

As a general rule, I do not tell interviewees who else I have interviewed or intend to interview. Usually, there's no reason to provide that information. If necessary, I can be nonspecific and say that other interviews have been conducted or that its part of my job to conduct other interviews. I don't usually make promises to other interviewees that I'll keep their names and information confidential either. It's my job as an investigator to collect information, not to tell others without a need to know who has or has not helped. I let the suspects worry about that.

Questions to Ask Employees and Former Employees

I've found it's much more effective to interview employees and former employees away from their current place of employment. I usually just show up on the doorstep of their home, dressed like a professional with proper identification in hand. If you call in advance to try to schedule the interview, one of two things (or both) will probably happen: (1) they will say they are too busy or (2) they will almost immediately inform the business owner, their supervisor, or other employees and others about the call. In fact, you should almost assume that right after you contact or interview a current employee that he or she will call or text the business owner, supervisor, and other employees before you even get to your car. That's less likely to be true if he or she has provided damaging information against the company or any of the company's employees.

If it's accurate to say so, you should probably tell the interviewee right off the bat that he or she is not suspected of doing anything wrong. That will relieve the heck out of him or her. Granted, that could change as your investigation progresses, but if it's accurate at the time of the interview, you might want to say so.

Author's Note: *Sometimes the suspect's company/corporation will employ legal counsel who will advise you that they represent the company/corporation and/or all the employees and that no interviews should be attempted of any current or former employees without first coordinating this through the attorney. Generally, they will not know about the investigation until you initiate some step or begin using an investigative tool(s) that allows them to learn of the investigation. The way you plan your investigation is important for a variety of reasons. The following questions for current and former employees assumes there is nothing prohibiting you from conducting those interviews. Also, former employees are sometimes more likely to provide information because they are not in fear of losing the jobs.*

The following is a list of questions that may be asked of employees or former employees of the suspect's company during an interview. It's not an all-inclusive list. The order of the questions can be rearranged as the interviewer deems appropriate. Before asking these questions, make sure you have properly identified the interviewee and introduced yourself (and your position). In the following scenario, it's assumed this is a contract and procurement fraud or perhaps collusion case. Many of the same or similar questions can also be utilized when interviewing someone about corruption.

Fifty Specific Questions for Employees and Former Employees

A.

1. Do you now or have you ever worked at _____ (*suspect's place of business*)?
2. What positions have you served there and when?
3. If you no longer work there, when did you leave and why?
4. Who was/is your immediate supervisor?
5. Do you know why I am asking you these questions?
6. I am asking these questions to determine if you are aware of any fraud or possible fraud that may have occurred at _____ (*suspect's place of business*). What do you know about any fraud or possible fraud committed there? (Elaborate.)

B1. *Ask these questions only if they know about fraud or possible fraud.*

7   How do you know about this fraud or possible fraud?
8   When did you first learn about the fraud or possible fraud?
9   How long has it been going on?
10 Is it still going on?
11 Who are the victims?
12 Who suffered the greatest financial loss?
13 What's the estimated dollar loss?
14 Are there any accomplices or others who helped facilitate the fraud? If so, name them and their positions.
15 Did they assist reluctantly, unknowingly, or did they intentionally assist in known fraud? Did *you* participate in any way? If so, explain.
16 (*Ask if the investigation concerns a defective product*) Is the product defective or is there a safety issue involving this product? If so, describe.

B2.

17 Do you have proof of the wrongdoing? If so, what is it, where is it, and how did you get it?
18 Can you get proof? If so, where from and how?

B3.

19 Who else knows about the fraud and how do you know this?
20 Who else has proof? What proof do they have and how do you know?
21 Who else can get proof?
22 Where else can proof be obtained?

B4.

23 Who else do you think will cooperate in this investigation and why?
24 Who else do you think will not cooperate in this investigation and why?
25 Who else have you discussed this fraud with and when?

B5.

26 Have you ever discussed this fraud with _____ (*the suspect[s]*)? If so, when, and what was said? Was anyone else present during this discussion? (Elaborate on all.)
27 Do you know if the suspect(s) knows what he/she did (or is doing) is illegal or wrong? If so, elaborate.

B6.

28 Do current or former employees know about the fraud? If so, what are their names and how do you know that they know about the fraud?
29 Do you have contact with any of the current or former employees outside the office?
30 Do you have or can you get their contact information?

B7.

31 Other than what you've already mentioned, how can what you've told me be proven?
32 What other evidence exists that can prove the fraud and who committed it?
33 Why (for what reason) do you suspect the fraud was committed?

B8.

34 Tell me how the system is supposed to work and how it was compromised so the fraud could be committed.
35 How could this fraud have been prevented?
36 How can this type of fraud be prevented in the future?

B9.

37 What happened to the money that was received as a result of the fraud?
38 What type of assets does the suspect own?

B10.

39 Why are you providing this information?
40 Why did you not provide this information earlier?
41 (*If the interview was scheduled*) Who did you tell about this interview?
42 Who do you plan on telling about this interview?

B11.

43 What else have we not discussed that you need or want to tell me about?

B12.

44 What is the best telephone number to reach you at?
45 Is it okay if I contact you in the future if I have some additional questions?
46 Do you have anything to add?

Author's Note: *If the interviewee provides you with names of people that you have already interviewed, act like the names are new to you. If you only ask for contact information about people you have not interviewed, the interviewee will logically assume that you've already talked to the others (and might even contact them). Interviewees actually pay close attention to what you write down and what you don't write down.*

C. Ask these questions only if the interviewee says that he or she does NOT know about fraud or possible fraud.

47 Specifically, I was wondering what you know about _____ (*the type of fraud that was alleged*). What do you know about that?
48 Are you saying that you are not aware of any fraud, possible fraud, or other wrongdoing regarding _____ (the *type of fraud that was alleged*)?
49 Is it okay if I contact you in the future if I have some additional questions?
50 What is the best telephone number to reach you at?

Toward the conclusion of the interview (if applicable) ask the interviewee if he or she has any documents or other proof that he or she wants to provide you with or said they would be provided during the interview. Also, make sure you provide your business card and ask the interviewee to contact you if he or she thinks of anything else or becomes aware of any activity that might be of interest to the investigation—including any attempts to obstruct or impede it.

You probably noticed that Part C of the interview questions specifically asks if the employee or former employee knew or knows of the fraud or possible fraud. If he or she was involved in the fraud and denies involvement, it makes it more difficult for him or her to later claim that he or she was reluctantly involved and only did so out of fear of losing his or her job. Factually, fraudsters often put their employees in tough positions where they must choose between doing the wrong thing and keeping their jobs or being unemployed. In short, even a denial of any knowledge can be of value to your investigation.

Interviewing Supervisors, Executives, Corporate Officers, and Business Partners

Supervisors, executives, corporate officers, and business partners may or may not know of the fraud. However, they might actually be part of it and/or the brains behind the scheme(s). If they are not personally involved in the fraud, they will often assist in the investigation. At the same token, they may not want the publicity (media coverage) that often results from such scandals (which often affects the value of their company's stock and/or future customer counts).

If you plan on interviewing executives and corporate officers, you should almost expect that they will have legal counsel present during the interview. If so, choose your questions and comments extra carefully and do not give up more information than you intend to. They will probably be fishing for information and, before you know it, they might start asking more questions than you.

So, after obtaining the needed information, you might want to excuse yourself *because you have to attend another meeting*. In fairness, even honest business executives and corporate officers have a right to be cautious and concerned if and when one of their employees commits fraud. Treat them and everyone else you come into contact during your investigation with respect. But that doesn't mean you have to answer all of the questions people ask during an interview that you scheduled.

Interviewing and Interrogating Suspects

Before the Suspect's Interview

This chapter led off by saying that an interrogation is accusatory (directly or indirectly). It's also been pointed out that an interview (non-accusatory) should usually precede the interrogation. The importance of building rapport before starting the interview has also been emphasized. The suspect is most often interviewed at or toward the end of the investigation. The reason for that is you first want to make sure that a crime and/or violation has actually occurred and that you've found evidence and/or identified witnesses that can prove it. If there is no evidence of wrongdoing, you probably have no reason to interrogate the suspect, but you can still interview him or her.

If you already know that the suspect is represented by legal counsel, you should request the interview through the legal counsel instead of arranging it through the suspect.

Author's Note: *In the real world, investigators don't tell the suspect or his or her attorney that they would like to conduct "an interview and interrogation." The word interrogation is seldom, if ever, mentioned. Even when summary reports are later written, they usually only reflect that the suspect was interviewed and the word interrogation is seldom included. Not long ago I read a book on interviewing written by a retired FBI agent in which he described how to conduct interrogations in great detail. But never once in the book was the word interrogation ever used. I can just about guarantee that all law enforcement officers (especially investigators) completed training titled "interview and interrogation." But when actually performed, the word interrogate seldom appears in any reports.*

If the suspect is not known to be represented by legal counsel, you could consider just showing up at the suspect's place of employment. If you call and schedule the interview in advance, you should expect that even if you agree on a time and place that you'll soon receive a call back from his or her attorney who will ask you a whole bunch of questions like, "Is my client a target? Is my client a suspect? What's this about? Blah, blah, blah."

Before interviewing and interrogating a suspect, you should already know the answers to all or most of the questions you are going to ask. It is extremely important that you prepare for this interview. Depending on the interview technique you are using, many interviewers will agree that you should bring a witness to this interview.

Prior to the interview you should properly identify yourself (preferably with credentials), and if the suspect is not in custody you should remind him or her that he or she is not in custody and is free to leave and/or terminate the interview at any time. If you are conducting the interview at the suspect's place of employment, instead say that he or she can terminate the interview and/or ask you to leave at any time. I usually also add that if the suspect doesn't like or understand a specific question, he or she doesn't have to answer it, or if he or she wants me to I will rephrase the question. All of this actually helps put the suspect more at ease, knowing that he or she has some control in the interview process. In a small way, it helps build rapport. In fact, usually after you tell the suspect all of that, you'll see him or her smile and sit more relaxed in his or her chair.

When I served as a federal agent, the policy was that if the suspect was in custody he or she had to be read his or her legal rights prior to initiating an interview. If the suspect was not in custody, the suspect did not have to be read his or her rights before the interview. The only exception was/is with U.S. military personnel. If they are suspected of a crime, prior to attempting to conduct an interview they must be read their Article 31 Rights under the Uniform Code of Military Justice, even if they are not in custody. You should check with your own legal counsel(s) and any applicable laws prior to conducting interviews and interrogations.

Questions to Ask a Suspect in a False Claims Case
Part I

1 If conducting a false claims investigation, you should ask the suspect to fully explain the entire document and data entry process used to generate and process an invoice. Also ask how invoices are completed and submitted. Ask him or her to provide the names and positions of all people involved in the process. Specifically ask what information (documents) is/are referenced or reviewed to complete or generate invoices.

After that, ask:

2 Who reviews the invoices before they are submitted?
3 Who reviews the invoices after they are submitted?
4 Who handles accounts receivable and reviews incoming payments?
5 How do they determine if the correct dollar amount was received?
6 After the invoices are submitted, does anyone check or audit to ensure that the information on the invoices was or is accurate?
7 What exactly are your responsibilities throughout this entire process?
8 How long has this process been used? (*If he or she says a different process was previously used, ascertain what that process was and when it was used.*)
9 Are there ever any exceptions or deviations from the process you have described?

Author's Note: *Specifically ask about the process previously described by any witnesses you already interviewed—particularly former and current employees. During the interview, avoid mentioning the names of anyone interviewed and if possible, don't even mention that interviews were conducted.*

10. Who is responsible for determining that the information on the invoices is accurate?
11. What is *your* responsibility to ensure that the information on the invoices is accurate?
12. When you provide _____ service (or provide a product), (*the service/product falsely billed*) how do you document it?
13. Who enters the description and quantity and prices?
14. Exactly how are the descriptions, quantities, and prices determined?

Author's Note: *The purpose of asking these questions is to lock the suspect in (with his or her own words) about how he or she says the system works and what role he or she personally plays in it.*

Part II

Author's Note: *In Part II, you will start by speaking in generalities (non-specific) and move to specific questions. One reason for that is you want to determine what information the suspect volunteers and when he or she volunteers it. This is kind of like gradually turning up the heat.*

15. Do you know of any invoices that were submitted for payment that were not accurate?
16. Do you know of any instances when payments were received that were for higher dollar amounts than services/products actually provided?
17. Has anyone ever informed you of or have you ever had any discussions with anyone about any invoices that were, or may have been, submitted with inaccurate information?
18. Has anyone ever informed you of or have you ever had any discussions about any payments received that were in excess of the dollar amount you should have received for the services/products provided?
19. If claims were submitted with inaccurate information for _____ service/products (*the service/product falsely billed*), whose responsibility would that be?
20. (*If necessary*) Would *you* bear any responsibility for this?
21. If overpayments were received for services, whose responsibility would that be?
22. (*If necessary*) Did you have any responsibility for this?
23. I'd like to show you some invoices now that seem to have inaccurate information, along with the corresponding records of payments made. (*Show a few invoices and records of payment.*) Can you explain how this happened?
24. Who caused or allowed this to happen?
25. Are *you* responsible? (If yes, why? If no, why not?)

26 It appears that approximately ___ invoices, totaling $ ____, were submitted that contained inaccurate information like the ones I just showed you. What are your thoughts about this?
27 How could this have happened?
28 Did you know about any of this prior to our meeting here today?

Part III

Author's Note: *In Part III, you will be establishing motive, intent, and what the suspect did with the money.*

29 Were these invoices generated and submitted with the intent to deceive?
30 Were these invoices generated and submitted with the intent to collect more money than you knew was deserved?
31 *(If the suspect admits involvement)* Why did you submit false invoices?
32 *(If the suspect admits involvement)* Did you know that submitting the false invoices was wrong when you did it?
33 What happened to the money after it was received?
34 Do you still have that money?
35 How do you think this matter should be handled?

Author's Note: *Do not suggest options, make any promises, or make any deals. Just ask that last question and document the answer. The suspect may say that he or she thinks the money should be repaid or that someone should go to jail. He or she may suggest it's another employee's fault.*

36 *(Optional question)* Do you think someone should be sent to prison for this?
37 Is there anything we have not talked about that you think we should?
38 Is there anything you would like to add?

Author's Note: *You may decide you want the suspect to write and sign a statement summarizing the key points of the interview, his or her involvement, and so forth. If the suspect takes full responsibility, that would be worth noting too. If the suspect says that he or she knew what he or she did was wrong while he or she was doing it, that fact should be included in the statement. In the real world, if the suspect's attorney is present, it's doubtful you'll get a written statement. In fact, if the suspect's attorney is there, it's doubtful you'll get answers to any of the questions listed in Part III above.*

It should be noted that if the suspect blames others, a computer glitch, or something else rather than taking responsibility for the false invoices, you'll later have the opportunity to try and determine if there is any merit to his or her statement. If the suspect was not telling you the truth, that means he or she just gave you his or her probable defense if the case were to go to trial. By disproving the suspect's excuse, you'll be more prepared if the case does go to trial. But you are only seeking the truth. How it plays out in court is usually out of your control.

Questions to Ask Those Suspected of Receiving Bribes or Kickbacks

It's assumed that, before conducting an interview with a suspect that may have received bribes or kickbacks, you actually have evidence of the bribes or kickbacks. If you are going on a fishing expedition, choose your words carefully.

Just as in Part I, Question 1 in the false claims case scenario, you'll want to get the suspect to lock him or herself in with his or her own words (box him or her in). The following is a list of questions that is similar to the ones I previously used when interviewing a suspect on a bribery case. That case involved a government contracting officer in Philadelphia, PA, who awarded government contracts to a contractor in Memphis, TN, to provide medical supplies. The Memphis contractor paid the government contracting officer thousands of dollars in bribes. Most were in the form of cashier's checks or cash. Before interviewing the contracting officer, I had already found the bribe payments in his bank account, which was held jointly with his wife.

Part I

1. Do you have any employment besides this job?
2. Are you collecting any disability, pensions, or other income like that?
3. Do you have any investments that you receive periodic payments from?
4. Did you receive any loans from non-financial institutions?
5. Where does your spouse (*or joint bank account holder*) work?
6. Is he or she collecting any disability, pensions, or other income like that?
7. Does he or she have any investments that he or she receives periodic payments from?
8. Did he or she receive any loans from non-financial institutions?

Part II

9. (*If the answers don't reflect they had any financial dealings with the bribe/kickback payer*) Can you explain the _____ dollars that was deposited into your account on _____ date?
10. (*If more than one payment was received*) Can you explain the _____ dollars that was deposited into your account on _____ date? (*Continue this questioning a couple more times if more payments were received.*)

Author's Note: *Watch the suspect's body language when you ask the above and below questions. You may even see him or her starting to sweat. In this case example, my suspect almost passed out!*

Part III

11. Who gave you this money?
12. Why was this money given to you?
13. How was the money provided? (*Provide details on shipping methods and cars used, and identify any personal assets used to transport/provide and receive the money.*)

14 What did you do in exchange or in return for the money?
15 What did you do with the money? (*Identify any assets purchased and/or where the money is now.*)

Regardless of what form the bribe/kickback was in, with some thought you will be able to develop a similar list of questions that takes away the suspect's probable defense before he or she gets a chance to offer it. In this example, prior to directly confronting the suspect, you'd almost expect that he or she would say that the money received was a loan or investment in the company, or that he or she worked part time for the company. By *heading him or her off at the pass*, you took away his or her defense before he or she had a chance to offer it. The suspect's own responses boxed him or her in. The information you receive about the current location of assets and what he or she did with the money could come in handy later if there are asset forfeiture provisions in the criminal or civil statutes used on your case and/or for other future financial recoveries.

Interview Notes

Your interview notes should be saved. If you took my advice and prepared a list of numbered questions for an interviewee, make sure you staple the list of questions to your notes. Many law enforcement manuals suggest/mandate that the interviewer initial and date the top and bottom of each page of notes. Typically, at the conclusion of the investigation, the interview notes will be placed in an envelope with the original official case file. However, check and comply with your own organization's policy.

Storage of Electronic Recordings of Interviews

If you recorded an interview (audio and/or video), you will need to comply with your organization's policies and procedures for copying and securing such recordings as evidence. My own suggestion is that if you think the item might be used in court and/or that the opposition's counsel might challenge the validity of it or would ask why the original was not secured, then you should secure it as evidence. But you'll need to follow your own applicable guidance/instructions on what to do with the recordings if you have them.

Interviewing Suspects Involved in Collusion, Bid Rigging, or Contract Award and Price Fixing

I think it's safe to say that suspects involved in collusion, bid rigging, or contract award fixing or price fixing will want to avoid providing incriminating information about themselves or others involved in schemes that circumvented or manipulated prices and/or fair and open competition in the contract or order award process. Those suspects know full well the seriousness and wrongfulness of their actions. They may have been able to rationalize their actions in the past, but once confronted by an investigator(s), most *bad guys* will realize their wrongful actions could send them to prison.

You should fully expect that suspects involved in such activity will initially deny any wrongdoing and any knowledge of it. They will most likely try to blame human and computer errors, honest mistakes, and coincidences. They'll probably accuse you of being on a fishing expedition. If they were involved in a conspiracy, they will not want to *rat out* their partners in crime and they can only hope that the others don't or didn't *rat them out*.

That said, before confronting a suspect for collusion, bid rigging, or contract award and/or price fixing, you should have at least some proof of the wrongdoing. Ideally, you'll also have proof of his or her involvement. But you don't necessarily have to have proof of the suspect's involvement when starting the interview. If he or she perceives that you have proof, might have proof, or are likely to get proof, he or she may very well tell you everything you want to know. Conversely, he or she may just tell you to *go pound salt*.

It's been my experience that the best way to obtain proof of collusion, bid rigging, or contract award and/or price fixing is two-pronged. You'll need physical evidence indicating or showing such wrongdoing occurred. Physical evidence can be obtained by reviewing and analyzing current and/or historic contracts and orders and all related documentation including requisitions, solicitations and advertisements, bids, quotes and proposals received and evaluated, notes, e-mails, price histories, and perhaps phone and text records and more. Legally obtained audio and/or audio-video recordings that provide incriminating information would probably be considered *the best* physical evidence. If illegal payments were made, you should have proof of those payments.

In addition, you'll need at least one person who can truthfully testify (if needed) that such wrongdoing did take place and provide specific information which can hopefully be corroborated.

Author's Note: *Physical evidence (or additional physical evidence) can also be obtained after an interview(s) has been conducted. For example, your suspect might confess and provide or direct you to additional evidence or proof. He or she may also be willing to make (legally) recorded calls to previous or current partners in crime (and/or wear a body wire when meeting with them) to obtain additional audio evidence.*

Author's Note: *Audio recordings do not always provide evidence implicating or incriminating suspects. Sometimes the second party (especially if he or she thinks he or she might be being recorded) will only say things (even if they are not true) that make him or herself appear innocent and/or that your cooperating party acted alone or is completely mistaken.*

After reading this section, you've probably concluded that's a whole lot of work to prove such wrongdoing. It *is* a whole lot of work! The good news is that after you obtain such physical evidence, and if just one suspect truthfully and honestly cooperates, the remainder of your investigation will be fun and exciting and worthwhile.

It is extremely important that all interviews in these types of cases be well planned and thoroughly conducted. (Electronically recording those interviews would probably also be in your investigation's best interest.) Once one suspect truthfully admits to his or her wrongdoing, especially if he or she "cooperates" after the interview, you'll probably uncover and gain proof that many others are or were involved.

It's been my experience that although people involved in such wrongdoing will initially be reluctant to admit their involvement, once they realize (or believe) that they've been caught, many will open up and tell you about more wrongdoing than you even thought was going on. But I should preface this by saying that it all depends on your demeanor and ability to conduct professional interviews. The wrong approach can screw everything up.

Author's Note: *I profess that investigators should always be "thinking plural" and not just trying to solve one case. Investigations involving collusion, bid rigging or contract award, and/or price fixing, by their very nature, involve two or more people/entities. But please don't stop there. Stay on the case and keep pursuing it until there is nothing left to pursue. You not only want to know who was involved but also how much historical impact they've had so that you can identify all victims and quantify the losses.*

Interviewing Other Suspects

Having read these descriptions of conducting interviews and interrogations, you know the importance of preparing for the interviews, privacy, and building rapport. Other suspect interviews should be conducted in a similar fashion as described in this chapter. Ideally, you will have already completed the majority of your investigation before interviewing the suspects.

You'll probably find that most employees that commit small-dollar fraud will confess relatively easily. In those types of cases, do not conduct suspect interviews solely with the intent of solving, proving, or gaining information about only one case. Instead, I strongly encourage you to "think plural," because even those small-dollar cases can lead you to additional cases involving fraud.

For example, if an employee embezzled some money from the company's checking account or stole some company property, there's a strong probability that he or she is or was involved in other crimes. The employee probably also knows others that are ripping off or have ripped off the company. I encourage you to plan your interviews accordingly. Keep in mind that the interviewee has no idea how much information you know about him or her. One thing the interviewee does know is that he or she is in trouble. By using the right approach, the information you obtain during your interview(s) can be very useful and can probably solve or lead you to more wrongdoing.

In Summary

As previously stated, an investigator who conducts interviews should continue to train on a regular basis to improve his or her interviewing skills. By preparing and planning for your interviews in advance, you will more often obtain more and better details. Your goal should be to conduct an extremely thorough and complete investigation in which as many facts as possible can be corroborated by as many witnesses and as much evidence as possible. You should also strive to obtain information that will be useful in identifying other instances of fraud or wrongdoing committed by the same suspect and/or others, and ways to improve the system so that future wrongdoing can be prevented and/or better detected. Don't just try to solve one case at a time. Instead, think plural.

The next chapter is on investigative reports and evidence.

Author's Note: Much of this chapter was derived, copied, and/or modified from Chapter 8 (Interviews and Interrogations) of *Healthcare Fraud Investigation Guidebook*, by Charles E. Piper, copyright 2016 by Taylor & Francis Group, LLC. CRC Press is an imprint of Taylor & Francis Group, an Informa Business.

10 Investigative Reports and Evidence

Investigative Reports

Writing detailed summary reports is an important part of the investigative process. However, you'll probably never hear anyone say it's the most fun part. During my more than 30-year career, I never once heard anyone say "I can't wait to write my report" or "The reason I became an investigator is to write reports."

When Reports Should Be Written and Types of Reports

Although investigative reports might be written by following an agency's or organization's mandatory guidelines and/or template outlines, it's worth mentioning that there are often several different types of investigative reports. Examples may include the following:

Case Initiation Reports

The case initiation report ordinarily details the who, what, when, and where and sometimes the why, how, and how much. For example, the report would include:

- Where, how, and when the referral/information was received/developed and by whom;
- Where the wrongdoing occurred (or is occurring);
- Who provided/developed the information;
- Who the suspect(s) is or might be;
- What the scam/scheme was;
- When the incident(s) took place;
- Who the victim(s) is;
- What the estimated dollar loss is or might be;
- Who the witnesses are or might be.

Author's Note: *If supportive documents/data or evidence were provided, these should also be included in the report and perhaps one or more of these documents attached to the report.*

In short, the case initiation report should contain sufficient information that describes the complaint/referral and information received or developed. At a minimum, it should provide an overview of the details received or obtained so that anyone who reads the report will have an understanding of why the investigation was initiated.

Author's Note: *Very often, most or all of the information contained in the case initiation will also be used (copied and pasted) in the final investigative summary report. That's another reason for the case initiation to be detailed.*

Interview Reports

Any time an interview (and/or interrogation) is conducted by an investigator, it should be documented in a report. Perhaps if the interview was electronically recorded (and the recording saved) the report could be written with less detail. But if there is no electronic recording, the report should be a detailed, accurate representation of what was communicated during the interview. Sometimes it's wise to also include information about what transpired or was said just before or after the interview if it could have investigative value.

Use of Investigative Tools, Sources, and Resources Reports

If you used investigative tools, sources, or resources during your investigation, they should be documented in a report. For example, if you performed surveillance, it should be documented and facts included about the time, date, location, and what was observed. If video or photographs were obtained, that should be mentioned and perhaps one or more of the photos/frames (or computer screenshots) should be included in or with the report—especially if they reflect their evidentiary value.

Another example of when reports should be written would include when you serve subpoenas. If a subpoena was to provide documents or records and the records were delivered to you, you should also document when and how they were provided, who provided them, and a description of what was provided. If items were not provided that should have been, also document that fact. This practice will often save you time in the long run because you'll eventually have to prepare an official report summarizing your investigation. When documenting your investigative activity shortly after it's performed becomes your standard practice, you'll always know with certainty when subpoenas were served, when they were complied with and by whom, what was provided, and perhaps what was not provided.

Another reason to document requests/receipt of documents and records is because you might find that what was provided contains false information and/or information that was created with the intent of obstructing or deceiving the investigator. If you document all the details as they occur, you can confidently testify to those facts.

Review or Analysis Reports

At the conclusion of the review and/or analysis of documents or data during your investigation, you should document your reviews of information (documents or data). The results of the review (findings) or analysis should also be documented in a report, not just in your working file.

Requests for Assistance and Related Responses Reports

Sometimes formal and informal requests are written for others (usually investigators) to provide assistance in the investigation. Reports should document when, how, and to whom the requests were made and what the requests were for. If the requests have deadlines for completion, that should also be documented. The same is true when responses are provided. If the responding party complies but doesn't write a report, you should write your own report describing the compliances. For example, let's say you formerly asked an auditor or analysts to review a bunch of invoices to determine if there was any evidence of duplicate submissions. If the auditor or analyst only verbally tells you the review found no evidence of double billings, either you or they should document that fact.

You might be wondering why you should document it if no evidence of wrongdoing was found. Well, what if you get transferred or the case gets transferred to another investigator? If the work and results are not documented, the newly assigned investigator might repeat the activity you already performed, which wastes valuable time and resources. Keep in mind that major fraud investigations can sometimes take several years to complete. Factually, many federal investigators get transferred or reassigned while working on such cases.

Other Reports

There is a variety of other reports that can also be prepared and/or obtained before the investigation is concluded, including the receipt of documents or evidence. This list is not intended to be all-inclusive.

Final Investigative Summary Reports

At the conclusion of your investigation, a detailed investigative summary report should be written. Law enforcement and other agencies have their own requirements for this and other reports, which usually also dictate the format the reports are written in. Templates and samples often prove very helpful. Very often, information that was included in previously prepared reports can be copied and pasted to the final report. Obviously, copying and pasting can save you time. But your end work product should be comprehensive and contain all the details a reader could want describing all aspects of the investigation.

Author's Note: *The best times to be thinking about the final investigative report is when you write your case initiation and while you are conducting your investigation.*

Since you know you are going to have to write the final report eventually, make plans for it well in advance and as you are investigating. This advanced planning will save you a lot of time and aggravation.

How Many Reports to Write

As a police officer, detective, and federal agent, I most often wrote separate reports for all or most of the occurrences/events listed in this section. However, now that I serve as a private investigator and consultant, my clients are charged by the hour or by the day. Understandably, clients usually want their costs kept to a minimum. To accommodate, I usually write one report and update it as the investigation progresses and when it is concluded. However, if I conduct non-recorded interviews, I often write separate reports describing the interviews and include them as attachments. Occasionally, other more detailed reports are also included as attachments but they are still referenced in the primary report. This obviously saves time (and money). But regardless of how or how often you or your organization decides to write reports, the investigative process should be well documented.

Attachments and Exhibits

I only know of one federal investigative agency that did/does not include attachments to their reports. Apparently, it's their agency's policy not to include attachments. Although I can understand wanting to keep attachments and exhibits to a minimum for filing space purposes, sometimes reports actually warrant and need attachments.

> **WAR STORY 10.1**
>
> During a joint investigation with a large federal investigative agency, a witness provided us with a one-page document that we considered a "smoking gun." That one document actually proved our case! The assisting agent wrote a report describing the document but did not include a copy of it as an attachment to his report. In fact, a copy of the "smoking gun" document was not even placed in that agent's official case file (at least that's what he told me). Instead, the original was placed in his evidence depository and a copy kept in the agent's "working file."

Author's Note: *If an attachment or exhibit will help the reader(s) understand the case or what was learned or established, the investigator should attach a copy of it to the applicable report. A less useful but possible alternative could be to include a scanned or photographed copy of the document(s) embedded into the narrative portion of the report. But to best prove your case, or to share information about your case, you must include (not exclude) essential information.*

Differing Opinions About the Content of Reports

Professional opinions often differ on what information should be included in investigative reports. One federal criminal prosecutor told me to write less in my reports. He said "The more you write in your reports, the more you have to defend in court." His theory was that the defense attorneys could question things I wrote, but couldn't question things I did not write.

> ### WAR STORY 10.2
>
> In one meeting, a senior agent from a highly respected federal investigative agency told me not to include details in an official report that described documents I reviewed which were obtained during our joint investigation. The federal prosecutor agreed with the agent. I asked how any of us would know or remember that the documents were obtained or reviewed, and what information they contained, if I didn't write a report. I was told to just write an official report reflecting that I had received the documents and then to write notes in my "working file" describing what I found during the review.
>
> The senior agent's and prosecutor's reasoning was that they did not want the defense counsel to know what we knew. I actually responded by saying something like, "Well, if the defense counsel can get their client off because of something I wrote in my report, then perhaps their client is innocent." That comment did not go over very well in that meeting and I was accused of not playing like a team member. Frankly, I don't want to be on those types of teams.

In contrast, when working with defense attorneys as a private investigator, one attorney emphasized "If it's not in the police report; it didn't happen!" Several defense attorneys have suggested to me that if a police officer took the witness stand and said he or she saw or did things that the officer did not previously document in their report, the defense attorneys would be all over the police officer *like stink on crap*. The defense attorneys would argue that if the cop did not document it, it didn't happen.

So which of these professional attorneys, methodology is correct? In my opinion, the defense attorney's approach makes more sense. Your investigative reports are certainly subject to be scrutinized by the opposition's counsel. But investigative reports should contain accurate descriptions of what transpired during the investigative process. If the accused is found innocent because of factual information, so be it.

Investigator's Remarks or Comments in Reports

While serving as a federal agent, I sometimes included remarks or comments in my reports which were preceded with the words "AGENT'S NOTE" in bold font. My agency permitted this and it was an opportunity for agents to include comments about things such as their observations. Each comment or remark was prefaced with "AGENT'S NOTE" so that the reader would understand that the information that followed was separate from other information included in the report. Examples might be as follows:

- **Agent's Note:** The information provided by John Smith during this interview greatly differed from what he said in a previous interview 1 month before.
- **Agent's Note:** Based on the analysis of documents, it appears that approximately 12 or more claims submitted by Dr. Jones contained false or inaccurate information.

You will notice that, in the second example, the words, "it appears that" were used and the word "approximately" was also used. In my opinion, both Agent's Notes helped the reader better understand the importance of certain information obtained and/or the investigator's observations. However, many of the criminal federal prosecutors insist that agent's notes should not be included in reports. Perhaps this stems from the belief that "The more you write, the more you have to defend in court."

So who is correct in this scenario? My belief is that it depends on what is written in the agent's note. It would be unacceptable for an agent to write "I think John Smith is guilty." That would really be taking a stance on the suspect's guilt and perhaps indicate that the investigator is no longer capable of being objective in the investigation. Agent's notes or similar comments or remarks should certainly be used sparingly.

Excluding or Omitting Information

I mention exclusions and omissions to illustrate that there are differing views as to what information should and should not be included in investigative reports. Ironically, when you attend training on report writing, the instructors will most likely tell you to include certain types of information and that there should be no exceptions. But seldom does anyone talk about information which should or should not be excluded from reports. Let me emphasize that information should not be omitted from reports for the purpose of intentionally withholding information to increase the chances that one side will win or one side will lose.

> ### WAR STORY 10.3
>
> As a private investigator and consultant, I was once hired to review a metropolitan police department's incident reports and subsequent internal affairs investigative reports that were written after the incident. The case involved an individual's complaint that he was injured by the police while in custody. My review found that the information in the police and internal affairs' reports appeared factual.

However, some extremely important information was completely omitted about things that occurred in the presence of the police officer who wrote the report. In fact, so much critical information was omitted that it appeared to be a cover-up. In my opinion, one of the police report's omissions appeared to be deliberate. I based my opinion on the fact that the officer's incident report included great detail about trivial things (like a picture falling off the wall during a scuffle). This demonstrated that officer's superb attention-to-detail skills and his ability to document his observations. But when important things happened at the scene which led to the injury of the complainant, all of a sudden the information lacked detail and excluded any mention of events before, during, and after the alleged injury. There was no mention at all of how the complainant was injured. But it was mentioned that the complainant refused medical attention.

Having written and reviewed thousands of police and investigative reports, it became apparent to me that the officer was trying to protect himself and/or another officer. He was careful not to include any false information in the report. But in my opinion, the omissions appeared deliberate. In short, intentionally omitting important information can sometimes have the same effect as intentionally including false information.

Another Source on Report Writing

My book, *Investigator and Fraud Fighter Guidebook, Operation War Stories** has a separate chapter titled "Summary Reports" that includes a useful section on common report-writing mistakes which I have learned over the course of my career. I highly recommend that you consider reading it.

In summary, reports serve as historical references of what transpired or was observed and learned during investigations. That's enough reason to ensure your reports are detailed, factual, and do not intentionally omit information.

Evidence

Conducting white-collar investigations often results in the collection of tangible evidence that may help prove your case. It's assumed in this writing that you and/or your organization have established policies and procedures for the legal identification, collection, and safeguarding of such evidence and the eventual return, disposal, and/or destruction of evidence before or after adjudication. It should be emphasized that it is important to establish and maintain the chain of custody of any evidence collected. Needless to say, whenever evidence is collected, a report should be written and/or this information should be included in some other report.

*Piper, Charles E., *Investigator and Fraud Fighter Guidebook: Operation War Stories*, John Wiley & Sons, Hoboken, NJ, 2014. (Copyright 2014, Wiley-VCH Verlag GmbH & Co. KGaA. Reproduced with permission.)

Keep in mind that some records and documents may be available from multiple sources. For example, if items were tested at an independent laboratory, the lab would have copies and the requestor and end user might also have copies. (Someone should have the originals.) During your investigation, you may want to obtain original and/or copies of the same documents from more than one source because vendors have been known to alter documents after receipt.

For example, test results can be altered to make it appear that failing samples actually passed. Some vendors have been known to copy and then alter the dates of testing to give the appearance that more batches, lots, or items were tested than actually were. Documents have also been known to be altered to increase or decrease quantities, dollars, and costs, to change names and addresses, etc. Some documents are 100 percent fraudulently created for the purposes of deceiving others. The takeaway point is that you may want to obtain documentary evidence from more than one source even if the information obtained is, or should be, the same.

It's been my experience that investigators in law enforcement and private sector agencies that conduct criminal investigations are more likely to collect and store evidence than private sector investigators who conduct civil and/or administrative investigations. Many prefer to just photograph items rather than collect the originals as evidence.

Many of the common types of items collected as evidence when conducting contract and procurement fraud, collusion, and corruption investigations are listed below. The list is not all-inclusive. Documentation may be paper copies and/or stored electronically.

Common Types of Evidence Collected During Contract and Procurement Fraud, Collusion, and Corruption Investigations

Contract File

The contract file should contain documentation from the inception until completion of the order. Documentation included in the contract file may include the following (*copied from Chapter 7*):

- Customer's request;
- Market research and/or price history search results;
- Requests for information (RFIs) (seeking information from vendors);
- Requests for bids (RFBs) (or solicitations or advertisements) that solicit bids/proposals;
- Records of vendors' price quotations received (telephonic or otherwise);
- Bid proposals received from bidders;
- Bid abstract (or similar listing of all vendors that submitted bids and their price quotes);
- Statement of value and/or cost and pricing data (pre-award) provided by vendor(s) with their proposals or soon thereafter;
- Contracting official's requests for additional information and/or supportive documentation;

- Vendor responses to the requests for additional information and/or supportive documentation;
- Bid proposal evaluations and ratings;
- Conflict of interest certifications (contracting officials, bid evaluators, and/or vendors);
- Buyer's pre-award surveys and/or inspection of bidder's premises, first articles, demonstrations, internal and external testing, and test results;
- Small Business Administration (SBA) requests for Certificates of Competency (CoC);
- SBA response approval/disapproval and/or issuance of CoC;
- If sole-source or set-aside—supportive documentation justifying the selection;
- Records of all pre-award conferences, meetings, source selection recommendations, and source selection decisions;
- Record and/or certification of price reasonableness and/or determination of best value;
- Contracting officer's certification that the selected vendor was deemed "responsible" and/or financially stable/sound;
- Signed contract;
- Protests and/or complaints from vendor(s) not awarded the contract;
- Results and/or responses to protests and/or complaints from vendors not awarded the contract;
- Signed amendments, modifications, and change orders;
- Documentation supporting request/need for amendments, modifications, and change orders;
- Records of requests for inspection and requests for testing;
- Records of inspection and test results;
- Records of acceptance (and/or refusal to accept);
- Customer (or end user) complaints;
- Resolution of customer (or end user) complaints;
- Vendor claims for payment (and supportive documentation if required);
- Statement of value and/or cost and pricing data (post award);
- Approvals and/or disapprovals of payments;
- Records of payment;
- Records of communication for any and all of the above;
- If contract was terminated before completion—supportive documentation justifying the termination, notice to contractor, response(s) from contractor, and official contract termination.

Author's Note: *The contract file could contain more or less of these documents and/or additional documents. Typically, only a few e-mail exchanges will have been printed and included in the contract file.*

Testing, Inspection, and Acceptance Documentation

The prime contractor, subcontractor, manufacturer, and/or buyer may have tested samples or end items. The items (or portions of them) may have been inspected.

The items may have also been signed for as being accepted. If so, those test or inspection results or official signatures for acceptance may be of evidentiary value.

Shipping and Receiving Records

If items were shipped and received, there should be records which support both. Those records may have evidentiary value.

E-mails, Text Messages, and Other Electronic Communication Exchanges

During your investigation, you may obtain or recover electronic communications of evidentiary value. You may want to print paper copies of the communication in addition to electronically storing it.

Electronic Data and Digital Photos and Videos

In major fraud cases, you may obtain or recover as evidence electronic data, digital photos and video, and other computer-generated or stored data or information. It's recommended that you gain assistance from experts to assist with any copying and storage of such items.

Hardware and Software

During some investigations, almost everything (including the kitchen sink) is obtained as evidence. I've participated in search warrants where federal agents that were specially trained in computer forensics obtained mirror copies of all data and files on business computers and/or their servers. Sometimes entire computers, cell phones, tablets, and other devices are secured as evidence. It's recommended that you gain assistance from experts to assist with any copying and storage of such items.

Billings, Invoices, and Payments

Original and copies of billings, invoices, and records of payment are often secured as evidence, especially in false claims cases. A good example where such evidence would be needed would be a double billing case.

End Items or Products

Some contract and procurement fraud cases will require securing as evidence end items or products which were provided by vendors that help prove fraud was committed. For example, if a contractor repackaged or changed the expiration dates on items to commit fraud, you may have to secure the items as evidence. If a contractor provided defective products, the products will need to be obtained as evidence.

Author's Note: *Occasionally, arrangements will have to be made to preserve evidence in a non-traditional environment, such as a refrigerator. With the approval of appropriate personnel (like the prosecuting attorney), sometimes evidence (or portions of evidence) will be retained, photographed, and released with a supportive chain of custody because it's impractical to store the evidence long term.*

Financial Records, Cash, and Gifts

If your case involved financial records or cash that are of evidentiary value, you'll have to secure those items as evidence. This would especially be true in bribery and kickback cases. Along those lines, there could be other items (especially in a bribery or kickback investigation) that help prove your case. Examples might be jewelry or other gifts given.

Other Items

Listed here are other items which may be considered evidence in contract and procurement fraud, collusion, and corruption investigations.

- Appointment files and calendars;
- Sign-in logs;
- Accounts payable;
- Accounts receivable;
- Interoffice messages;
- Phone records;
- Company policies and procedures;
- Current and former employee personnel files;
- Employee payments and paid commissions;
- Contractor payments and paid commissions;
- Consultant payments and commissions;
- Photographs and video;
- Audio-recorded interviews;
- Handwritten or signed confessions;
- Social media and related sites;
- Websites.

The next chapter provides insight and suggested guidance on investigative case planning, goals, and strategies to consider when conducting contract and procurement fraud, collusion, and corruption investigations.

Author's Note: Much of this chapter was derived, copied, and/or modified from Chapter 9 (Investigative Reports and Evidence) of *Healthcare Fraud Investigation Guidebook* by Charles E. Piper, copyright 2016 by Taylor & Francis Group, LLC. CRC Press is an imprint of Taylor & Francis Group, an Informa Business.

11 Investigative Case Planning, Goals, and Strategies
(The Piper Method of Conducting Thorough and Complete Investigations*)

You've probably heard Benjamin Franklin's famous quote, "If you fail to plan, you are planning to fail." But what should your plans and goals be when conducting a contract and procurement fraud, collusion, or corruption investigation? Perhaps you answered by saying, "To learn the truth" or "To establish the facts." Maybe you answered, "To put the dirtbags in jail."

Although all of those answers might be acceptable *(of course, the dirtbags should only go to jail if they are guilty)*, let me suggest that you should have much bigger and better plans and goals.

To be a highly successful fraud fighter in this arena, you should be "thinking plural." You should be trying to identify as much fraud, collusion, and corruption as possible as well as attempting to identify any waste and abuse while maximizing the use of time, tools, resources, techniques, and legally obtained information.

One of my sayings is, "A good investigator can connect the dots, but a great investigator can find the dots to connect."*

Author's Note: *The beginning of this book includes a diagram of The Piper Method of Conducting Thorough and Complete Investigations* which outlines how to conduct as many as ten case-related investigations simultaneously. Using this method has resulted in identifying more wrongdoing by more people, even with fewer resources. Some people say, "Don't work harder; work smarter." I suggest that you should strive to do both.*

Listed here are the ten simultaneous investigations that I suggest can be conducted when conducting almost any investigation—especially contract and procurement fraud, collusion, and corruption investigations.

The Piper Method—Ten Simultaneous Investigations*

1. Investigating for criminal violations;
2. Investigating for civil violations;
3. Investigating for administrative violations;
4. Investigating to determine if the same suspect committed similar wrongful acts;

---

*Piper, Charles E., *Investigator and Fraud Fighter Guidebook: Operation War Stories*, John Wiley & Sons, Hoboken, NJ, 2014. (Copyright 2014, Wiley-VCH Verlag GmbH & Co. KGaA. Reproduced with permission.)

5 Investigating to determine if the suspect committed other somewhat related wrongful acts;
6 Considering whether others might have or might be committing the same type of wrongful acts;
7 Considering how others might commit the same or similar acts in the future;
8 Investigating for indications of waste/abuse;
9 Investigating for indications of systemic weaknesses;
10 Considering ways the system can be improved to prevent future occurrences.

Author's Note: *Whenever investigating any one individual, the investigator should always be mindful of possible involvement of accomplices, co-conspirators, and others who may have assisted before, during, or after the offense(s).*

How to Conduct Ten Simultaneous Investigations on One Case

Listed in the following are brief descriptions on how each of the ten simultaneous investigations can be conducted on investigations involving contract and procurement fraud, collusion, and corruption.

1 Investigating for Criminal Violations and

2 Investigating for Civil Violations

These two investigations can very easily be conducted simultaneously and are often performed by federal and state investigators. It's simply a matter of knowing the criminal and civil statutes that may apply to the investigation that you are conducting and the elements that need to be proven to consider using these statutes for prosecutorial considerations. Of course it's the criminal and civil prosecutors' responsibility to determine what charges (if any) to bring. By following the above guidance, you certainly can present your case in a manner that best proves your case.

One important factor to consider, however, is the use of federal grand jury subpoenas to obtain documents/records and/or testimony. Using grand jury subpoenas on a criminal case can more than just muddy the water if trying to also prove a civil case. Using grand jury subpoenas can make it almost impossible (or at least difficult) for certain information obtained in the criminal case to be used in the civil case. Therefore, the investigator should think long and hard about which tools he or she has at his or her disposal, and if and when to use them. Ideally, both the criminal and civil prosecutors will simultaneously allow for both the criminal and civil investigation to be conducted in a manner that will result in a successful conclusion.

Author's Note: *Please see Chapter 2, which describes "The Yates Memo." On September 9, 2015, Deputy Attorney General Sally Q. Yates signed a seven-page memorandum sent to all U.S. attorneys' offices nationwide (criminal and civil) and to the FBI and others with the subject "Individual Accountability for Corporate Wrongdoing." The memo includes six key steps to "strengthen our pursuit of individual corporate wrongdoing ..."*

146 Chapter 11

Three of the key steps are:

- Criminal and civil corporate investigations should focus on individuals from the inception of the investigation;
- Criminal and civil attorneys handling corporate investigations should be in routine communication with one another;
- Absent extraordinary circumstances or approved departmental policy, the Department will not release culpable individuals from civil or criminal liability when resolving a matter with a corporation.

Author's Note: *The Piper Method was released in publication long before The Yates Memo. Obviously, the Department of Justice (DoJ) and the FBI now also understand the importance of the criminal and civil division of the U.S. attorneys offices working together as a team—at least concerning corporate investigations.*

3 Investigating for Administrative Violations

Many law enforcement investigators and agents are only concerned about getting convictions on criminal cases. Some are also interested in pursuing civil investigations. Not too many are interested in investigating administrative violations. In my opinion, the main reason for this is because many law enforcement officers, their supervisors, their offices, and/or their agencies are often evaluated (directly or indirectly) on making arrests and getting indictments, convictions, and dollar recoveries.

But what should you do if you are investigating and find wrong or improper activity that's not considered criminal or civil, yet contributes to the detriment of the contract and procurement system which you have concerns about? Should you just dismiss it? I don't think so, and I don't think the taxpayers, business owners, possible stockholders, and others think so either.

4 Investigating to Determine if the Same Suspect Committed Similar Wrongful Acts and

5 Investigating to Determine if the Suspect Committed Other Somewhat Related Wrongful Acts

It's been my experience that when you identify contract or procurement fraud, collusion, or corruption, those same players have also committed other and/or additional similar and/or somewhat related violations. If you approach your investigation with this mindset, and are actually alert for and/or on the lookout for additional fraud schemes and wrongdoing, you will probably find them. Sometimes those additional schemes that you identify will be more serious and/or have caused higher dollar losses than what you were originally investigating.

Author's Note: *Some investigative agencies have internal high-dollar threshold policies that allegations/complaints must meet before they will initiate investigations.*

An example might be that there must be a loss of at least $50,000 or even one million dollars before a case is opened. In my opinion, those policies must be extremely flexible and not carved in stone. Too often, good cases are dismissed by willing investigators just because of their agencies' short-sighted policies. A good investigator knows that, with further investigative effort, many or most of those original tips, allegations, and/ or complaints will lead to identifying much more fraud, collusion, and/or corruption. Just as police departments can't dismiss calls about "shots fired" and say that they only investigate homicides, fraud investigators should not totally dismiss provided information regarding fraud, waste, and abuse just because it doesn't meet a high-dollar threshold.

Regarding contract and procurement fraud, collusion, and corruption (especially involving the federal, state, and local governments), if the person or company caused such harm to your agency or organization, they probably did the same to others. In my opinion, it is your responsibility to try to determine who those others are. I emphasize the word "try" because in the real world you can inform other investigators and investigative agencies about the wrongdoing and they just won't react. There's not much you can do about that except to document who you informed, when you informed them, and what you informed them about. Hopefully at least some of the other investigators or investigative agencies will react and join in the investigation if their participation is warranted.

Proving additional criminal and/or civil wrongdoing makes it less likely that the suspect (or the suspect's attorney) will be able to convince others (a judge or jury) that the wrongdoing that occurred was an accident or attributable to others. It also makes the case more appealing for prosecutors when you identify additional wrongdoing because the dollars involved will probably be higher.

In short, by proving that the individual(s) or company(s) committed many instances of fraud and/or different types of fraud (perhaps affecting more than one entity), it will be more difficult for the suspects and/or their attorney(s) to present a plausible defense. You are also more likely to hold the wrongdoer accountable for all or most of their misdeeds rather than just a small amount of them. If you conduct a less-thorough investigation, the individual(s) or company(s) will still have profited from the wrongdoing that you failed to identify.

6 Considering Whether Others Might have or Might be Committing the Same Type of Wrongful Acts

Usually after you've invested considerable amounts of time investigating and proving contract or procurement fraud, collusion, or corruption that was perpetrated by a suspect(s), you will have developed somewhat of an expertise on (1) the wrongdoing and how it was accomplished and (2) how to investigate it (and perhaps how not to investigate it).

While conducting almost every major fraud, collusion, or corruption investigation, there is a learning curve. By the time you've concluded the investigation that you are working on (or probably before), you will become knowledgeable enough to search for and identify others who have committed the same wrongful acts and you will be capable of completing those investigations in less time. I'll go so far as to say that you would probably be able to make an entire career out of investigating that one case's scheme(s) if there were no limits on where you could investigate.

However, in the real world, most investigators are forced not to follow the trend because of their own supervisor's or agency's direction and/or an existing heavy caseload. Instead, investigators are often instructed to work entirely brand new cases (or existing cases) and start learning everything from scratch all over again. However, my philosophy is if "there's gold in them thar hills," keep digging!

7 Considering How Others Might Commit the Same or Similar Acts in the Future

Based on what you've learned and/or are learning during your investigation, your insight, wisdom, and foresight may allow you to surmise or speculate that the same scheme (or a variation of it) might happen somewhere else and/or will happen in the future. Don't dismiss your intuition, because you are probably correct! Your goal should also be to try to prevent the fraud, collusion, and corruption from happening and/or prepare for it to happen and take appropriate action.

8 Investigating for Indications of Waste/Abuse

As previously stated, many law enforcement investigators and agents are only concerned about investigating criminal and/or civil violations. Even some of the "most respected" and best known investigative agencies do not investigate waste and abuse. The sad truth is that many of those investigators will come across waste and abuse during their investigations and intentionally dismiss it because they are not required to investigate it and/or their own agency will not allow them to investigate it.

Consider the following questions while thinking objectively (not like your own agency's policy dictates). If you learned that the government was paying three times more for something than they should *(hmm, that does sound familiar, doesn't it?)*, shouldn't you try to do something about it? If you learned that your payment office was accidently double-paying vendors because of a fault in their computer system, shouldn't you address that? If you learned that your contracting office was routinely ordering an extraordinary amount of a specific item and those items were not needed, shouldn't you bring that to someone's attention? *(Yes, you should also think that someone might be receiving bribes or kickbacks for ordering so many of those items that are not needed.)*

As far as I am concerned, any investigator or investigative agency that is not also searching for waste and abuse while conducting criminal and/or civil fraud, collusion, or corruption investigations is not conducting thorough enough investigations. It is unacceptable for knowledge or suspicion of waste and abuse to be dismissed or *kicked to the curb* just because it's not a criminal or civil violation. Some might say, "But that's the way we've always done it." My response is, "Exactly, that's why the problems keep getting worse, the taxpayers keep losing money, the costs of products and services keep rising and many company's value or stocks are not what they should be.

Author's Note: *If you are conducting this more thorough ten-step approach during your investigation, you will have to ask more questions during your interviews and perhaps conduct some interviews that you would not have otherwise conducted. You may also have to look at additional documents and data. But the return on investment, although difficult to quantify, will be worth it in the long run.*

9 Investigating for Indications of Systemic Weaknesses

While conducting your investigation, you should also be investigating what caused or allowed the wrong that you are investigating to occur in the first place. There could be deficiencies in management, policies and procedures, security, oversight, checks and balances, and so forth.

Chapter 9, which was on interviewing, included a couple of suggested interview questions about what caused or allowed wrongdoing to occur and how it could be prevented. The people you are interviewing who actually work in the field usually know about deficiencies and how improvements can be made. It only takes a minute to ask them. Those types of questions should be part of your plan when preparing for interviews.

10 Considering Ways the System can be Improved to Prevent Future Occurrences

As mentioned earlier, you can acquire good insight on how the system can be improved to prevent future occurrences simply by asking the people in the field. They know, and are usually never asked. Based on your own knowledge acquired during the investigation and/or from your own prior experience or training, you too will have ideas on how to fix what's broken or in need of repair. No later than at the conclusion of every investigation, you should prepare written reports describing any and all systemic or other weaknesses and/or deficiencies that you've identified during your investigation and then make written recommendations as to how to fix or correct the problem(s).

Think about it. If you could prevent the wrong from reoccurring in the future, wouldn't that be a good thing? Wouldn't we all be better off and the wrongdoers worse off?

Drafting Investigative Plans for Investigative Efforts

Having outlined the overall most-thorough approach to investigating contract and procurement fraud, collusion, and corruption, attention will now focus on things to consider when developing a plan to investigate such matters. Because there are so many possible variables on the types of schemes conducted and people investigating, the following should only be used as a generic guide for consideration.

Author's Note: *Factually, all investigators and examiners reading this book do not have the same authority, power, jurisdiction, or responsibilities. Therefore, they do not all have access to the same resources, tools, and techniques. Keep in mind, however, that if everyone is working together, that becomes less problematic.*

Staying Organized

When conducting high-dollar or complex fraud, collusion, or corruption investigations, you'll usually obtain and accumulate large amounts of documents and electronic data. It's important to stay well organized. Consider keeping a log describing what and when items or information were requested; what, when, and if they were obtained; where and from whom you obtained them; and, just as importantly, when you've reviewed and where you stored them.

Another reason you must stay organized is because you'll probably also be assigned other unrelated cases during this same time frame and therefore might be away from some cases for extended periods. Also, sometimes investigators and agents get reassigned. It would be great if a case transfer could be completed in an orderly fashion rather than handing off or receiving a big mess. In the real world, messy case transfers often result in those cases getting closed.

Filing and Storing Investigative Reports

It is important to be thinking about your final investigative summary report when you first start your investigation. The better you prepare for the final report in advance, the easier it will be to write, and the better quality it will be too.

This means that your official investigative case file should contain all original investigative reports written during the course of the investigation. You should ensure that all reports are also provided and saved electronically. (*Since many agencies are becoming paperless, perhaps that's the only way you file and store reports anyway.*) The benefit of having the reports saved electronically is that the information can easily be copied and pasted into the final report if necessary and easily electronically shared with others.

Author's Note: *If you've never worked a nationwide large-scale investigation before, you might be thinking that the above is fairly obvious advice. But if you have other investigators assisting at various locations (perhaps in different states), you've got to set the ground rules from the very beginning. If you don't, it will haunt you when trying to compile all of the information to write the final report.*

Saving and Storing Interview Notes

At the conclusion of the investigation, you must ensure that all interview notes are retained (preferably with the original case file). Make sure that's the rule from the start. Follow (or improve upon) your own organization's policy if needed.

Saving and Storing Audio and Video Recordings and Photographs

It's my opinion that not all original audio and video recordings and photographs need to be secured as evidence. However, copies should be retained. For example, if you took photographs of a building while on surveillance and nothing happened, I don't think the original photos need to be secured as evidence. (Check with your agency and/or legal counsel for their policies and/or opinions.)

However, if you have audio, video, or photographs that you do think will be used as evidence or that the defense might question or want for evidence, you should safeguard them and secure them as evidence. Since most recordings and photographs are digital, it can become costly to save memory discs in evidence rooms. Some recording devices do not even use memory discs (such as many digital audio recorders). In those cases, many investigators consider the first copy as evidence.

Saving and Storing Evidence

See the previous point on audio, video, and photographic evidence. You may also have additional electronic evidence (especially e-mails). You'll need to make arrangements to secure those too. Paper documents will undoubtedly also be considered as evidence. Occasionally in fraud, collusion, and corruption cases, you'll obtain and secure other tangible items as evidence. A great example is a bribery case where you might obtain cash, cashier's checks, or others items of value as evidence.

Proactive and Reactive Investigations

Proactive Investigations

Analysis and Data Mining

Many business entities and government agencies take proactive steps in the attempt to detect fraud with the use of computer analytics, data mining, professional analysis, and/or other methods. These are great ways to identify potential fraud. The next step for many is to conduct their own preliminary investigation or inquiries, often without conducting any interviews or using typical investigative tools or methods. Frequently, their objective is to determine if there is probable fraud or just accidental mistakes. Some law enforcement investigative agencies also follow the same process to identify possible fraud.

Investigative Projects

Fraud fighters should consider opening proactive investigative projects with the goal of identifying fraud, collusion, or corruption in specific areas. Investigative projects are an example of how an investigator can accomplish the sixth type of simultaneous investigation listed above (*considering whether others might have or might be committing the same type of wrongful acts)*. One way to start would be by analyzing your contracting office's bid abstracts which summarize all the bid proposals submitted on individual contracts and comparing them to contracts actually awarded. Most investigators never think to examine information about which entities did not get awarded the contracts, but this information can be very valuable, especially when large amounts of historical information are available. By doing this, you may identify bid rotation schemes, favored contractors, and perhaps wrongfully inflated prices. The more you study and identify patterns, the more "bad guys" you'll probably catch.

Undercovers

Some law enforcement agencies also perform undercover activities in an attempt to identify and gain evidence against fraudsters and those that pay or receive bribes or kickbacks. Undercovers can also be utilized as a tool during an existing investigation, not just before it. Federal undercovers are usually titled under an operation name like "Operation Ill Wind" described in Chapter 2.

Reactive Investigations

It's been my experience that most investigations are initiated in a reactive manner based on information received from the above proactive type efforts, hotlines, or other complaints and so forth. Sometimes the assigned investigator knows nothing at all about the case until it is assigned to him or her.

Developing Investigative Plans and Strategies

It's good to have a handy list of all of the investigative tools, resources, and techniques that are at your disposal which you could use during any of your investigations. If you are not a law enforcement investigator, you might also want to have a sub-listing of the tools, resources, and techniques that law enforcement has that you do not. In fact, you could also have a listing of the tools, resources, and techniques that other investigative agencies have that you often work with (or could work with). Many of those sources, resources, tools, and techniques are listed in Chapters 7 and 8.

Factually, some organizations have bigger budgets and more resources than others. I know for a fact that one of the best-known federal criminal investigative agencies has many more resources to investigate government corruption and fraud, even though they do not investigate waste or abuse or try to identify systemic weaknesses or other deficiencies and are under no obligation to make recommendations for improvement.

Author's Note: *Politics aside, it's a good idea for all investigators of contract and procurement fraud, collusion, and corruption to know and become acquainted with others' abilities and resources and their willingness to assist in investigations so that all efforts can be maximized and investigative costs kept to a minimum.*

Investigative Planning Steps to Consider

Below are some steps to consider when drafting your investigative plan and strategy. Realize that the plan will need to be updated as your investigation progresses because of new information that has developed and for a variety of other reasons.

1. After grasping the information in the allegations or complaint received, determine if you have answers (or partial answers) to the seven questions: who, what, when, where, how, why, and how much. You'll probably be able to relatively quickly obtain additional information on the known suspect(s) if working a contract fraud case.
2. Consider what criminal and/or civil statutes may have been violated.
3. Consider where the case can be (or should be) prosecuted: federal and/or state (and which federal district and/or state), criminal, and/or civil.
4. Consider which other government agencies, companies or company branches, and/or others may have been victimized by the same suspect(s) using the same schemes.
5. Consider what tangible evidence you know or believe should/could exist.
6. Consider who should/might possess information that will assist in the investigation. Think about witnesses and then think about which of them may be cooperative or uncooperative and would probably tell or not tell the suspect(s) of your investigation.
7. Consider what sources and resources are available to assist in your investigation.
8. Consider what investigative tools and techniques will be (or could be) at your disposal.
9. Consider your existing work and personal calendars and existing caseload and how your time can be best used to conduct and complete this investigation.
10. Consider the best order to utilize the sources, resources, tools, and techniques that will provide the most benefit in the most time-efficient and cost-effective manner without jeopardizing the results of the investigation or any of your (or others') existing investigations. Also take into consideration any of your other personal and professional commitments.

As stated, your plan is probably going to change. Do not lock yourself into a course of action as if it's written in stone. You will update your plan and strategy as the investigation progresses. Most investigators maintain a working file in addition to an official file. Your investigative plan should be maintained in your working file.

By having written investigative plans on all of your assigned investigations, you will be able to stay intimately familiar with all of your cases at any given time. In all probability, you won't be able to work on one or more cases for a significant amount of time. Drafting a well-thought-out plan will serve as your roadmap to successfully completing the investigation regardless of when you are working on the case.

In addition, should the case be transferred to another investigator, your updated well-thought-out plan, combined with your previous written reports, will greatly assist whoever takes over the case and should allow for a smooth transition.

Your supervisors will probably also ask you to provide periodic briefings on your cases and you will probably be required to type periodic case summaries. By having a written plan (and your case reports), you can easily provide the information describing what you've done as well as what and when you plan on doing other things.

Murphy's Law

Murphy's Law is: Whatever can go wrong will go wrong. That happens a lot during investigations. Examples might be:

- You travel to conduct an unscheduled interview of a key former employee and he or she isn't home, or worse yet, went on vacation;
- You plan on conducting surveillance and the video camera battery dies;
- You plan on conducting a suspect interview with another federal agent, and the assisting agent calls you moments before and says he or she can't make it;
- You plan on reviewing recently received documents, and your supervisor assigns you two new cases.

But knowing about Murphy's Law in advance allows you to make or consider contingency plans to avoid disaster. Sometimes all you can do is postpone or delay your plans. It's usually not the end of the world. Just remember, investigations never go as smoothly as you think they will. President Dwight Eisenhower once said, "Farming looks mighty easy when your plow is a pencil and you're a thousand miles from the corn field."

Timing Is Everything

Sometimes, many steps in your investigative plan can be in progress at the same time. It doesn't always have to be, "First I'll do this, and then I'll do that." A good example of this is when agents execute search warrants or serve subpoenas. You can often also conduct interviews (even if they are just preliminary interviews) while you are there.

I often used a tactic as a federal agent when I was going to serve a grand jury subpoena. I'd interview an individual *before* letting him or her know about the subpoena. After the interview was completed, I'd hand the individual the grand jury subpoena that he or she did not realize I was going to serve him or her with. That way, the information I obtained prior to serving the subpoena was not considered grand jury material. Some might argue that if I handed the grand jury subpoena to the individual first and then asked that same individual questions, the information I obtained would be considered grand jury material.

Another advantage to this approach was that if the subpoena was for testimony, I would have already documented what the individual told me in person before he or she was scheduled to appear before the grand jury. This information can be useful to prepare the questions that will later be asked of the person when he or she appears before the grand jury. I would also be able to use the information I obtained in my interview in the civil case and/or for administrative purposes whereas if I did not interview the individual first, I'd have to wait to hear (or learn of) his or her responses when he or she testified, and then the results would be considered grand jury material.

> ### WAR STORY 11.1
>
> A fellow senior agent in one of my offices often tasked other agents to assist by conducting interviews of employees of a suspect company during the evening hours. He arranged for each of us to simultaneously knock on the doors of different employees' houses and ask them questions about fraud that may have occurred at their workplace. Some agents complained that the particular agent was making us do his work for him. There was some truth to that.
>
> But the senior agent knew that as soon as one employee was interviewed, that employee would most probably tell his or her supervisor, which would trigger the calling of the company's legal counsel. The company's legal counsel would in all probability immediately call the case agent and tell him that the attorney represented the company and all employees and that no further employee interviews should be conducted without the approval of the legal counsel.
>
> By having many interviews conducted simultaneously before the company (or their attorney) became aware of any investigation, the case agent increased the likelihood of obtaining useful information for the investigation before the attorney could close that door.

Author's Note: *Consider what effect the timing of your use of investigative tools will have on your investigation before initiating or using those tools.*

A Sample Investigative Plan

Listed below is a sample law enforcement investigative plan for use after receiving a referral on a contract or procurement fraud case.

Author's Note: *Whenever possible, report writing should take place shortly after each step is completed or when it is most practical.*

1 Interview the complainant;
2 Get/request records, documents, and information from public sources and your contracting office or wherever the order(s) was placed;
3 Review and analyze all information obtained thus far (at least start the process);

4 Perform surveillance;
5 Request a mail cover and perhaps perform a trash cover;
6 If necessary, conduct simultaneous interviews of current employees;
7 If permissible, interview former employees;
8 Interview any other witnesses, suppliers, subcontractors, etc.;
9 Serve subpoenas for records and/or testimony;
10 Review all information obtained thus far and prepare for suspect interviews;
11 Interview suspect(s);
12 Ensure all subpoenas and other requests have been complied with and follow up as needed;
13 Prepare for case presentation(s) to prosecutor(s);
14 Brief prosecutor(s);
15 Complete anything else that's needed.

In Summary

This chapter has described the importance of making plans to achieve investigative goals and emphasized that investigations should be conducted thoroughly to identify all fraud, collusion, corruption, waste, and abuse involving as many suspects as possible while pursuing criminal and civil violations, identifying systemic weaknesses and other deficiencies, and making recommendations for improvement. (*Sorry, I forgot to include leap tall buildings in a single bound and bend steel with your bare hands.*)

Can you really do all of this in all of your investigations? Perhaps not always. But I think you will agree that most of us can strive to do much more than we have been doing. We can easily identify more wrongdoing by the same suspects that we are already investigating and we can certainly try to figure out how to prevent contract and procurement fraud, collusion, and corruption and also make recommendations to try to fix known or potential problems.

Football teams have lots of plays in their playbooks which they first study and then practice. Not every play gets used during every game. But the players need to be knowledgeable about the plays they can execute so that those plays can be called into action with a moment's notice. Similarly, contract and procurement fraud, collusion, and corruption investigators should approach each investigation with a plan and know what their capabilities and goals are. In football, the goal is not to just make first downs and not to just make touchdowns. The goal is to win and to defeat those wrongdoers in an ethical manner.

The next chapter describes case presentations and testifying.

Author's Note: Much of this chapter was derived, copied, and/or modified from Chapter 10 (Investigative Case Planning, Goals, and Strategies) of *Healthcare Fraud Investigation Guidebook* by Charles E. Piper, copyright 2016 by Taylor & Francis Group, LLC. CRC Press is an imprint of Taylor & Francis Group, an Informa Business.

12 Case Presentations and Testifying

While serving as a private investigator and consultant, I often receive telephone calls from individuals needing investigative assistance. Many callers have never before had to relate case facts to others and they tend to ramble on and on before getting to the point. I understand that many callers are nervous and some don't have any idea what they really want. By asking questions, I can eventually draw out sufficient information to make sense of what happened, what they know or suspect, and/or their goals. My point is that it takes practice or experience to effectively communicate to others information about possible wrongdoing.

I received training on courtroom testifying while attending federal, state, and military investigative academies. In fact, one academy actually videotaped each student separately testifying in mock trials and then showed each student's video in front of the class to be critiqued by the instructors and fellow students. This type of training is very beneficial. We all learned from each others' strengths and weaknesses. I've also testified at numerous adjudicative hearings across the United States.

However, during my 30-year law enforcement career, I never received formal training on how to present case facts about a completed investigation to an attorney, supervisor, or others. Perhaps it was assumed that if you could conduct an investigation, write reports, and testify then you should be able to verbally present case facts to others. When presenting simple street crime cases (burglaries, robberies, assaults), that's probably a valid assumption. However, presenting the facts about a major fraud, collusion, or corruption case to others who have no previous knowledge about the case should not be taken lightly. It not only takes preparation but often some creativity.

Different Briefings for Different Folks

The type of presentation you provide as well as what information to share will depend on who you are briefing and the purpose of the briefing. Your second and third-line supervisors may only want to know what type of case you are working, the statutes and violations, who and where the suspects are, the estimated dollar loss, and when you'll be finished with the case. Higher-ranking superiors are often more interested in learning the results, not the details. Of course, some senior leaders might demand much more detail and question your every move and/or perhaps offer valuable (or not-so-valuable) input.

Corruption cases, on the other hand, seem to get everyone excited. Perhaps that's because of the anticipated media coverage that will be generated when the case is complete. If you are working a corruption case, you can almost expect that your superiors will be requiring more briefings and updates than usual and will constantly ask when you will be finished.

Providing Quality Briefings

> ### WAR STORY 12.1
>
> When I was a relatively new federal agent and briefing federal prosecutors, my case briefings contained factual information which essentially detailed how I first got the case, what I did, and the most recent developments. One day, a federal prosecutor, who I successfully worked cases with in the past, immediately interjected with a smile before I started talking, "Is this going to be one of those briefings where I don't find out what the case is all about until the end of your story?"
>
> Because we got along so well, we both laughed. The prosecutor knew that I did good work but, apparently, I got long-winded and took too long to get to the point. As time passed, I improved my fraud case presentation skills. In fact, I often interject some humor while briefing because fraud cases can often be dry, with facts and figures.

During the 1980s, I watched a television interview of President Ronald Reagan, who was known as "The great communicator." Reagan was asked how he was able to communicate so effectively. He replied by saying something like, "First, I tell people what I'm going to tell them. Second, I tell them. Third, I tell them what I told them."

Subsequently, I adopted a similar approach when providing written and oral summaries of investigations. Cases are much easier to understand when a brief summary is provided right from the onset followed by a presentation of the case facts and then a brief summary of what was covered.

Investigator's Voice, Appearance, and Bearing

We've all sat through presentations provided by monotone speakers where, no matter how good the information was, the speakers almost put their audiences to sleep. You definitely don't want to be one of those speakers. Provide some degree of excitement and energy when making your presentation. But be careful not to speak a mile a minute. Just because you can speak fast doesn't mean the information you're providing can be absorbed as quickly. Keep in mind that when you are briefing a prosecutor or law enforcement officer/investigator (and hoping they will consider accepting your case) they are probably thinking about how your case would play out in court and perhaps how *you* would play out in court. Strive to demonstrate that you are a professional and can communicate information effectively.

Physical appearance and bearing during presentations can also make a difference. You don't always have to wear your Sunday best suit, but don't dress down like you are going to clean out the attic either. It's been said that 50–90 percent of communication is nonverbal. That means that, regardless of the great information you are verbally providing, only a small portion of it may actually be received and people might be receiving more information from you by what is not coming out of your mouth. Since that's the case, make sure that you sit or stand up straight and be conscious of your nonverbal communication too.

Visual Aids

Visual aids are also a form of nonverbal communication. It's said that a picture is worth a thousand words. Studies have also shown that people remember pictures. Therefore, when providing a detailed briefing about a complex fraud, collusion, or corruption case, it's in your interest to develop and create some visual aids and/or take some photographs to help illustrate case facts. (*The Appendix of this book includes samples of case presentation visual aids for such cases.*)

Providing Copies of Reports and Documents

If you believe your case is worthy of acceptance for prosecution consideration and/or by a law enforcement agency for further investigation, during your verbal presentation you should provide them with a copy of a summary investigative report which contains much (or all) of the information/documents obtained to date. If you've already completed much or most of the investigation, you'll have to decide how much information and documentation to initially provide.

If it's a solid case, you might want to consider putting the entire case together, tabbed and indexed, so that they can take the case and run with it. Alternatively, you could provide a shorter summary report and offer to provide a more detailed report after acceptance. But provide them with some form of a written summary report which they can refer to in the future. Sometimes, prosecutors and law enforcement agencies can't immediately accept a case but they might be able to accept it later. If they have your report in hand, it will make it much easier for both you and them.

It's been my experience that it's often best not to provide the report until after your verbal briefing unless you will be referring to information or graphics in the report while you are talking. If you hand someone a three-ring binder while you are speaking, they will often start flipping through the pages while you are talking (and not really listening to what you are saying). On the same token, if you hand them a three-ring binder at the conclusion of the briefing and never reference it, they might just toss it in their working files after you leave and never even look at it.

Near the conclusion of the briefing, you could opt to provide copies of your report along with a brief verbal description of the information your report contains. You could also point out where certain information can be found in your report. Your case is more likely to get accepted if you can impress upon your audience that you have a good case and that it is well organized, and you present it well. However, it should be emphasized that potential dollar loss, harm, existing caseloads, and other factors are also considered before cases are accepted.

Author's Note: *Just like you wouldn't try to sell or trade in your used car before vacuuming and washing it, don't present a case that you want to be accepted until you have it in good condition.*

Testifying

Days before you are scheduled to testify in court, the prosecuting attorney will probably discuss with you what questions you will be asked. Even if that doesn't happen, if you are a witness for the prosecution, the questions will ordinarily be straightforward and only asked because it's known or assumed that you have the answers. But remember what I just said about nonverbal communication. You have to dress appropriately for a courtroom setting and speak clearly and confidently about your answers. If you don't understand a question, ask that it be repeated or rephrased.

Some say it's best to just answer the question that was asked and not to elaborate unless told to do so. A defense attorney once said that, when you are on the stand, "If you are asked if you know what time it is, answer yes. Don't offer the time because that's not what you were asked."

Keep in mind that the defense attorney's job is not the same as the prosecutor's. Expect that, during cross-examination, the defense attorney might try to twist your words around and challenge anything or everything you testified about earlier. Remember that he or she is just doing his or her job and is usually very good at it. Try to use the same tone and demeanor when answering all questions, regardless of who asks them—or at least don't *fly off the handle* just because you don't like the question or the way it's being asked.

If you will be testifying about facts and figures, make sure you review and verify the accuracy of them before testifying so that you are comfortable and confident about the information before getting on the stand. The better prepared you are, the smoother it will be. But be prepared to be challenged about the accuracy of the information you provide.

The prosecutor will be the one deciding whether any graphics or visual aids will be used in court. It's been my experience that visual aids often help jurors and judges to better understand or grasp the information provided in fraud cases. If you will be testifying about information contained in visual aids, triple check to ensure all the information is accurate and that you can confidently testify about that information, even if challenged by the opposing counsel.

If you've never testified in court before, it would be great if you could see the courtroom and where you will be sitting before actually testifying. In sporting events, teams usually have a higher winning percentage for home games than they do road games. Granted, the cheering fans might help, but perhaps it's because they are more comfortable with the playing field and surroundings.

The next chapter details post-adjudicative action.

Author's Note: Much of this chapter was derived, copied, and/or modified from Chapter 11 (Case Presentations and Testifying) of *Healthcare Fraud Investigation Guidebook* by Charles E. Piper, copyright 2016 by Taylor & Francis Group, LLC. CRC Press is an imprint of Taylor & Francis Group, an Informa Business.

13 Post-Adjudicative Action

Watching guilty suspects get sentenced to prison sentences, witnessing financial judgments being imposed, and submitting press releases about the successful adjudicative action on your contract or procurement fraud, collusion, or corruption case does not conclude the investigator's work. There are many things that must be done and should be considered once the adjudicative action is completed against an individual or entity. In fact, at the time the case is officially opened, the investigator should actually start thinking about what he or she should/will do after the investigation is completed.

Media coverage alone that publicizes guilty verdicts, fines, fees, and judgments does not prevent the same type of criminal activity from reoccurring in the future. If it did, there would be no crime today and the jails would be less crowded. Although publicity about the adjudicative action can be beneficial (usually more so to the prosecutors and investigators), it is not the end-all solution to preventing criminal activity.

Fraud Vulnerability and Deficiency Reports

Every federal and state law enforcement investigator and agency, as well as investigators and their organizations in the private sector, that investigates contract and procurement fraud, collusion, or corruption has (or should have) an obligation to also search for systemic weaknesses and deficiencies (and possible weaknesses and deficiencies) that caused or may have caused or contributed to any fraud, waste, and abuse (not just fraud), and to document their findings.

This responsibility actually takes very little additional time. Although it may pain some investigative agencies' ears to hear, taxpayers' and other sources' funds should not continually be directed to fund the growth of investigative agencies and organizations to catch criminals when the money could more appropriately be used to try to prevent, detect, and deter such wrongdoing from reoccurring or occurring in the first place.

All investigators that investigate contract and procurement fraud, collusion, or corruption should also be required to include in their final investigative reports whether they identified any systemic weaknesses (or possible systemic weaknesses), deficiencies, and/or indications of waste or abuse during their investigation and indicate if they made any recommendations for improvement. Copies of those deficiency reports and recommendations should be included in the official investigative case file and should include a listing of all those who were on the distribution.

It is paramount that the investigators' deficiency reports and recommendations be provided to the responsible personnel (decision-makers) of the victim agency(s) so that those individuals can become aware of the problems and possible solutions and be held accountable for making improvements to reduce the probability that the wrongdoing will occur again in the future. The investigators' documentation and appropriate distribution will make it impossible for those in responsible positions to later say they were unaware of such deficiencies.

The Importance of Recognition and Rewards

Investigators, examiners, and others should be officially recognized and rewarded when they identify such weaknesses, deficiencies, waste, and/or abuse—especially when they make useful recommendations for improvement and those recommendations (or parts thereof) are implemented. If there is no incentive for the investigators and others to do this type of work, it will not get done. Consequently, the wrongdoing will continue and funds will continue to be lost to fraud, waste, and abuse and additional funds that could have been saved or better spent will have to be spent to conduct investigations.

Storing and Archiving Investigative Case Files

Investigative agencies and organizations have their own policies and procedures regarding how to retire a closed investigative case file. As previously stated, it's recommended that all interview notes be placed in the official file before placing it in archives. Remember that sometimes cases are appealed and even retried. When cases are "unsolved" or no adjudicative action is taken or considered, sometimes information or evidence are later obtained which could help prove wrongdoing that couldn't be proven before.

During my 35-plus years of conducting investigations, I've often pulled old, closed case files to obtain useful information and sometimes to solve old cases. So don't assume that once your case file is placed in storage that it's in its final resting place. If the case file is well documented and well organized during the investigation and at closing, all that hard work may also be very useful in the future.

Suspensions, Debarments, and Integrity Agreements

The equivalent of a financial death sentence for many government contractors is to be banned from or excluded from government programs. These forms of exclusion are often temporary (called suspensions) or permanent (debarments). Typically, when excluded from one government program, they are often (perhaps always) automatically excluded from others.

Government contractors who are suspected of criminal or civil violations (and the attorneys that represent them) know that being suspended or debarred essentially means, "game over." Therefore, they often attempt to negotiate settlements in which the contractors agree to reimburse losses and perhaps pay fines and/or the cost of investigation as long as they are not excluded from government programs. Sometimes the government prosecutors and investigators don't really want to see the suspects go out of business because if that happens, they may not be able to repay the losses and fines.

During my federal law enforcement career investigating fraud, I found it's not unusual for a government contractor or individual that has committed fraud, to plead guilty to a misdemeanor or Internal Revenue Service violation and/or agree to some civil statute violation and repayment to avoid having a felony conviction.

Corporate Integrity Agreements

A government contractor that has committed fraud (or possible fraud) can sometimes still stay in business if they are afforded the opportunity to sign a corporate integrity agreement with the victim agency in which the contractor has to implement and abide by strict policies and procedures to ensure they won't go astray again in the future.

Author's Note: *For additional information, see the Government Accountability Office (GAO) website on "Suspended and Debarred Businesses and Individuals Improperly Receive Federal Funds" (http://www.gao.gov/products/GAO-09-174).*

The information which follows was copied from the GAO's website on June 7, 2016:

> To protect the government's interests, any agency can exclude (i.e., debar or suspend) parties from receiving federal contracts or assistance for a range of offenses. Exclusions of companies or individuals from federal contracts or other funding are listed in the Excluded Parties List System (EPLS), a Web-based system maintained by GSA. Recent allegations indicate that excluded parties have been able to receive federal contracts. As a result, GAO was asked (1) to determine whether these allegations could be substantiated and (2) to identify the key causes of any improper awards and other payments detected. GAO investigated parties that were excluded for offenses such as fraud, theft, and violations of federal statutes and received awards in excess of $1,000.
>
> Businesses and individuals that have been excluded for egregious offenses ranging from national security violations to tax fraud are improperly receiving federal contracts and other funds. GAO developed cases on a number of these parties and found that they received funding for a number of reasons, including because agency officials failed to search EPLS or because their searches did not reveal the exclusions. GAO also identified businesses and individuals that were able to circumvent the terms of their exclusions by operating under different identities.

GAO's cases include the following: (1) The Army debarred a German company after its president attempted to ship nuclear bomb parts to North Korea. As part of the debarment, Army stated that since the president "sold potential nuclear bomb making materials to a well-known enemy of the United States," there was a "compelling interest to discontinue any business with this morally bankrupt individual." However, Army told GAO it was legally obligated to continue the contract and paid the company over $4 million in fiscal 2006. In fact, the Army had several options for terminating the contract, but it is not clear if these options were considered.

(2) The Navy suspended a company after one of its employees sabotaged repairs on an aircraft carrier by using nonconforming parts to replace fasteners on steam pipes. If these pipes had ruptured as a result of faulty fasteners, those aboard the carrier could have suffered lethal burns. Less than a month later, the Navy improperly awarded the company three new contracts because the contracting officer did not check EPLS. Most of the improper contracts and payments GAO identified can be attributed to ineffective management of the EPLS database or to control weaknesses at both excluding and procuring agencies. For example, GAO's work shows that entries may contain incomplete information, the database has insufficient search capabilities, and the points of contact for information about exclusions are incorrect. GAO also found several agencies that did not enter exclusions and others that did not check EPLS prior to making awards. Finally, GAO found that excluded parties were still listed on GSA's Federal Supply Schedule, which can result in agencies purchasing items from unscrupulous companies. To verify that no warnings exist to alert agencies that they are making purchases from excluded parties, GAO used its own purchase card to buy body armor worth over $3,000 from a company that had been debarred for falsifying tests related to the safety of its products.

In summary, once the investigation and adjudicative action has been completed, the investigator usually has some additional work to do before the case file can actually be retired.

The next chapter provides a sample (fictional) case study-story in which readers can get an idea of how information provided in this book can be applied to an investigation after the receipt of a complaint.

Author's Note: Much of this chapter was derived, copied, and/or modified from Chapter 12 (Post-Adjudicative Action) of *Healthcare Fraud Investigation Guidebook* by Charles E. Piper, copyright 2016 by Taylor & Francis Group, LLC. CRC Press is an imprint of Taylor & Francis Group, an Informa Business.

14 Sample Case Study
Story #1

This chapter provides a fictional case study-story to demonstrate how the previous chapters' information and guidance can actually be applied in the field. Many fraud fighters serve as auditors, analysts, examiners, consultants, or in similar investigative-type positions, and very often their information is provided to field investigators to prove (or disprove) if fraud occurred and/or perhaps is still occurring. Many of the referrals end up in the hands of federal and/or state law enforcement investigators. Often those same professionals provide valuable assistance during such investigations.

In this fictional case study-story, the assigned investigators assume the roles of senior federal agents that routinely investigate contract and procurement fraud, collusion, and corruption. This case study provides insight as to how investigators (in this case federal agents) might go about conducting such an investigation while utilizing *The Piper Method of Conducting Thorough and Complete Investigations*.*

This case study-story is intentionally written to serve as a less-detailed overview of the previously described suggested investigative process. It does not include all possible investigative steps and/or details that would ordinarily be completed and documented in an official investigation. As you may know, actual high-dollar fraud investigations often take years to complete. Contributing factors to some delays are caused by the investigator's other responsibilities, including simultaneously investigating other existing unrelated cases, the opening of other new cases, participation in training, preparing for office inspections and supervisory case reviews, assisting other agents, waiting for supervisory approval of the investigator's drafted reports, and other requests. In many cases, delays are caused by waiting for others to complete assigned or requested tasks such as complying with subpoenas and so forth. However, in this sample, the investigation will proceed at almost lightning speed as compared with a real-life case.

All names of persons, entities, agencies, and organizations listed in this case study are fictional. Any resemblance to actual cases and/or individuals, entities, or others is purely coincidental.

*Piper, Charles E., *Investigator and Fraud Fighter Guidebook: Operation War Stories*, John Wiley & Sons, Hoboken, NJ, 2014. (Copyright 2014, Wiley-VCH Verlag GmbH & Co. KGaA. Reproduced with permission.)

Background Information

The assigned investigator is Special Agent Dan Durbin. SA Durbin is employed by a federal investigative agency named the Federal Investigative Service (FIS). Durbin was raised in the South Side of Chicago and has served as a federal agent for over 10 years. He works in a small one-agent office in Memphis, TN. His immediate supervisor's office is located in Nashville, TN.

The referral sent to SA Durbin is dated January 8, 2015. It's from the FIS audit agency located in Baltimore, Maryland. Durbin received it on January 12, 2015. The referral pertains to a contractor located in Memphis, TN that provides office supplies to various federal agencies, including FIS. The name of the entity is Plenty of Office Stuff, Inc. (POSI).

The referral reflects that POSI has been awarded numerous federal contracts since October 2001 to supply various office products. But many complaints have been received about POSI's shipments. Some shipments contained less quantity than ordered, some contained the wrong items, and some items were never delivered at all. However, POSI submitted invoices for all those orders and the invoices have all been paid. There has been a noticeable increase in complaints about POSI's shipments in the last 3 months.

During its first 10 years of operation, POSI received approximately $10 million in government contract awards each year. But in the past few years, POSI has been awarded many more contracts. More recently, the total dollar amount of government contracts awarded to POSI was

- 2012: $15 million
- 2013: $18 million
- 2014: $22 million

The referral includes a CD with an Excel spreadsheet which lists information about the POSI contracts that received complaints. The information provided includes:

- Federal contract numbers (and dates awarded);
- The contracting offices where the contracts were awarded from;
- Each contracting officers' name, work address, e-mail address, and telephone number;
- Each contract's total award price;
- Descriptions of items ordered and individual prices per item;
- The location where shipments were supposed to be delivered;
- The dates complaints were documented, with descriptions of the discrepancies.

POSI is owned by Mr. Paul P. Pane. POSI's office manager is Ms. Lucy L. Lightweight.

Monday, January 12, 2015

(Memphis, TN)

The Case Initiation

SA Dan Durbin sits at his desk after opening the new referral that was delivered via an overnight delivery service. After giving it a quick overview, he steps to his copy machine and makes a working copy of the referral and the attachments. Next, he grabs two manila folders and with a black marker writes "POSI Working File" on one. The second folder will be his official file. He uses a two-hole punch to punch holes in the top of the referral documents and places them inside the official file. Durbin has been through the case initiation drill hundreds of times. He next types a case initiation report, obtains a case number through his agency's intranet case log system, and scans a PDF version of his report into the case log system. He then e-mails his supervisor in Nashville advising that he has just opened a new case.

The Investigative Plan

Durbin takes a couple sips of coffee, grabs a blank legal notepad, and scribbles on the top: *POSI: Draft Investigative Plan*, and he starts drafting his plan. About 20 minutes later, Durbin receives an e-mail from Janice Slow, his Nashville supervisor. Durbin reads the e-mail, shakes his head in disbelief, and whispers out loud to himself, "Who the heck cares how many spaces are supposed to be in between sentences?!"

Durbin tosses aside his draft investigative plan and makes minor corrections to his previously drafted case initiation report. After saving the report, he resubmits it for approval and whispers, "Just let me work the case, would ya'?"

After taking another sip of coffee, Durbin continues writing his investigative plan. From under his desk mat, he removes two sheets of paper. One sheet has a list of investigative tools and techniques and the other sheet lists frequently used federal criminal and civil statutes. Referencing each sheet, Durbin completes drafting his plan and then checks his e-mail. There's a new one. It's from his supervisor, Janice Slow.

Exhaling deeply, Durbin opens the e-mail and reads that his supervisor approved his report but wants him to draft an investigative plan. Durbin shakes his head in disbelief, grabs the pad of paper that already has his plan written on it, holds it up to the computer screen and says out loud, "Dahhhh!"

SA Durbin is assigned to a one-agent office and he has no secretary or administrative support. He has successfully investigated more contract and procurement fraud, collusion, and corruption cases than most other agents in his agency. His immediate supervisor (Janice Slow) has only worked a few simple contract fraud cases during her career, and even those were worked jointly with other agencies where she played a supportive role. She has never investigated a bid rigging or corruption case. Janice Slow was selected to be a supervisor by another less-experienced manager because of her administrative skills.

Durbin types a label with the newly assigned case number and places it on the official case folder. Next, he prints two copies of his approved case initiation and puts one copy in his work folder and one in his official file. After gulping down the last of his coffee, Durbin stands up and glances outside of his office window, located on the tenth floor of a downtown commercial office space. He watches vehicles heading to and from Arkansas on a bridge over the Mississippi River.

Contacting Other Federal Agencies

Knowing that other federal agencies may have also been victimized by POSI, Durbin sends e-mails to his investigative contacts with those agencies informing them of the referral and the opportunity to join the investigation if their agency may have been harmed.

As usual, few respond. One agent who Durbin has worked with before does reply. Her name is SA Tina Thomas and she works with the Federal Fraud Bureau. SA Thomas' office is located on the third floor in the same building.

Thomas' e-mail reads: "Danny Boy, count me in! Let me know when you want to meet."

Durbin replies: "Cool, how about my office tomorrow morning at 9? I'm going to work out before I come in to the office. I've attached my case initiation. Make sure I get a copy of yours."

Thomas responds: "Ditto on working out first. Will do."

Tuesday, January 13, 2015

Joint Agents Meeting

The next morning at 9:00 AM sharp, SA Tina Thomas knocks on SA Dan Durbin's office door. Holding a fresh cup of coffee, Durbin opens the door and the two agents shake hands.

Durbin asks, "Hey Tina, how come you're the only agent that ever answers e-mails about working joint cases?"

Tina takes a sip from a can of highly caffeinated soda, smiles, and replies, "Because I'm the only one who will put up with you Danny Boy!" They both laugh.

SA Thomas was raised in New York City. She's been a federal agent for a little over 9 years. Both Durbin and Thomas previously served as street cops before becoming federal agents.

The two sit at Durbin's desk and Durbin runs a computer aerial view search of POSI's address. He tilts the large desktop computer's screen so both agents can see.

Tina replies, "Man, it's a little tiny place. How the heck is he shipping so much stuff out of there?"

Durbin replies, "He must have another facility somewhere else."

Durbin minimizes the computer screen and searches the internet for additional information about POSI. He clicks on POSI's company website and the two agents view the home page, which has several photos on it. "Paul Pane is a heavy man, isn't he?" Tina remarks.

Durbin replies, "Well, his office manager, Lucy Lightweight, looks like she could be a model."

Tina holds four fingers in front of her face while still looking at the computer screen and jokes, "I wonder what they'd look like behind bars."

"Pane might be the first one to have to worry about that," Durbin jokes.

The two agents share responsibilities. Tina will request a 30-day mail cover on all mail addressed to all occupants at POSI's mailing address. She will also check the social media profiles on Paul Pane and Lucy Lightweight. Durbin will obtain background information on the company and the owner. He'll obtain a Dun & Bradstreet report on POSI and search Tennessee's Secretary of State records for corporations and corporate officers to see if additional information can be found on POSI, Paul Pane, and Lucy Lightweight.

Wednesday, January 14, 2015

SA Tina Thomas and SA Dan Durbin speak on their cell phones.

Durbin: *Get this! The state's corporate records show Pane uses his home address for two other active companies! There's nothing else on the internet about either company. One's named P.P. Supplies and the other is just Paul Pane, Enterprises.*

Tina: *What's P.P. Supplies do? Sell diapers!?*

Durbin: *(Laughing) Actually, the company has a Cage Code and it also does business with the G.*

Tina: *How much business is P.P. Supplies doing with the government?*

Durbin: *Not as much as POSI, but about half a million a year since 2012. Both of these companies list Paul Pane as the president. Guess who the vice president and treasurer are?*

Tina: *Don't tell me. It's Lucy Lightweight the pretty model girl, right!?*

Durbin: *You got it! And P.P. Supplies also has complaints against them for not shipping items on their contracts.*

Tina: *Dang! Now I have to update my report and add P.P. as a subject.*

Durbin: *Dang paperwork! Did you get that mail cover request sent out?*

Tina: *Sure did. Now I'd better do one on Paul Pane's and Lucy Lightweight's houses too. I'll get them out by the end of the day.*

Durbin: *Great idea. I'll make a request to get a breakdown on all of P.P.'s government contracts and complaints against them. You think we should do a trash cover?*

Tina: *Dang, Durbin! Give me a break! I hate digging through people's trash.*

Durbin: *Tell ya' what; since you're doing the mail covers, I'll get the trash from Pane's house. He lives in a mansion in a gated community. I pass the front gates on my way to work. I think his trash day is tomorrow.*

Tina: *It figures. He's living the life of the rich and famous. Don't dent your G-car sneaking through the gates like you did last time!*

Durbin: *Shhhh. You must have me mistaken with someone else. That never happened.*

Thursday, January 15, 2015

11:00 AM

SA Tina Thomas and SA Dan Durbin speak on their office phones.

Durbin:	Tina, I should have asked you to come with me to get this guy's trash. Stinky! Crappy! Nasty!
Tina:	(Laughing) What did you expect? You think the rich guy's garbage is cleaner than yours?
Durbin:	Very funny. I lucked out and got Lucy Lightweight's trash too. She tossed some good stuff. I got about 6 months' worth of bank statements from P.P. Supplies and Paul Pane Enterprises.
Tina:	She's careless! What address is on the bank statements? Anything good in them?
Durbin:	She smothered them in coffee grounds but you can still read everything. The address on the bank statements is for Paul Pane's house. I guess he gave them to her. I haven't read them yet. Why don't you come up to my office and we can look at the bank statements together.
Tina:	I'll be right up.

11:45 AM

(Both agents are wearing blue disposable gloves, sitting at Durbin's desk looking at dirty bank statements.)

Tina:	My Gosh! Look at all these big deposits into Paul Pane Enterprises' account. $10,000! $20,000, $50,000!
Durbin:	Yea, and they write checks from that account the same way. $3,000! $5,000! $10,000! Almost every deposit and check is for high-dollar, even-numbered dollar amounts that end in zeroes.
Tina:	(Pretending to be waiving a small flag with one hand) Red flag! Red flag! Red flag!
Durbin:	(Leaning back in his chair) We're going to have to subpoena these banks. We need to find out where that money's coming from that's being deposited into Paul Pane Enterprises' account and who those checks are going to.
Tina:	Here's my prediction. The money is coming from POSI and the checks are going to Paul Pane and Linda Lightweight.
Durbin:	Probably. But maybe some money is coming from P.P. Diapers.
Tina:	(Laughing) It's not P.P. Diapers; it's P.P. Supplies.
Durbin:	Dang! You started it! Now I can't get P.P. Diapers out of my brain.
Tina:	(Laughing) Were there any pee-pee diapers in the trash cans?
Durbin:	Very funny! Next time you can do the trash covers!
Tina:	(Sitting up straight and acting serious) I'm only kidding. You did a great job! You are the best trash cover man in Memphis, Tennessee.

Durbin: (Sarcastically) *Ha! Ha! You know what? I'll bet Pane is paying off some people too.*

Tina: *You mean bribes!? That makes sense to me. Every time I've seen even-numbered high-dollar amounts ending in zero coming out or going into bank accounts, they were either for bribes, kickbacks, or drugs.*

Durbin: *How about we do this? I have to photocopy and then log these bank statements as evidence. You start finding out which contracting office has awarded the most contracts to POSI and P.P. Diapers and if the same contracting officers kept awarding contracts to them.*

Tina: (Holding her hand over her mouth while trying to hold back laughter.)

Durbin: *What's so funny?*

Tina: (Laughing) *Nothing.*

Durbin: *No, what's so funny!*

Tina: *You said P.P. Diapers again.*

Durbin: *No I didn't! I said P..P ... P.P. ... P.P. ... Dang! What's the name of that stupid company!?*

Tina: (Laughing) *P.P. Supplies.*

Durbin: *This is all your fault! I'll probably be saying diapers when we go to trial!*

January 16–March 30, 2015

During the next couple of months, SA Tina Thomas and SA Danny Durbin continued gathering and analyzing contract award information and delivery complaints against POSI and P.P. Supplies.

The mail cover results came back and identified possible financial institutions that the individuals and companies might be affiliated with along with some probable customers.

The two agents met with prosecutors from the criminal and civil divisions at the U.S. Attorney's office in downtown Memphis. Grand jury subpoenas were obtained for 3 years of bank statements for the following:

- Plenty of Office Stuff, Inc. (POSI);
- PP Supplies;
- Paul Pane Enterprises;
- Paul Pane;
- Lucy Lightweight.

After reviewing the bank statements, additional subpoenas were served on the same banks to obtain copies of deposits, withdrawal slips, and checks that were for high-dollar, even-numbered dollar amounts.

The awarded contracts review found that one government contracting officer was responsible for awarding all of the contracts awarded to P.P. Supplies and many of the contracts awarded to POSI. That contracting officer's name is Stephanie Steinback. Her office is in Philadelphia, PA.

Sample Case Study: Story #1   173

Wednesday, April 1, 2015

10:30 AM

SA Dan Durbin and SA Tina Thomas are sitting at a large table inside Durbin's office with banker boxes full of documents surrounding them and piles of documents and files on top of the table.

Tina: (Munching on pretzels from a bag on the table while reviewing documents). *Find anything?*

Durbin: *Yea, I find your crunching pretzels and reaching back and forth into that noisy paper bag very annoying.*

Tina: (Sarcastically) *Well, excuse me! I didn't eat breakfast so I could sit at this stupid messy table with you.*

Durbin: *I know. Sorry. Give me one of those pretzels* (Durbin reaches in the bag and starts munching on a pretzel.)

Tina: (Looks up from the documents she's reviewing) *Dang, those pretzels are noisy.*

Durbin: (Intentionally crunches louder and then holds up a check) *Who the heck is Anthony Polanski!?*

Tina: *He's obviously a half-Italian and half-Polish guy? Why?*

Durbin: *Well, Paul Pane Enterprises has been paying him about fifty-K a month for the past 3 years.*

Tina: *Fifty thousand a month!?* (Tina removes a computer tablet from her purse and searches for Anthony Polanski.)

Tina: *The internet says Anthony Polanski of Las Vegas, Nevada, is a consultant that specializes in federal government contracting.* (Tina turns the tablet toward Durbin showing a photograph of Anthony Polanski.)

Durbin: *He looks dirty!*

Tina: *I'll bet he crunches his pretzels real loud too!*

Durbin: *Looks like we're also going to Vegas!*

Tina: *Whatever goes in Vegas; stays in Vegas.*

Durbin: *Maybe not this time.*

Saturday, April 4, 2015

Memphis, TN

9:15 AM

SA Tina Thomas and SA Dan Durbin are dressed in professional attire and each is holding a leather notebook while standing on the front porch of Lucy Lightweight's house in Memphis. SA Durbin rings the front doorbell. The front door opens and both agents hold up their credential cases showing their badges and federal agent identification.

Lucy Lightweight:	It's awfully early. Can I help you?
Durbin:	My name is Special Agent Durbin. This is Special Agent Thomas. We'd like to talk to you about some business matters that have been taking place at Plenty of Office Stuff. Can we come in for a few minutes?
Lucy Lightweight:	Am I in trouble? Do I need a lawyer?
Tina:	You are not in custody and we can't advise you whether you need a lawyer or not. But if you decide you don't want to talk to us after we tell you what this is about, we'll leave. How's that?
Lucy Lightweight:	Okay then. I wasn't expecting company, but come on in.

During the interview, Lucy Lightweight tells all. She said that she knew that Paul Pane was paying Anthony Polanski several thousands of dollars each month to help Pane get awarded government contracts. She only met Anthony Polanski once when he came to Memphis and he kept trying to get her to go on a date with him. She refused. Lightweight didn't know what Polanski did to help get government contracts but it seemed to work because POSI's business had increased tremendously.

She said Pane opened another company named P.P. Supplies, which also was awarded government contracts, and that sometimes P.P. Supplies and POSI both submitted bids for the same contracts. If POSI didn't get the contract, very often P.P. Supplies did.

Lightweight didn't know Stephanie Steinback, but Lightweight heard that she drives a fancy sports car and likes to go on vacations in Europe. Steinback got divorced a few years ago from a banker. Lightweight knew nothing about short shipments or invoicing. She said Paul Pane handled all that.

The agents asked Lightweight if she was willing to record some future conversations and telephone calls she has with Paul Pane. Although initially reluctant, Lightweight agreed.

The agents later obtain approval from both of their own agencies to have Lucy Lightweight record calls and meetings with Paul Pane. Lightweight also signed forms showing she voluntarily consented to have her conversations and calls with Paul Pane recorded.

Tuesday, April 7–Friday, April 10, 2015

Lucy Lightweight's conversations with Paul Pane were recorded. Pane admitted that he paid Anthony Polanski high dollars so that Polanski could assist in getting federal contracts awarded to POSI and P.P. Supplies. Pane deposited funds from both of his companies into Paul Pane Enterprises' bank account. Pane wrote checks from that account to Polanski.

Pane told Lightweight that he believed Polanski probably has given money and gifts to Stephanie Steinback to sway her to award contracts to both companies.

Sample Case Study: Story #1

It was Steinback who suggested Pane open a second company so it could provide complementary or alternate bids to get contracts awarded at higher prices. During a meeting, Pane showed Lightweight a copy of Steinback's e-mail suggesting he open the company. Unknown to Pane, Lightweight took a cell phone photograph of the e-mail and forwarded it to SA Tina Thomas.

Friday Night, April 10, 2015
7:30 PM

SA Durbin and SA Thomas are eating at a famous barbecue restaurant in downtown Memphis.

Durbin:	So it looks like we've got three interviews to do.
Tina:	Paul Pane, Anthony Polanski, and Stephanie Steinback.
Durbin:	Who do you think we should do first?
Tina:	Pane can give us Anthony Polanski and Polanski can give us Stephanie Steinback.
Durbin:	Yea, and then who knows who Stephanie Steinback can give us.
Tina:	Exactly.
Durbin:	You ready to move to Vegas?
Tina:	I will if you will.
Durbin:	(Laughing) What, and give up this barbecue? (Durbin licks fingers.)

Saturday, April 11, 2015
Memphis, TN
9:15 AM

SA Tina Thomas and SA Dan Durbin are dressed in professional attire and each is holding a leather notebook while standing on the front porch of Paul Pane's house in Memphis. SA Durbin rings the front doorbell. The front door opens and both agents hold up their credential cases showing their badges and federal agent identification.

Paul Pane:	(Pane's eyes open wide when he sees the badges.)
Tina:	My name is Special Agent Thomas. This is Special Agent Durbin. We'd like to talk to you about some business matters that have been taking place at Plenty of Office Stuff. Can we come in for a few minutes?
Paul Pane:	What kind of business matters?
Tina:	Mr. Pane, we can stand on this front porch for all your neighbors to see and start gossiping or you can invite us in and we'll tell you all about it.
Durbin:	Sir, you're not in custody so if you change your mind and don't want to talk to us, we'll leave.
Paul Pane:	I'd still like to know what this is all about.

Durbin: It's about Anthony Polanski and Stephanie Steinback.
Paul Pane: (Acting confused) *Am I supposed to know them?*
Durbin: (Removes copies of two checks payable to Anthony Polanski from his notebook and holds them in front of Paul Pane to read.) *We just want to hear your side of the story. Now, would you like to invite us in or not?*
Paul Pane: (Speaking sadly) *I guess you two would find this out eventually. Come on in.*

Paul Pane confessed to submitting bids from his two companies to compete against each other to get awarded government contracts. Pane said he gradually increased his bid prices and was surprised that he kept getting awarded contracts no matter how high he bid. Pane said he paid Anthony Polanski to facilitate everything with Stephanie Steinback. Polanski told Pane that he gave Steinback cash and paid for some of her trips to and from Europe.

Pane said that when he first opened POSI, it was difficult to get awarded government contracts. Then, out of the blue, he received a call from Anthony Polanski who said he owned a consulting company that helped contractors increase their chances of getting awarded contracts. His fees were high, but he came through.

Regarding the short shipments, Pane said that although his company made a lot of money, Polanski's consulting fees were pretty expensive. Sometimes Pane directed his employees to include a few less items in the shipments and sometimes Pane submitted invoices first and planned on shipping the orders after receiving payment. He admitted that sometimes he never got around to shipping all the orders even after getting paid. Pane said any wrong items delivered were honest mistakes.

When asked who else knew about all of this, Pane said no one else knew and that his office manager, Lucy Lightweight, was kept in the dark. She didn't know about any of the short shipments or payments to Polanski. Pane said that Lightweight might have suspected some shenanigans were going on but she was smart enough not to ask questions until recently. Pane asked if the agents spoke with Lightweight and was told they don't provide the names of people they interview. Durbin clouded the issue by saying they would probably need to talk with Lightweight sometime in the future to corroborate Pane's statements.

Pane provided a computer printout of all the checks and payments he made to Anthony Polanski which went back to 2012.

Pane agreed to make recorded telephone calls to Anthony Polanski. The agents again obtained their own agencies' approval to have the calls recorded.

Wednesday, April 15, 2015

In the presence of the two agents, Paul Pane placed a recorded call to Anthony Polanski who told Pane he's been providing Stephanie Steinbeck with cash and has paid for her trips to Europe. Polanski suggested that Pane not ask too many questions because Pane would be better off not knowing how he "worked his magic."

Sunday, April 19, 2015
(Las Vegas, NV)
8:15 PM

After checking into separate rooms at the MGM Casino and Hotel in Las Vegas, NV, SA Tina Thomas and SA Dan Durbin walk together to the Bellagio Hotel's fountains and watch a few water shows with Frank Sinatra songs playing in the background.

Tina:	So how do you think Anthony Polanski's going to react when we knock on his door in the morning?
Durbin:	To tell you the truth, I think good ole Tony is going to crap in his Las Vegas pants.
Tina:	(Laughing) How do you know he wears Las Vegas pants?
Durbin:	What other kind of pants would he wear in Las Vegas?
Tina:	Does that mean you're wearing Las Vegas pants?
Durbin:	(Stretching the hips of his pants outward) I'll be darned. I guess I am wearing Las Vegas pants! But I'm not going to crap in mine.
Tina:	(Laughing) Well, I certainly wouldn't want to be in his shoes.
Durbin:	You mean his Las Vegas shoes?
Tina:	Let's not do this anymore.
Durbin:	You started it.
Tina:	No, you started it …

Monday, April 20, 2015
(Las Vegas, NV)
8:15 AM

SA Tina Thomas and SA Dan Durbin are dressed in professional attire and each holding a leather notebook while standing on the front porch of Anthony Polanski's house. It's a big house and, unlike most nearby homes that have desert landscaping, has an artificial green lawn. SA Durbin rings the front doorbell. The front door opens and both agents hold up their credential cases showing their badges and federal agent identification. Anthony Polanski answers the door sporting a deep tan and wearing shorts, sandals, and a dress pullover shirt.

Anthony Polanski:	Yes, officers, what can I do for you?
Durbin:	Mr. Polanski, my name is Special Agent Durbin. This is Special Agent Thomas. We'd like to talk to you about the work you do for Mr. Paul Pane from Memphis. Can we come in for a few minutes?
Anthony Polanski:	Well, I was just getting ready to play some golf.
Durbin:	(Looks up at the blue sky) It doesn't look like it's going to rain and I'm sure the golf course will still be there later today.

178   Chapter 14

Anthony Polanski:	Well, I guess you can come in as long as this doesn't take too long.(Polanski opens the door and lets the two agents inside.)
Durbin:	Those are nice pants. Did you get those in Las Vegas? (Tina shakes her head in disbelief that Durbin asked the question.)

When confronted with copies of the check payments to him by Paul Pane, Anthony Polanski said he wanted to speak to his attorney and did not want to answer any more questions. The agents left their business cards and thanked him for his time.

9:30 AM

SA Dan Durbin drives their rental car down the Las Vegas Strip with SA Tina Thomas riding in the front passenger seat.

Durbin:	Well, ole Tony lawyered up?
Tina:	Guess we're going to Phili to interview Stephanie Steinback, huh?
Durbin:	Man, I hate East Coast time. It's 3 hours later there.
Tina:	And you'll have to put on your Philadelphia pants.
Durbin:	(Slamming his fist into the steering wheel) Oh crap!
Tina:	Now what's the matter?
Durbin:	This is the only suit I brought. I don't have any Philadelphia pants.
Tina:	They'll be Philadelphia pants when you get there. After all, what other kind of pants would someone wear in Philadelphia?

Wednesday, April 22, 2015

(Philadelphia, PA)

6:30 PM

SA Tina Thomas and SA Dan Durbin are dressed in professional attire and each is holding a leather notebook while standing on the front porch of Stephanie Steinback's house. SA Durbin rings the front doorbell. The front door opens and both agents hold up their credential cases showing their badges and federal agent identification. Stephanie reacts with complete silence and just stares blankly at the agents.

Tina:	My name is Special Agent Thomas. This is Special Agent Durbin. We'd like to talk to you about some contracts that you awarded. Can we come in for a few minutes?
Stephanie Steinback:	Why couldn't you just ask me about that while I was at work?
Tina:	We thought you might prefer to talk to us here. If we talked to you at work, people might get the wrong impression.
Stephanie Steinback:	Oh I see. Am I in some sort of trouble?
Tina:	We're just trying to get a better understanding of things.

Stephanie Steinback invited the two agents inside. When confronted with the evidence, she cried and said that her ex-husband wasn't required to pay the high alimony she thought she would get when they got divorced. Steinback said she needed to keep her income up so she could pay for her two children's college. Steinback admitted that it was her idea for Paul Pane to open P.P. Supplies because her supervisors started asking why she was awarding so many contracts to POSI.

Steinback admitted that she dismissed others' bids whenever possible to show favoritism to Pane's companies and that Anthony Polanski paid her to award those contracts. She said Polanski paid her cash and paid for many of her trips to and from Europe.

When asked if she had proof of any of this, Steinback said she saved all of her e-mail exchanges with Polanski and kept a log of all the contracts she awarded to Pane's companies in return for the payments. She said that all the deposits into her bank account with cash were from money that Polanski gave her.

Stephanie Steinback voluntarily allowed the agents to download and copy her e-mail exchanges with Polanski onto a flash drive. She also provided the agents with the log of contracts she awarded to Pane's companies and copies of her bank statements.

The rest of the interview was also interesting:

Tina:	Other than your regular pay, have you received any other gifts, money or anything else of value from anyone else for work you did in contracting?
Stephanie Steinback:	No, just from Anthony.
Tina:	Have you favored any other contractors in contract award decisions?
Stephanie Steinback:	No, just Pane's companies.
Tina:	Why did you keep awarding Pane's companies more contracts when there were complaints that he wasn't shipping what was required?
Stephanie Steinback:	I didn't know anything about that. My job was to award contracts. Nobody ever told me he wasn't delivering.
Tina:	Are any other contracting officers favoring Pane's companies?
Stephanie Steinback:	Just me, as far as I know. I award all the contracts for office supplies.
Tina:	What other vendors does Anthony Polanski represent to help get government contracts?
Stephanie Steinback:	Oh, he represents lots of companies! He's paying almost everyone I work with!
Durbin:	You're saying that Anthony Polanski is paying other government contracting officers in your office to favor other contractors?
Stephanie Steinback:	Sure! I thought you knew that.
Durbin:	(Bluffing) Yea, we know a lot! We just want to see if you are going to tell us everything you know or if you'll try to hold back

180   Chapter 14

	on us. So far you've been very honest and cooperative and I'm glad to see that.
Tina:	How do you know that other contracting officers in your office are favoring certain vendors and that Anthony Polanski is paying the contracting officers?
Stephanie Steinback:	It's no secret in our office. We talk about it all the time. Even our supervisors are in on it ...

Thursday, April 23, 2015
(Philadelphia, PA)
9:00 AM

The two agents are eating large, soft pretzels while standing in front of the Rocky Balboa statue by the stairs of the Philadelphia Art Museum.

Tina:	I like these soft pretzels.
Durbin:	Yea, they are much quieter than the ones you were munching on in my office.
Tina:	So what are we going to do now?
Durbin:	You mean after we run up those Rocky Stairs?
Tina:	Yea, after we run up those Rocky Stairs.
Durbin:	(Exhales forcefully) Well, for starters, we got a zillion reports to write, evidence to lock up, and recordings to get transcripts made of. I guess we'll have to turn this new information over to our Philadelphia offices.
Tina:	I hate giving up good cases. But you're right, there's no way our agencies will let us continue to work on this Philadelphia nest of corruption from Memphis.
Durbin:	Wait a second. I got a text from Janice Slow.
Tina:	Gosh, she's such a pain! Now what does she want?
Durbin:	(Reading the text on his phone) She's asking when I'm going to give her my case planning sheet on this case.
Tina:	You're joking, right?
Durbin:	I wish I was joking. Watch this. (Durbin speaks out loud as he types a text response.) I'm still working on the investigative plan. (Durbin hits the send button.)
Tina:	(Laughing) You're going to drive her nuts! (Tina hands Durbin her half-eaten pretzel). Hold my pretzel and time me. I'm running up the Rocky Stairs first.
Durbin:	(Imitating Rocky Balboa) Yo Tina! You want to have a good time, you got to have a good watch!
Tina:	(Running up the Rocky Stairs) You mean a good Philadelphia watch!
Durbin:	Yea, until we get back to Memphis.

The two agents returned to Memphis, completed all of the paperwork, processed the evidence, and briefed the criminal and civil prosecutors. They quantified the dollar losses for all the short shipments and other complaints against Pane's companies for which Pane received payments. The agents next sent referrals to their agency's Philadelphia offices to continue the investigative effort.

As a result of the two agents' work, criminal charges were brought against many current and recently retired government contracting officers, including Stephanie Steinback, for circumventing contract procedures and receiving bribery payments. Also charged were Paul Pane and Anthony Polanski. Lucy Lightweight was considered a key witness and not charged. Civil judgments were also made against Anthony Polanski, Paul Pane, Plenty of Office Stuff, Inc., P.P. Supplies, and Paul Pane Enterprises.

The two agents later made recommendations for improvement to prevent such wrongdoing in the contract award process from reoccurring.

After their investigation, SA Tina Thomas transferred agencies and went to work as an SA for the FIS. Tina and SA Durbin then worked full time together in the same office in Memphis, TN.

Author's Note: Some of the introduction of this chapter was derived, copied, and/or modified from Chapter 13 (Sample Case Study Utilizing *The Piper Method*) of *Healthcare Fraud Investigation Guidebook* by Charles E. Piper, copyright 2016 by Taylor & Francis Group, LLC. CRC Press is an imprint of Taylor & Francis Group, an Informa Business.

15 Sample Case Study
Story #2

Case study-story #2 is a fictional story and a spin-off from case study-story #1. Special Agents (SAs) Dan Durbin and Tina Thomas are both senior federal agents from the Federal Investigative Service (FIS). The agents routinely investigate contract and procurement fraud, collusion, and corruption. This case study provides insight as to how investigators might go about conducting their investigation while utilizing elements of *The Piper Method of Conducting Thorough and Complete Investigations*.*

All names of persons, entities, agencies, and organizations listed in this case study are fictional. Any resemblance to actual cases and/or individuals, entities, or others is purely coincidental.

Monday, July 6, 2015

(Memphis, TN)

9:15 AM

SA Dan Durbin and SA Tina Thomas of the FIS are sitting at their desks, which face each other inside their small office on the tenth floor of a commercial building located in downtown Memphis, TN.

Durbin flips through files while continuously glancing at his computer's monitor. He frequently sips from a cup of coffee. SA Thomas drinks from a can of highly caffeinated soda and holds the almost empty can up high, trying to sip the last drop of soda.

Durbin: (Watching Tina trying to get the last drop) *I think there's one more drop in that can. Tilt it a little higher! Higher! Higher!*

Tina: (Brings the empty can down, slams it on her desk and squeeze crushes it). *What's your problem, Mr. Coffee Cup Glued to Your Fingers?*

Durbin: *Nothing. I just find it amusing that every morning you go through the same ritual of trying to get every last drop out of that can of soda.*

---

*Piper, Charles E., *Investigator and Fraud Fighter Guidebook: Operation War Stories*, John Wiley & Sons, Hoboken, NJ, 2014. (Copyright 2014, Wiley-VCH Verlag GmbH & Co. KGaA. Reproduced with permission.)

Tina: What's the difference? You just keep refilling your coffee cup over and over and running back and forth to the men's room all day. I drink one can of this and I'm good to go! What are you working on that has you so bored that you have to watch me?

(Durbin points down to a thick file folder on his desk and replies) It's a cost-mischarging case. I've been working on it for about 2 years now.

Tina: Oh, I hate cost mischarging cases! They are so time consuming and confusing.

Durbin: Well the good news is I'm about finished with the document review part and I'm getting ready to interview some company employees. Our auditors have done a great job sorting through everything and they've concluded there is no way in the world this company used all the labor hours and material they claim to have used on this cost-plus project. The auditors said it looks like they were actually working on several firm-fixed-price contracts and charged extra time and materials to the cost-plus contract.

Tina: Thank goodness for auditors. They save us a lot of headaches.

Durbin: Actually, I could use a hand doing the interviews. Do you think you can work this weekend with me? All you have to do is be a witness to the interviews, I'll write the reports.

Tina: Sounds like easy overtime to me. I've got some interviews on one of my cases that I'd like you to sit in on too. So you can return the favor.

Durbin: What kind of case is that?

Tina: It's a progress payment fraud case. The contractor's been in business for about 10 years and has several open contracts that he's receiving progress payments on. The Government Quality Assurance Representative, aka the QAR, said the contractor has only completed about 25 percent of one contract, but they've submitted progress payment claims reflecting they are 75 percent finished with the work!

Durbin: Where is the company located?

Tina: Well, we are not stopping by Wrigley Field to watch the Cubs play, but it's in your hometown—Chicago, Illinois.

Durbin: (Jumps to his feet and yells) Chi-Town! Holy Cow! I'm definitely in! Don't worry about stopping by Wrigley; I'm a White Sox fan anyway. But I will buy you the best hot dog you've ever had in your life!

Tina: No you won't! I'm from New York and the best dogs in the world are in N-Y-C!

Saturday, July 11, 2015
(Memphis, TN)
9:15 AM

SA Durbin and SA Thomas ride in Durbin's unmarked government vehicle (a blue Jeep Cherokee). While driving, Durbin briefs Thomas on the interviews they will attempt this morning.

Durbin: The first two interviews we are going to try to do are with former employees of the target company, named Warehouses, Buildings & Sheds, Inc., or WBS for short.

Tina: WBS. It sounds like a television station! (Imitating a news reporter and holding an imaginary microphone up to her mouth.) *This is Tina Thomas from WBS reporting live from Memphis, Tennessee ...*

Durbin: Yea, Yea, Yea. Anyway .... The first guy we'll visit is named Tony Tribune. Tony was a laborer on this contract. His time cards reflect that he worked almost exclusively on a cost-plus contract number ending in 999 that was awarded in 2013. We think he was working on a bunch of other firm-fixed-priced contracts.

9:35 AM

The two agents are dressed in professional attire and each is holding a leather notebook while standing on the front porch of Tony Tribune's house in Memphis. SA Durbin rings the front doorbell. The front door opens and both agents hold up their credential cases showing their badges and federal agent identification.

Tony Tribune: *You guys with Chicago P.D.?*

Durbin: *No sir. My name is Special Agent Durbin. This is Special Agent Thomas. We're with the Federal Investigative Service. We'd like to talk to you about some projects you worked on when you were employed by Warehouses, Buildings & Sheds, Inc. Can we come in for a few minutes?*

Tony Tribune: *Everybody's still sleeping and the house is a wreck. Can we just talk out here?*

Durbin: *Sure that's fine. Let me ask you first of all, can you explain how you logged your work hours every day? Did you fill out time cards and list the number of hours you worked on each project or what?*

Tony Tribune: *That's how we used to do it and I think that's how we were supposed to do it. But starting in early 2014, we got a new management and office staff. I was told by my boss that I no longer had to complete time cards because that would be handled by the front office. So they took care of my time cards. I just showed up, did my job and made sure they paid me correctly.*

Tina: *Who told you to stop using the time cards?*

Tony Tribune: *My immediate supervisor was Sammy Shooter. He started in about February 2014 and told me to stop using time cards. The new office manager's name is Nancy Tagler. She also started in February 2014 and took care of the time cards.*

Tina: *How do you know Nancy Tagler took care of the time cards?*

Tony Tribune: *That's what Sammy Shooter told me and one day I walked into the office and I saw her filling out everybody's time cards.*

Durbin: *What do you know about a contract number that ended in 999? Did you work on that?*

Tony Tribune:	I remember that contract because the last digits were all the same. I put about 8 hours on the project—total. I just had to fix some loose ends that someone else couldn't do. I spent most of my other time working on smaller projects.
Tina:	So contract 999 was a big contract?
Tony Tribune:	Oh yeah, that was a huge contract! It was worth several million bucks. Management was all excited about it and said it would be a huge moneymaker for them. I remember Sammy saying it was going to save the day!
Durbin:	How do you know you worked on contract 999 and that you only worked 8 hours on it?
Tony Tribune:	I remember it because it was on my birthday, March 18, 2014, and I wasn't feeling very well because I celebrated Saint Pat's Day with some friends the night before. Sammy came to me and said he needed me to work that day on the big project. I was hoping to take it easy that day but I couldn't.
Durbin:	Mr. Tribune, are you aware of any mischarging of labor time or materials at WBS?
Tony Tribune:	Well, you know, I just did what I was told. But the rumor mill had it that there were some shenanigans going on in the office. The company wasn't making the profits they used to. I guess that's why they fired the old managers and brought in the new managers.
Tina:	Back when you did complete time cards, were you ever instructed to log your hours to projects that you didn't actually work on?
Tony Tribune:	It's funny you ask that because right before Sammy Shooter started working there, my old boss, Billy Best, asked me to use pencil on my time cards instead of ink like we usually did. One week I forgot and I used pen and he was furious. He grabbed the time card and told me he'd do it himself.
Durbin:	What happened to Billy Best?
Tony Tribune:	They fired him right before Christmas in 2013. I heard he's still looking for work.
Durbin:	Why did you leave WBS?
Tony Tribune:	After they fired Billy right before Christmas, I started not trusting management. Then, when I got that e-mail about not completing time cards, I knew something wasn't right. I stayed quite a while longer because I had to make a living. But I turned in my resignation on June 1, 2015. So did a few other employees, including my buddy Johnny Priest.
Durbin:	Did Johnny Priest quit for the same reason you did?
Tony Tribune:	Yes sir. Johnny is a straight arrow. He's by the numbers all the way. He didn't like what they were doing at all. Johnny's my business partner now. We work together every day. He'll be glad to talk to you.
Tina:	Mr. Tribune, do you happen to have any printed e-mails or company memos or anything like that which instructed you to use pencil on your time cards or saying that you didn't need to keep time cards anymore?

Tony Tribune: As a matter of fact, I printed and saved the e-mail back in February 2014 that Nancy Tagler sent out about not completing time cards and that the office would take care of it. I made three copies of it because I wanted to C-Y-A. Let me go inside the house and get you one of the copies.

The agents obtained the printed e-mail from Tony Tribune as evidence and had him initial it and place the date and time on it. Durbin gave Tribune one of his business cards and asked him to call if he thought of anything else.

Next, the two agents interviewed Johnny Priest, who essentially told them the same thing that Tony Tribune did. Priest said he worked on contract 999 the same day as Tribune and that that was the only time he worked on that contract.

(Taking a lunch break at a fast food restaurant)

Tina: So, were those interviews as helpful to you as they seemed?
Durbin: Oh yea! The company is screwed! In particular, Sammy Shooter and Nancy Tagler! From what I recall, they logged that Tony Tribune and Johnny Priest both charged at least 30 hours a week to contract 999 for several months. But now we know the only day they worked on that project was the day after Saint Patty's Day, for 8 hours. The company is so busted!
Tina: So do you want to interview Billy Best next?
Durbin: If you are up for it, I'd love to do that.
Tina: Ya' know our boss, Janice Slow, is going to want all those reports of interviews on her desk first thing Monday morning.
Durbin: In her dreams! (Both agents laugh)

After eating their lunch, the two agents drove to Billy Best's house. Best told the agents he was fired because he wouldn't go along with his supervisor's instructions to mischarge time. Best said that, in late 2013, he was told to charge as many labor hours as possible to contract 999 because it was a cost-plus contract. He was told to alter employees' time cards and record that they worked on contract 999 even if they did not. Best said he did what he was told and even instructed his employees to use pencil on the time cards so he could switch the hours.

Best related that he felt terrible about doing it but had no choice because they threatened to replace him if he didn't do what he was told. Right before Christmas 2013, Best told his supervisors that he wasn't going to continue mischarging time anymore. He was fired right on the spot and was told it was for poor work performance.

When asked if he had any proof, Best said he kept some of the original time cards that the employees first turned in before they started using pencil. He provided the original time cards to the agents which were secured as evidence.

Best said that the name of his supervisor who ordered the falsification of time was Joseph Heartless. Heartless is the company's Chief Financial Officer (CFO).

Best said that, to his knowledge, the 999 contract was the only one that had time mischarged to it. He did not know anything about any materials being mischarged to the contract.

During the rest of the week, SA Durbin wrote up the reports of interviews, copied, logged, and secured the evidence, and wrote a separate report summarizing his review of information on the original time cards provided by Billy Best.

Monday, July 20, 2015
(Memphis, TN)
10:15 AM

SA Dan Durbin and SA Tina Thomas are at their desks. Durbin is speaking on the phone with his supervisor, Janice Slow, in her Nashville office.

Durbin: (Speaking into the phone) *Yes, Janice.* (pause) *Yes, Janice.* (pause) *Yes, Janice, will do.* (Durbin hangs up the phone.)
Tina: *Another nice Monday morning call from Janice Slow?*
Durbin: *I swear she's going to drive me nuts! She said that after each interview I should come back to the office and type up the report of interview so she can know what happened as soon as possible.*
Tina: *And you said yes to that?!*
Durbin: *I said yes to get her off the phone. I'm not going to do that!*

The office phone rings and SA Thomas answers: *FIS, Agent Thomas. Can I help you?* (pause) *Yes, Janice.* (pause) *Yes, Janice.* (pause) *Will do, Janice.* (SA Thomas hangs up the phone.)

Durbin: *Well, what did she want?*
Tina: *She said I shouldn't follow your example and that I should always return to the office and type up the reports of interviews right after they are conducted.*
Durbin: *And you said yes to that?!*
Tina: *She's off the phone, isn't she?*

The agents later interviewed WBS' former office manager at her home who stated that Joseph Heartless instructed her to falsely charge materials and employees' time from fixed-price government contracts to cost-plus government contracts. She refused, and quit the same day.

Monday, August 10, 2015
(Memphis, TN)
9:00 AM

Additional SAs from the FIS Central Field Office assisted in executing a search warrant at WBS to search for and obtain evidence of cost mischarging. SA Dan

188   Chapter 15

Durbin was the lead agent. FIS computer forensic agents obtained mirror image copies from the computers inside the office. One agent videotaped the entire inside of the building after they arrived and again just before they left.

While there, SA Durbin and SA Thomas teamed and interviewed office manager Nancy Tagler and project supervisor Sammy Shooter. Both admitted their part in mischarging labor hours and materials to contract 999 and to several other cost-plus contracts. Tagler provided a list of the other government contracts which had false charges made to them. Both Tagler and Shooter said they received orders from Joseph Heartless, the CFO, to mischarge the time.

The agents attempted to interview Heartless, but he said he wanted a lawyer. Right after that, the company's corporate attorney showed up and said he represented the company and all employees and that no other interviews could be conducted without his approval.

Executing the search warrant took most of the day. They obtained as evidence many boxes of documents, including contracts, invoices, payments received, time cards, e-mails, memorandums, and other information. They had to rent a small truck to haul everything back to the FIS Memphis office. SA Durbin gave an itemized inventory of all items seized as evidence to the corporate attorney.

After loading all of the documents and evidence into the FIS evidence room, Durbin ordered pizzas and sodas for the assisting agents.

Just as Durbin took his first bite of pizza, his cell phone rang. Chewing quickly and swallowing, he answered his phone, "Durbin!"

Durbin: (Pauses while listening) *Everything went fine Janice. I think we got some good stuff.* (pause) *Yes, Janice.* (pause) *Yes, Janice.* (Durbin hangs up his phone and shakes his head in disbelief.)

Tina: *That sounded familiar.*

Durbin: *She asked me if I left an itemized inventory of evidence seized at the company and if I secured the evidence.*

Tina: (Sarcastically) *It was nice of her to show up to assist. After all, agents came in all the way from Chicago to help out and she couldn't make the 3-hour drive here?*

Durbin: *Frankly, I'm glad she didn't show up.* (Durbin bites an angry chomp from his slice of pizza.)

Tina: *How many times do I have to tell you my name is not Frankly?* (Both agents laugh.)

During the next several months, Durbin gained valuable assistance from his audit team, which analyzed the evidence and helped quantify the false time and material charges to various federal cost-plus contracts awarded to WBS.

Durbin wrote a detailed summary report which included the auditors' reports, reports of interviews, and other exhibits. He also created some visual aids using Microsoft PowerPoint to help present the case facts. He provided copies of everything to both the criminal and civil prosecutors at the Western District of Tennessee's U.S. Attorney's office in Memphis.

Both the criminal and civil prosecutors accepted the case against WBS, Joseph Heartless, Sammy Shooter, Nancy Tagler, and Billy Best. Best's cooperation was taken into consideration.

SA Dan Durbin and SA Tina Thomas continued working on their other cases.

16 Sample Case Study
Story #3

Case study-story #3 is a fictional story and a spin-off from case study-stories #1 and #2. Special Agents (SAs) Dan Durbin and Tina Thomas are both senior federal agents from the Federal Investigative Service (FIS). The agents routinely investigate contract and procurement fraud, collusion, and corruption. This case study provides insight as to how investigators might go about conducting their investigation while utilizing elements of *The Piper Method of Conducting Thorough and Complete Investigations.**

All names of persons, entities, agencies, and organizations listed in this case study are fictional. Any resemblance to actual cases and/or individuals, entities, or others is purely coincidental.

Tuesday, September 1, 2015
(Memphis, TN)
9:15 AM

SA Dan Durbin and SA Tina Thomas of the FIS are sitting at their desks which face each other inside their small office on the tenth floor of a commercial building located in downtown Memphis, TN.

Durbin:	Do you still need me to go to Chicago with you to assist on some interviews on your progress payment fraud case?
Tina:	Funny you should ask because I just completed putting together some interview folders and wondered if you could still help out. This doesn't look like a big case, but the Government Quality Assurance Representative said the contractor has only completed about 25 percent of one contract, but they've submitted progress payment claims reflecting they are 75 percent finished with the work. We may only have to do one interview. If the suspect confesses, we might be done.

---

*Piper, Charles E., *Investigator and Fraud Fighter Guidebook: Operation War Stories*, John Wiley & Sons, Hoboken, NJ, 2014. (Copyright 2014, Wiley-VCH Verlag GmbH & Co. KGaA. Reproduced with permission.)

Sample Case Study: Story #3   191

Durbin: What's the name of the company and what part of Chicago are they in?
Tina: The company's name is South Side Manufacturers. Guess what part of Chicago it's in?
Durbin: I'd say they are White Sox fans, like me, on the South Side.
Tina: (Sarcastically) Bingo! You should be an investigator!
Durbin: (Sarcastically) I have my moments. Do you really think that Janice is going to approve my travel request? I think she'll say that you can go because it's your case but that an agent from Chicago can witness the interviews.
Tina: Well, it's September and getting close to the end of the fiscal year. She loves spending our region's money as the FY gets closer to ending.
Durbin: Yea it's funny how my requests for travel during the early parts of the year get scrutinized and then in September they spend money like drunken sailors!
Tina: They know that if they don't spend it this year ...
Durbin: Yea I know, they won't get it next year. Do you think they'll authorize us to fly up there or will we have to drive?
Tina: I guess it depends how much money they've got. My fingers are crossed that we can fly and rent a car.

Friday, September 4, 2015

(Midway Airport: Chicago, IL)

6:30 PM

SA Thomas is driving a white Chevy Cruze rental car and SA Durbin is riding in the front passenger seat.

Durbin: I know a great pizza place right around here. You okay for that?
Tina: Sounds good to me, but it won't be as good as New York's pizza!
Durbin: Why do you always say that? It's good. I don't know if it's better than New York's or not.
Tina: Ok, I didn't know you were so sensitive.
Durbin: I'm not. But the White Sox are better than the Yankees.
Tina: Oh, don't even start ...

Saturday, September 5, 2015

(Chicago, IL)

9:30 AM

The two agents are dressed in professional attire and each is holding a leather notebook while walking from their parked car to the front door of Rita Durkin's house. Durkin is the vice-president of South Side Manufacturers.

Tina: (Walking next to SA Durbin) So this is how the other half lives.

Chapter 16

Durbin: It's a frigging mansion! You think Alfred the butler is going to answer the door?
Tina: That wouldn't surprise me at all.

SA Thomas rings the front doorbell. The front door opens and both agents hold up their credential cases showing their badges and federal agent identification. A uniformed maid answers.

Maid: Oh my! Can I help you with something?
Tina: My name is Special Agent Thomas. This is Special Agent Durbin. We'd like to speak with Ms. Rita Durkin.
Maid: Can I say what it's in reference to?
Tina: It's in reference to South Side Manufacturers.

The maid invites the two agents inside the house. SA Durbin stares up at the magnificent chandelier hanging from the ceiling. After the maid steps away, he whispers to SA Thomas, "Well, now we know where the progress payment money went." SA Thomas then puts her index finger to her mouth, advising Durbin to be quiet.

A few minutes later, the sound of high-heeled shoes striking the shiny tiled floor is heard approaching. A woman dressed in business attire approaches SA Thomas with a smile and her hand is extended to shake.

Rita Durkin: (Shakes hands with both agents) Hi, I'm Rita Durkin. What can I do for you?
Tina: (Holds up her badge and federal agent identification) My name is Special Agent Thomas and this is Special Agent Durbin. We work for the Federal Investigative Service and would like to ask you a few questions about some federal contracts awarded to South Side Manufacturers.
Rita Durkin: (Smiling). Oh, that would be fine. But I am curious why you didn't just stop by my office.
Durbin: We thought we'd give you the option. Sometimes people are more comfortable talking about some things away from work. I must say that you sure do have a beautiful home. We'll try to be done quickly.
Rita Durkin: Thank you. Let's go into the front room where it's more comfortable.

The agents follow Rita Durkin to the front room and she asks the agents if they would like something to drink. SA Thomas answers for both, "No thanks, we're good." The agents sit across from Rita Durkin and SA Thomas begins the interview.

Tina: We were reviewing some recent progress payment requests that you made for payment. Can you tell us how you determine the dollar amounts to put on progress payment claims?
Rita Durkin: Well, as you know, South Side Manufacturers has a long, excellent history of filling the federal government's contractual needs. You'll find few if any complaints about the quality of our work.
Tina: Yes, that's true Ms. Durkin, but I was wondering if you could tell me

	how you determine the dollar amounts to put on progress payment claims.
Rita Durkin:	I review the amount of work completed and the expenses we've incurred and then complete the claim forms to get reimbursed for that work.
Durbin:	You do all that by yourself? On every claim?
Rita Durkin:	Yes, I do. Actually, I get the numbers from our office staff and inquire with the floor supervisors as to how much work has been completed.
Tina:	How far along is contract 301 to manufacture 100 large widgets?
Rita Durkin:	It's just about completed.
Tina:	How much would you say? 50 percent complete? 60 percent? 75 percent?
Rita Durkin:	If I recall correctly, I'd say it's about 80 percent completed right now.
Tina:	(Removes ten signed progress payment claims forms from contract 301 from her folder) Ms. Durkin, the last progress payment you submitted indicated the contract was 75 percent complete and because you certified to this, your company was paid. Did you read the certification before signing these claim forms? (SA Thomas hands the claim forms to Rita Durkin.)
Rita Durkin:	(Reviews the signed claim forms and nervously laughs) *I'm sure I did. The forms are pretty standard so I knew I was certifying even if I didn't read the certification each time.*
Tina:	Well here's what I'm trying to figure out. The Government Quality Assurance Representative said he's inspected your plant and you are actually only about 25 percent completed with that project but you've submitted claims for and received payment for 75 percent of the total cost of the contract. Can you explain that discrepancy?
Rita Durkin:	(Suddenly turns cold and seems angry) *The QAR is mistaken! That's all there is to it!*
Tina:	Well that's what I was hoping too. But our auditors have also found that you have not purchased enough, and don't have enough current inventory to manufacture the remaining large widgets. You've provided the government to date with 18 large widgets, and the QAR says you have 7 in progress. That's 25 in total. But your progress payments indicate or infer that you've completed or incurred costs for about 75 large widgets.
Rita Durkin:	Hmm. I don't see how this could have happened.
Tina:	I have to be honest with you. I don't think this is the first time this has happened. I think perhaps you sometimes need a little extra cash flow to finish your projects, which you've always come through on in the past, so you collect the money in advance and then finish up the work. Is that what happened on this contract?
Rita Durkin:	Well, as I said, we always provide excellent quality for the government and we are never late on our deliveries.
Tina:	But in this case, you knew you had not yet completed 75 percent of the contract yet. Correct?

Rita Durkin:	Yes, that's true. We were getting behind on some of our other contract work and I just needed the money up front so we could finish everything up. I am hoping to get awarded a few more contracts in the very near future and that will keep the cash flow coming in.
Durbin:	I'm just curious. What would happen if you didn't get awarded those future contracts and get that extra cash flow? Would that mean you would not be able to complete some of the contracts your company has already been awarded?
Rita Durkin:	I'd find a way somehow. I could get a second mortgage on my house if I needed to.
Tina:	But the bottom line is, you've been submitting progress payment claims indicating you were further along in completing the contracts so you could collect money in advance. Is that right?
Rita Durkin:	Yes, but we always deliver.
Tina:	And you submitted progress payments on contract 301 which you knew contained inaccurate information. Right?
Rita Durkin:	Yes, I did. But nobody got hurt. The work will get done.
Tina:	I'm sure it will. But was the reason you submitted those claims to collect money because you didn't have enough money in-house to get what was needed to complete this and other contracts?
Rita Durkin:	Yes it was. You see my business partner left last year and he took half the money from our company bank account so I really had no choice.
Durbin:	Why did your business partner leave?
Rita Durkin:	He got divorced and was kind of living some fancy new lifestyle. He moved up to New York.
Durbin:	I hear they've got the best pizza up there in New York.

(SA Thomas frowns at Agent Durbin. He shrugs his shoulders and smiles.)

Tina:	So how far along are you really with the contract to manufacturer 100 large widgets?
Rita Durkin:	Probably 25 percent, just like you said.
Tina:	How about we do this? (SA Thomas hands Ms. Durkin a copy of the last progress payment claim submitted indicating the contract was 75 percent completed.) This is the last progress payment claim you submitted. If it's accurate to do so, why don't you write on it that you've only completed about 25 percent of the work? Can you do that?
Rita Durkin:	Will I get in trouble if I do that?
Tina:	Well, it's the truth, right? We do need to establish the truth. You want to tell the truth, don't you Ms. Durkin?
Rita Durkin:	Of course I do. Will I have to pay that money back?
Tina:	I'm not exactly sure how this all plays out. We are federal agents. We just establish the facts and learn the truth and then brief the people that need to be briefed. If you don't want to write anything, you don't have to.
Rita Durkin:	Ok, I'll write it. (Ms. Durkin writes across the bottom that the contract is only about 25 percent completed.)

Tina: Now, can you sign your name under that and put the date and time down next to it?

(Ms. Durkin does as asked and SA Thomas collects the signed paper from her.)

Tina: So let me tell you what will happen next. I'm going to brief my bosses and the United States Attorney's office on what we've established here today and I'll tell them how cooperative you've been with us today. Does that sound okay?

Rita Durkin: Yes, I suppose that's best. I appreciate you telling them that I've cooperated.

Durbin: Ms. Durkin, you can probably save us a lot of time here. About how many other federal contracts have you submitted progress payment claims on that contained inaccurate information so you could collect money in advance?

Rita Durkin: I'd say all of the ones submitted in the past year. But I always completed the projects on time.

Durbin: But you needed the government's money in advance, otherwise you would not have been able to complete the contracts. Is that right?

Rita Durkin: Yes, but only because my former business partner took money out of our company account. I'd still try to find the money elsewhere if necessary.

Durbin: I understand. It's a shame that he did that.

Rita Durkin: Yes it is. It caught me completely off guard.

Tina: Ms. Durbin, I think we are pretty well done here. Do you have any questions for us?

Rita Durkin: So you will call me and let me know what happens next?

Tina: (Hands Ms. Durkin her business card.) You can call me anytime you want and I'll try to keep you informed.

The two agents stand up and shake Ms. Durkin's hand. She escorts the agents to the front door and the agents enter their car and depart.

While riding in the car back to the airport, SA Durbin comments to SA Thomas, "Now, that was the most non-confrontational confession I've ever witnessed."

Tina: Well, there was no reason to yell and scream. She knew that she lied. And you just had to make that comment about the New York pizza, huh?

Durbin: I couldn't resist."

Tina: (SA Thomas' cell phone rings and she answers) *Thomas!* (pause while listening). *But Janice, we just now finished the interview! I planned on updating you when we got to the airport!* (SA Thomas rolls her eyes at SA Durbin while talking on the phone.) *I'll call you from the airport, okay?* (pause). *Oh really?! Good luck with that! Goodbye Janice.*

Durbin: Some things never change.

Tina: (Smiling) Actually they might.

Durbin: What do you mean?

Tina:	Janice just told me she's up for promotion!
Durbin:	You're kidding me, right?
Tina:	(Laughing) No, I'm not kidding! Hey, you said you were going to buy me a hot dog on this trip!
Durbin:	Yes, I did! I know another good place right by the airport. Let's stop there.
Tina:	Sounds good. It won't be as good as a Coney Island Dog but ...
Durbin:	There you go again ...

Upon returning to their Memphis office, SA Thomas copied the progress payment claim form that Rita Durkin wrote on and then logged it into the evidence room. SA Thomas later wrote a detailed summary report detailing the interview of Rita Durkin. She included a copy of the progress payment claim form that Rita Durkin wrote on during the interview as an attachment to the report.

SA Thomas requested and subsequently obtained copies of all of the progress payment claim forms submitted by South Side Manufacturers for the past 18 months along with records of payment. She also obtained a complete list of federal contracts awarded to South Side Manufacturers during the past 5 years.

SA Thomas completed a summary report which included the Government Quality Assurance Representative's original referral, the report of the interview of Rita Durkin along with the attachment, and a copy of federal contract 301 for the 100 large widgets along with all of the signed progress payment claim requests and records of payment on that contract. Thomas also included an Excel spreadsheet listing all of the federal contracts awarded to South Side Manufacturers during the past 5 years and annotated which ones progress payments were submitted on and paid during the past 18 months. She also created some visual aids using Microsoft PowerPoint to help present the case facts. One of them included a bar graph showing the percentage of work certified as being completed on contract 301 and the amount of work that had actually been completed.

Thomas provided the report and exhibits to both the criminal and civil prosecutors at the Western District of Tennessee's U.S. Attorney's office in Memphis. Both the criminal and civil prosecutors accepted the case against South Side Manufacturers and Rita Durkin.

SA Tina Thomas and SA Dan Durbin continue working other cases together. Janice Slow got promoted but remains in their chain of command.

Conclusion

Contract and procurement fraud, collusion, and corruption are worldwide problems. Too often, red flags are dismissed or ignored either out of ignorance, misguided trust, or just "going-along-to-get-along." Resources to detect and investigate such wrongdoing are often insufficient.

The information and guidance in this book should greatly assist those responsible for investigating, prosecuting, and maintaining the integrity of private and public sector contract and procurement systems.

Utilizing *The Piper Method of Conducting Thorough and Complete Investigations** will help detect and identify more wrongdoing and hold accountable those unscrupulous individuals and entities involved. Using this method will also help identify waste and abuse as well as systemic weaknesses which caused and/or contributed to the wrongdoing. Also, the recommendations that you make for improvement will help to prevent such wrongs from reoccurring.

Your efforts help ensure the integrity of contracting, procurements, and other acquisitions, which allows for fair and open competition. Your efforts also help to keep prices from unnecessarily rising. This benefits consumers, taxpayers, business entities, stockholders and investors, and government agencies.

When investigating, always remember to *think plural; not singular* and to find the dots to connect. It's important to share information with other fraud fighters and to work as a team.

To those who continue to strive for perfection in this arena, I thank you and wish you continued success.

---

*Piper, Charles E., *Investigator and Fraud Fighter Guidebook: Operation War Stories*, John Wiley & Sons, Hoboken, NJ, 2014. (Copyright 2014, Wiley-VCH Verlag GmbH & Co. KGaA. Reproduced with permission.)

Appendix: Samples of Visual Aids for Presentations on Contract and Procurement Fraud, Collusion, and Corruption Investigations

SAMPLES
OF

CONTRACT & PROCUREMENT FRAUD,
COLLUSION & CORRUPTION

CASE PRESENTATION
VISUAL AIDS

SAMPLE
CASE
PRESENTATION
VISUAL AIDS

Fictitious Illustration Intended for Demonstration Purposes Only
Prepared by and photos by: Charles E. Piper, CFE, CRT

Figure 1

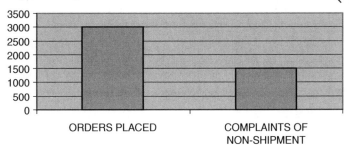

Figure 2

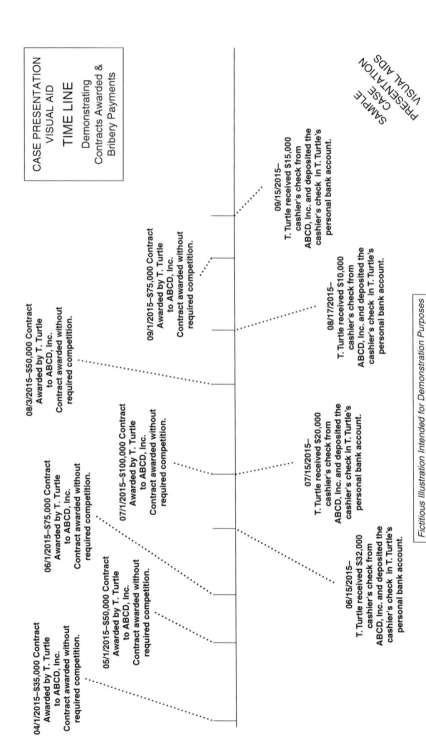

Figure 3

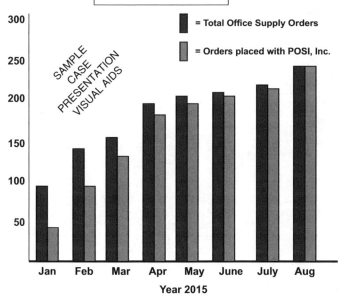

Figure 4

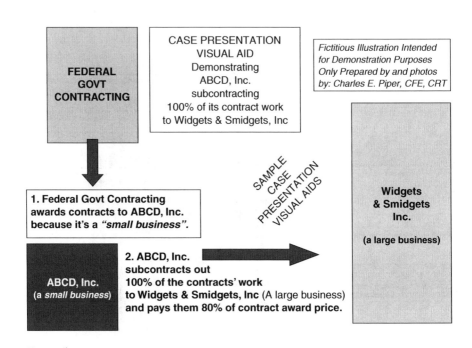

Figure 5

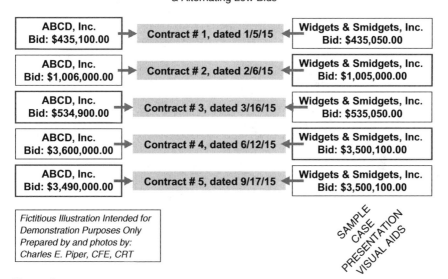

Figure 6

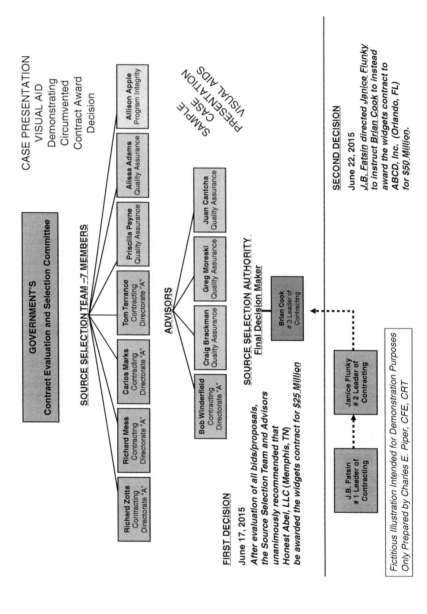

Figure 7

Index

Administrative Contracting Officer (ACO) 4
Agnew, Spiro 35
Alaska Native Corporations (ANCs) 23
analysis reports 135
asking for information 110
Association of Certified Fraud Examiners (ACFE) 97, 101
audits 107
Authorized Civil Investigative Demands (AIDs) 105

bank statements, requesting and reviewing 98–9
bid-rigging 40–5; bid rotation 40–1; bid suppression 44; complimentary bidding 41–2; fictitious vendors 43; market division 44; price fixing 44–5
Blanket Purchase Agreement (BPA) 16–17
bribery 32, 97, 128
Buy American Act violations 66–7

case initiation reports 133–4
case planning, goals, and strategies (reports and evidence) (investigative) 144–56; administrative violations 146; civil violations 145–6; conducting ten simultaneous investigations in one case 145–9; criminal violations 145–6; development of investigative plans and strategies 152; drafting of investigative plans 149–51; Murphy's Law 154; others committing the same acts in the future 148; others committing the same type of wrongful acts 147–8; Piper method 144–5; planning steps 153–4; proactive investigations 151–2; reactive investigations 152; sample plan 155–6;

suspect committed wrongful acts 146–7; systemic weaknesses, indications of 149; system improvement 149; timing 154–5; waste/abuse, indications of 148–9
case presentations and testifying 157–61; briefing differences 157–8; investigator's voice, appearance, and bearing 158–9; providing copies of reports and documents 159–60; quality briefings 158; testifying 160–1; visual aids 159
Clayton Antitrust Act 45
Commercial and Government Entity (CAGE) Code 89
competition schemes *see* source selection and competition schemes
complimentary bidding 41–2
computers 104
conflicts of interest 33
consumer scams 68
contract file contents 91–3
contracting, corruption in 28–39; bribery 32–3; case samples 34–8; conflicts of interest 33; corruption, forms of 30; Foreign Corrupt Trade Practices Act 37–8; gratuities 33; kickbacks 33; Operation Ill Wind 34; players in contract fraud and corruption schemes 29–33; Procurement Integrity Act 34; quid pro quo 31–2; U.S. Air Force Contracting Scandal, Darleen Druyun and 35; U.S. Air Force Thunderbirds $50 million contract scandal 35–7; Vice President Spiro Agnew accepted bribes for contracts 35; Yates memo 38–9
contracts, procurements and related fraud (introduction to) 1–27; Blanket Purchase Agreement contract 16–17; Business Development Program 22–3; certification of cost and pricing data

14–24; checking price histories 12; contract award process 4; contract fraud, collusion, and corruption (categories) 27; contract fraud and corruption schemes, occurrence of 27; contractual modifications and change orders 25–6; cost-plus contract 13; definition of contract 8; Federal Acquisition Regulation 4–7; firm-fixed priced contracts 9–10; FOB origin and FOB destination 17–18; guaranteed maximum price contract 15; Historically Underutilized Business Zones 24; not to exceed contract 15; procurement and administrative contracting officers 4; procurements, paper and electronic 26–7; purchase order contracts 15–16; research and development contract 18–20; Schedule of Values 15; set-aside contracts and the SBA 22; shipping costs 17; sole source contract 20–1; terminating contracts 26; types of contracts 8–14; urgent need contract 21

contractual right to review 106
corporate integrity agreements 164–5
corporate officers, interview of 123–4
cost mischarging 70–1
cost-plus contract 13
credit card fraud 75
criminal history checks 99–100

Data Universal Numbering System Number (DUNS NUMBER) 89–90
deception detectors 109
defective pricing 48, 73
defective products 65
Defense Contract Audit Agency (DCAA) 101
Defense Criminal Investigative Service (DCIS) 79–80
Defense Federal Acquisition Regulation Supplement (DFARS) 5
Defense Logistics Agency (DLA) 89
Department of Defense (DoD) 5, 79, 89
Department of Justice (DoJ) 38, 81
Druyun, Darleen 35
Dun and Bradstreet (D&B) 96–7

e-mail 95, 142
employees, questions to ask 119–23
enforcement 81–6; Department of Justice Antitrust Division 81; Project on Government Oversight 83; U.S. Attorneys' offices 82–3; U.S. Federal Trade Commission 82

evidence collection: billings, invoices, and payments 142; contract file 140–1; electronic communication exchanges 142; electronic data 142; end items or products 142–3; financial records 143; hardware and software 142; miscellaneous items 143; shipping and receiving records 142; testing, inspection, and acceptance documentation 141; *see also* reports and evidence (investigative)

expense reimbursement fraud 74–5

false claims case, questions to ask suspect in 125–7
Federal Acquisition Regulation (FAR) 4–7; clause example 6; description 5; limitations on subcontracting 6–7; pricing policy 10; supplements 5–6
Federal Bureau of Investigation (FBI) 34, 80
federal investigative agencies 79–81; Defense Criminal Investigative Service 79–80; Federal Bureau of Investigation 80; Government Accountability Office 79–81; Military Criminal Investigative Organizations 80; Offices of Inspector General 79
Federal Procurement Data System-Next Generation (FPDS) 20
federal statutes 83–6
fictitious vendor fraud 43, 72
final investigative summary reports 135–6
firm-fixed priced (FFP) contracts 9–10
FOB origin and FOB destination 17–18
Food and Drug Administration (FDA) 18
Foreign Corrupt Trade Practices Act (FCPA) 37–8
fraud: credit card 75; expense reimbursement 74–5; fictitious vendor 72; interviews and interrogations 114–23; progress payment 75

General Services Administration (GSA) 24
ghost shipments 63–4
Government Accountability Office (GAO) 79–81, 100, 164
government public websites 100
gratuities 33

Index   207

guaranteed maximum price (GMP, GMAX) contract 15

Historically Underutilized Business Zones (HUBZones) 24, 48
hotlines 103

inflated hours 70
informants 103–4
integrity agreements 163–4
internet: as investigative tool 110; as resource for obtaining information 101–2
interview reports 134
interviews and interrogations 112–32; before the suspect's interview 124–5; bribes or kickbacks, questions to ask suspects of receiving 128–9; collusion, bid rigging, or contract award and price fixing (suspects involved in) 129–31; complainants and whistleblowers 114–15, 117; contact and procurement fraud, collusion, and corruption 114–23; electronic recording of interviews, storage of 129; false claims case, questions to ask suspect in 125–7; interview notes 129; preparing for the interview 116; questions to ask 117–23; recordings 115–16; supervisors, executives, corporate officers, and business partners 123–4; suspect interview and interrogation 124–9; time duration and interview settings 115
investigators, enforcers and statutes 79–87; Defense Criminal Investigative Service 79–80; Department of Defense contracting 79; Department of Justice Antitrust Division 81; enforcement 81–6; Federal Bureau of Investigation 80; federal investigative agencies 79–81; federal statutes 83–6; Government Accountability Office 79–81; Military Criminal Investigative Organizations 80; Offices of Inspector General 79; Project on Government Oversight 83; task forces 81; Title 5 U.S. Code 86; U.S. Attorneys' offices 82–3; U.S. Customs violations (common) 86–7; U.S. environmental law violations (common) 87; U.S. Federal Trade Commission 82
invoices, duplicate 69–70
items never ordered, shipment of 64–5

kickbacks 33, 128–9

Lincoln Law (False Claims Act) 69; *see also* payment schemes (contractor and vendor)
losing bidders' files 94

mail covers 107–8
Military Criminal Investigative Organizations (MCIOs) 80
Murphy's Law 154

National Institute of Allergy and Infectious Diseases (NIAID) R&D contracts 18–19
NATO: Codification System (NCS) 89; Commercial and Government Entity (NCAGE) Codes 89
Naval Criminal Investigative Service (NCIS) 34
non-government websites 101
not to exceed (NTE, NTX) contract 15

Office of Federal Contract Compliance Programs (OFCCP) 95
Office of Inspector General (OIG) Act 79
Operation Ill Wind 34
overnight delivery services 94

payment schemes (contractor and vendor) 69–78; cost mischarging 70–1; credit card fraud 75; defective pricing 73; duplicate invoices 69–70; expense reimbursement fraud 74–5; fictitious vendor fraud 72; inflated hours 70; Lincoln Law (False Claims Act) 69; progress payment fraud 75
performance schemes (contractor and vendor) 62–8; Buy American Act violations 66–7; consumer scams 68; defective products 65; false certifications or test results 67; ghost shipments 63–4; items never ordered, shipment of 64–5; performing unnecessary services 67; providing fewer materials than invoiced 67; short shipments 63; wrong items, shipment of 64
Piper method of investigation 144–5, 197
polygraphs 109
post-adjudicative action 162–5; corporate integrity agreements 164–5; fraud vulnerability and deficiency reports 162–3; recognition and rewards,

importance of 163; storing and archiving investigative case files 163; suspensions, debarments, and integrity agreements 163–4
pricing, defective 48, 73; FAR policy 10
prime contractors' files 93
proactive investigations 151–2
Procurement Contracting Officer (PCO) 4
Procurement Integrity Act 34
procurements, paper and electronic 26–7
progress payment fraud 75
Project on Government Oversight (POGO) 83
public records 95
purchase order contracts 15–16

quid pro quo 31–2

reactive investigations 152
reports of discrepancies (RODS) 93
reports and evidence (investigative) 133–43; attachments and exhibits 136; case initiation reports 133–4; differing opinions about content of reports 137; evidence 139–40; excluding or omitting information 138; final investigative summary reports 135–6; how many reports to write 136; interview reports 134; investigator's remarks in reports 137–8; invoices, as evidence 142; report writing, additional source on 139; requests for assistance and related responses reports 135; review or analysis reports 135; types of evidence collected 140–3; types of reports 133–5; use of investigative tools, sources, and resources reports 134; when reports should be written 133
request for bid proposals (RFP) 57
request for bids (RFB) 92
request for information (RFI) 92
requests for assistance and related responses reports 135
research and development (R&D) contract 18–20
review reports 135
Robinson-Patman Act of 1936 45

sample case study (story #1) 166–81; background information 167; case initiation 168; contacting other federal agencies 169; investigative plan 168–9; joint agents meeting 169–70

sample case study (story #2) 182–9
sample case study (story #3) 190–9
Schedule of Values 15
search warrants 104–5
set-aside contracts 22
Sherman Antitrust Act 45
shipping costs 17
short shipments 63
Small Business Association (SBA) 48; Business Development Program 22–3; Certificate of Competency 49
social media 96, 101, 109
sole source contract 20–1
source selection and competition schemes 40–61; accepting late bid proposals 54; bid-rigging 40–5; buyer schemes 49–61; change order and modification manipulation 61; changing of bid prices and blank bids 54; consultants, middlemen, and "10 percenters" 45–6; contractor and vendor schemes 40–8; contracts awarded without required SBA Certificate of Competency 49–52; defective pricing 48; excluding qualified bidders 55–6; false surety bonds 47–8; making unnecessary purchases 54–5; overly broad specifications or contract requirements 60; overly specific specifications or contract requirements 59; release of bid information 53; reposting the same need 54; Sherman Antitrust Act 45; splitting purchases 52–3; unjustified sole source 60; vague specifications or contract requirements 56–8
sources and resources (investigative) 88–102; bank statements, requesting and reviewing 98–9; bribery payments, finding evidence of 97–8; Commercial and Government Entity Code 89; contract file contents 91–3; in contract and procurement fraud and collusion investigations 90; in corruption investigations 97; criminal history checks 99–100; Data Universal Numbering System Number 89–90; Dun and Bradstreet report 96–7; e-mails 95; federal government's exclusion list 95–6; from the contracting office 91; from the requestor, customer, or buyer 90; funding requests and approval 91; Government Accountability Office 100; government public websites 100;

internet, websites, and social media sites 101–2; losing bidders' files 94; miscellaneous customer-related files 93; miscellaneous investigative and law enforcement agencies and units 97; NATO Commercial and Government Entity Codes 89; non-government websites 101; overnight delivery services 94; previous investigation checks 99; prime contractors' files 93; public records 95; social media 96; subcontractors' files 93; telephone records 95; text messages 95; third-tier contractors' files 94; trucking companies 94; U.S. Postal Service 94
splitting purchases 52–3
statutes *see* investigators, enforcers and statutes
subcontractors' files 93
subpoenas 105
surety bonds, false 47–8
surveillance 108

task forces 81
telephone records 95
testifying *see* case presentations and testifying
text messages 95
thinking plural 31, 131, 197
third-tier contractors' files 94
Title 5 U.S. Code 86
tools and techniques (investigative) 103–11; analysis and audits 107; asking for information 110; Authorized Civil Investigative Demands 105; computers, hardware, and software 104; consensual monitored recordings 108–9; contractual right to review 106; hotlines 103; informants 103–4; internet 110; mail covers 107–8; polygraphs and deception detectors 109; search warrants 104–5; social media 109–10; subpoenas 105; surveillance 108; trash covers 107; undercovers 108; websites 109
trash covers 107
trucking companies 94

undercovers 108
unnecessary services 67
urgent need contract 21
U.S. Air Force Contracting Scandal, Darleen Druyun and 35
U.S. Air Force Thunderbirds $50 million contract scandal 35–7
U.S. Attorneys' offices 82–3
U.S. Customs violations (common) 86–7
U.S. environmental law violations (common) 87
U.S. Federal Trade Commission (FTC) 82
U.S. General Services Administration (GSA) 5
U.S. Postal Service 94, 107

visual aids, samples of 198–202

websites: government 100; as investigative tool 109; non-government 101
whistleblowers, interviewing of 114–15, 117
wrong items, shipment of 64

Yates, Sally Q. (memo) 38–9